Iroquois Land Claims

Iroquois Books

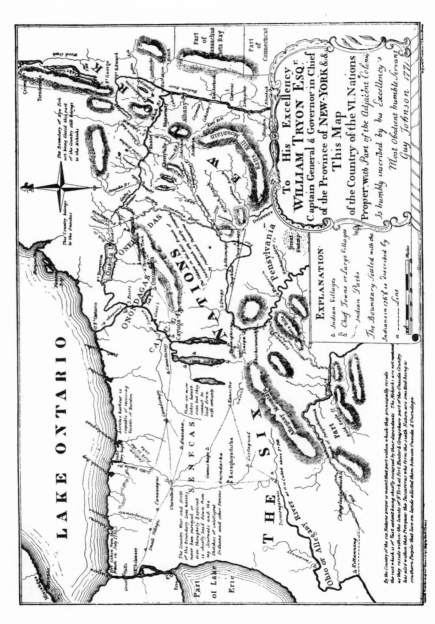

Map 1: The country of the Six Nations, 1771

IROQUOIS
LAND CLAIMS

Edited by
Christopher Vecsey
and
William A. Starna

Syracuse University Press

First Published 1988

First Edition

95 94 93 92 91 90 89 88   5 4 3 2 1

Iroquois Land Claims is published with the generous support of the John Ben Snow Foundation.

The paper used in this publication meets the minimum requirements of American National Standard for Information Sciences—Permanence of Paper for Printed Library Materials, ANSI Z39.48-1984.∞™

Library of Congress Cataloging-in-Publication Data

Iroquois land claims / edited by Christopher Vecsey and William A. Starna. — 1st ed.
    p.   cm. — (Iroquois books)
    Includes bibliographies and index.
    ISBN 0-8156-2434-4 (alk. paper). ISBN 0-8156-0222-7 (pbk. : alk. paper)
1. Iroquois Indians—Claims—Congresses. 2. Iroquois Indians-
-Land tenure—Congresses. 3. Indians of North America—New York (State)—Claims—Congresses. 4. Indians of North America—New York (State)—Land tenure—Congresses. I. Vecsey, Christopher.
II. Starna, William A. III. Series.
KFN5940.A75I76 1988
346.74704'32—dc19   87-33621
[347.4706432]   CIP

Manufactured in the United States of America

Contents

MAPS

Contributors

JACK CAMPISI has taught anthropology and education at a number of State University of New York colleges: New Paltz, Albany, and Oneonta. His publications include articles in the Smithsonian Institution's *Handbook of North American Indians: Northeast* (1978) and Imre Sutton's *Irredeemable America* (1986). He is co-editor of *Extending the Rafters* (1984), a multi-disciplinary book in Iroquois studies, and he has served as consultant to many American Indian tribes.

WILLIAM T. HAGAN is Distinguished Professor of History, State University of New York, College at Fredonia. His many books include *The Sac and Fox Indians* (1958), *American Indians* (1961), *Indian Police and Judges* (1966), and *The Indian Rights Association* (1985). He is on the Board of Directors of the Darcy McNickle Center for the History of the American Indian at the Newberry Library in Chicago.

LAURENCE M. HAUPTMAN is Professor of History, State University of New York, College at New Platz. From 1972 to 1984 he directed the Annual Eastern Regional Conferences on the Native American, and has written many books and articles, including *The Iroquois and the New Deal* (1981) and *The Iroquois Struggle for Survival* (1986). He received a Nelson A. Rockfeller Institute of Government Senior Fellowship in 1985 to study relations between the Iroquois and New York State.

CHRIS LAVIN is executive city editor of the Rochester *Times-Union*. As a reporter for the *Times-Union* and the *Finger Lakes Times* in Geneva, New York, he covered Iroquois land issues for several years and authored an award-winning series of articles, "The Iroquois: A People Apart," in the *Times Union*.

ARLINDA F. LOCKLEAR is Directing Attorney for the Washington office of the Native American Rights Fund. A Lumbee Indian, she is the first Indian woman lawyer to appear before the United States Supreme Court, where she has won two cases. She has won numerous awards for her work, and is on the Board of Directors of the American Civil Liberties union.

IRVING POWLESS, JR., is one of the chiefs of the Houdenosaunee (Iroquois Confederacy) Grand Council, and is a lifelong resident of the Onondaga Nation. He serves frequently as legal and historical advisor to Iroquois and other American Indians in dealings with non-Indian authorities.

WILLIAM A. STARNA is Professor of Anthropology and Chairman of the Department, State University of New York, College of Oneonta. In addition to many publications in journals such as *American Antiquity, Man in the Northeast, Ethnohistory,* and *New York History,* he has written technical reports on Native American history and culture for Indian tribes, museums, and universities. He received a Nelson A. Rockefeller Institute of Government Senior Fellowship in 1986 to study Iroquois land claims in New York State.

ALLAN VAN GESTEL is a partner in the Boston law firm of Goodwin, Procter & Hoar, a member of the Massachusetts bar and the bar of the Federal Court in Massachusetts, the United States District Court for the Northern District of New York, and First and Second Circuit Court of Appeal and the Supreme Court of the United States. He has served as defense counsel representing private landowners and municipal and county governments in Oneida and Cayuga land claims.

CHRISTOPHER VECSEY is Associate Professor of Religion and Native American Studies at Colgate University. He is the author of *Traditional Ojibwa Religion and Its Historical Changes* (1983), editor of *Belief and Worship in Native North America* (1981) and *The Study of American Indian Religions* (1983), and co-editor of *American Indian Environments* (1980).

Acknowledgments

Chapter seven is reprinted with permission from *Rockefeller Institute Working Papers*, Number 20, Fall 1985, The Nelson A. Rockefeller Institute of Government, State University of New York. An earlier version of chapter eight was published in April 1981 in the *New York State Bar Journal*.

The maps found in this volume were prepared by Ronald E. Embling, Instructional Resource Center, State University College at Oneonta.

We appreciate the support of the John Ben Snow Memorial Trust and its director, Professor Vernon Snow, for funding the *Iroquois Land Claims* symposium at Colgate University in April 1986. Colgate's Native American Studies Program provided the organization that made the conference, and this book, possible.

Finally, we are indebted to the contributors and their efforts in making the complex nature of Indian land claims understandable.

Iroquois Land Claims

1

Introduction
The Issues Underlying Iroquois Land Claims

CHRISTOPHER VECSEY

When newspapers report on American Indian land claims, including those made by Iroquois nations, many Americans respond in bewilderment, or bemusement. To most non-Indians, the claims represent an anachronism, a novelty, perhaps an annoyance, at the very least a mystery, or to those in the claimed areas, a threat. A suit is filed, a speech is made, a court decision is reached, a settlement is negotiated, and people ask: Who are these Indians? How do they have the right to make such claims? Why are these claims treated with such seriousness? What might be their outcome?

To an American Indian, or to one who deals with Indian issues, to the reporter, lawyer, or scholar who studies Indian affairs, the importance of these claims seems incontrovertible, maybe even pre-eminent. Regarding the claims, there exists a remarkable divergence in awareness between the general populace and those who have investigated the issues underlying the claims. Even the scholar or lawyer who disagrees with the claims' rationale at least understands the historical and legal contexts from which they arise, knows their importance, and recognizes the range of possible directions in which they may lead.

The following series of essays is designed for those who know that these claims exist, but are unsure of their origin, nature, or import. The collection includes essays first presented in a symposium at Colgate University in April, 1986, within the Oneida land claim area. Sponsored generously by the John Ben Snow Memorial Trust, with the personal interest of its Director, Professor Vernon Snow, the symposium reached a large audience of Iroquois, students, scholars, representatives of municipal and county governments, journalists, and

I

non-Indian residents of the disputed territory. *Iroquois Land Claims* is meant to communicate what informed persons know, in language relatively free of jargon, to an expanded audience of students, teachers, and other open-minded persons who want to learn what the land claims are about.

There already exists a substantial literature on Indian land claims, epitomized most recently and ably by Imre Sutton's edited work, *Irredeemable America*,[1] which delineates the basic and numerous issues common to most Indian land claims. The purpose of the present work is to examine the claims of one diverse group of Native Americans—the Iroquois—in order to see a particular set of issues in the round. By drawing upon the varied viewpoints of those who have a direct stake in the claims' outcome—Iroquois, lawyers representing or defending against the claims, expert witnesses—and those who have extensive knowledge of the claims through long observation, the book may serve to reveal the coherence and complexity of the issues.

At the same time, *Iroquois Land Claims* adds a dimension to the published literature on Iroquois history and a culture, a dimension concerning the past, present, and future of the Iroquois land base, presently missing in a book-length treatment. As such, the editors hope that the work will make a contribution to the Iroquois Books series of Syracuse University Press. Hence, the book is directed to those interested in the Iroquois—the Senecas, Cayugas, Onondagas, Oneidas, Mohawks and Tuscaroras—as well as those who wish to study Indian land claims.

When confronted by reports of Indian land claims, non-Indians often ask: What is the legal basis for such claims? Underlying this question are frequently unspoken uncertainties: Why can Indians make claims for land, when other American groups cannot? Do Indians have special rights in regard to land ownership, or special legal status as members of Indian nations? Do these Indian nations have special status in regard to the legal system of the United States? William T. Hagan, Distinguished Professor of History and author of many books on Indian legal history, explains in his article that Indian land claims arise from a special set of historical and legal relations that are particular only to Indians, including the Iroquois.

The readers of his essay will learn that Indians in the United States are admitted to possess an inherent right to land that precedes the existence of the United States, and that the nation has promised repeatedly to uphold Indian land rights. Readers will learn that one must regard the Indians' national (or tribal) existence apart from and

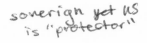
sovereign yet US
is "protector"

transcendent to the existence of individual Indians. The United States recognizes these Indian nations as sovereign entities to whom the United States is legally bound to carry out its "Trust Responsibility," i.e., act as protector. Finally, readers will learn that a number of legal processes exist through which Indian nations may pursue claims for land.

Hagan states that "improprieties" occurred on the part of the U.S. federal system in Indian relations, particularly in the making of land transfer treaties in the century following the American Revolution. Although a Court of Claims made possible in 1855 redress against the federal government for perceived wrongs, Indian nations were explicitly excluded from the process in 1863. Only through special legislation did Indian nations achieve rare success in making claims, until in 1946 Congress created the Indian Claims Commission (ICC).

The ICC has been a flexible mechanism for resolving Indian claims against the nation—determining the justice of particular claims, deciding suitable recompense, and apportioning the sources of payment—but the mechanism has not served those Indian nations whose claims are primarily against individual states of the Union, rather than the national government. These exceptions take place within the thirteen original states, where state governments dealt directly—and, it is asserted, illegally—with Indian nations during the early history of the Republic. For such Indians, including the Iroquois in claims within the State of New York, the courts have served as mechanisms and forums for such claims, although the federal guardian-ward relation has posed an alternative path toward negotiated resolution of claims. Thus, although the ICC opened the way for claims, some Indians have bypassed that method and have gone to the courts, Congress, and the President (and even to the international community, through the United Nations), to seek justice.

To date, the following claims to land (see Map 2) have been filed (although future claims are not precluded). These include a series of Oneida claims, the first filed in 1970, which can be generally grouped into pre-1790 and post-1790 suits. For the pre-1790 period, the claim is for approximately 5.5 million acres of land occupying a 12-county area 50 miles wide extending from Watertown south to the Pennsylvania border. The post-1790 claim is for 250,000 acres of land lying in Oneida and Madison counties. In addition to these Oneida claims, the Cayugas, in 1980, filed a claim for 64,000 acres of land at the northern end of Cayuga Lake in Seneca and Cayuga counties; the Mohawks brought an action in 1982 for 10,500 acres which adjoin the existing

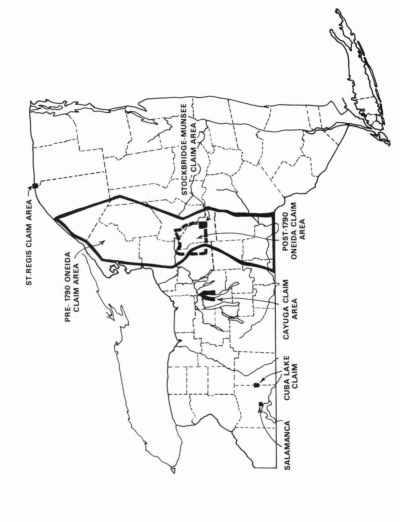

Map 2: Indian land claims in New York State, with area of Salamanca leases

reservation on the American side in Franklin and St. Lawrence counties, including two islands in the St. Lawrence River and lands along the Grass River; the Senecas, in 1985, sued for about 50 acres of state-owned property in Allegany and Cattaraugus counties (the Cuba Lake claim); and in October, 1986, the Stockbridge-Munsee tribe of Wisconsin filed a claim to six square miles of land they formerly occupied in Madison and Oneida counties.

Based on the same legal theory as the claims that have been filed, i.e., New York State's violation of Nonintercourse Acts, are several potential claims. These minimally involve the Onondaga Tribe, the Seneca, and the Shinnecock, a state-recognized tribe occupying a reservation in the Hamptons area of Long Island.

Once readers have assessed the premises of Indian land claims, a second question occurs: How can Indians justify their claim to specific areas of land? Informing (or misinforming) such a question may be the idea that Indians were nomadic, with no sense of property or territoriality, or at least that without surveyors' maps, fences, and other means of securing rights of possession, their claims have little substance. When Indians shifted village sites, overlapped in their land-use patterns, and conquered each other in wars, so that there may be conflicting Indian claims to the same land, how can aboriginal title be established?

William A. Starna, who has written extensively on Iroquois culture before contact with Euroamericans, presents a case for Iroquois aboriginal title based upon the use Iroquois made of their environment, or land. In so doing, he draws a picture of the Iroquois economy in the seventeenth century, an economy grounded in a land base, as any future Iroquois economy would be grounded in expanded territory.

Starna depicts the slash-and-burn horticulture of the seventeenth-century Iroquois as well as their hunting, fishing, and gathering routines that helped provide their sustenance. He puts a lie to the notion that Iroquois were nomadic, without a concept of territoriality; to the notion of "virgin land"; to the suggestion that Iroquois title covered only lands where villages were situated. Given their economy at the time of their first contact with Euroamericans, their land base was far more extensive than just that occupied by their villages. There were boundaries among the various Iroquois nations, marked by natural signposts: rivers, ridges, and the like. Their holdings were extensive, and known by themselves and their neighbors, both Indian and non-Indian.

Starna demonstrates that Iroquois land tenure did not regard the land as personal real estate, but as territory inhabited by politically interrelated kinship groups who granted usufructuary privilege (the right to use resources) to families within the Iroquois nations. As a result, today's land claims are not made by individual Iroquois, but by representatives of the Iroquois nations that held the land title 300 years ago. The nations are making these claims based on their aboriginal title.

In short, Starna's article serves to establish Iroquois aboriginal title because of their exclusive "use and occupancy" of a territory "from time immemorial," the major criterion upon which Indian land claims are built. Nevertheless, the language of maps made by Euroamericans, and of treaties made between the State of New York, the United States, and the Iroquois nations signifies a centuries-old recognition of Iroquois title to specific lands now being claimed. The Iroquois claim to aboriginal title is corroborated in the documents of the sovereignties that took the land.

If Indian nations, including the Iroquois, can make land claims, and if the Iroquois can establish their aboriginal title to land, upon what bases can they prove that their land was taken from them improperly? Were Iroquois lands transferred in such a fashion as to justify these claims? Can the land transfers be proven to have been flagrantly wrong, not only according to moral principles, but also according to U.S. federal law? Answers to these questions can be reached only by answering the question: What were the historical circumstances of the land transfers?

Iroquois and other American Indian nations have made their land claims in an attempt to right the wrongs that they perceive to have been perpetrated and perpetuated upon them. These assertions of wrong-doing appeal to a common conscience of the American people; thus there is the assumption of a moral argument underlying all claims. Nevertheless, the claims do not proceed according to a purely moral rationale, the way they might if they were textbook cases in ethics.

A moral debate regarding the facts and processes of Indian dispossession might commence with an espousal of principles against dispossessing Indians from their land, and would surely arouse the oft-repeated justifications for that dispossession: that the United States was destined (by God, presumably) to inhabit and possess its present territory; that laws of discovery by Christian nations superceded rights of aboriginal possession; that Indians were not using the land to its greatest potential; that laws of evolution decreed that Indians must give *moral and legal questions?*

social darwinism

way to superior Euroamericans; that the U.S. conquered Indians and took their land as spoils; that a dwindling Indian population had to give way to a proliferating Euroamerican one; that in the American Republic, minorities had to submit to the will of the majority; that the blessings of Euroamerican civilization were proper payment for land; and so on. These justifications undergird defenses against Indian land claims, and are sometimes voiced. Nevertheless, Indian nations bypass such defenses and proceed to specific arguments based on history and law.

The transfer of much of Iroquois land took place between the 1760s and the 1840s. Most crucial in setting the pattern for dispossession were the years immediately following the American Revolution. During this time, three major types of sovereignties—the six nations of Iroquois, the State of New York, and the new American Republic under the Articles of Confederation and later the U.S. Constitution— vied for the same territorial jurisdiction.

Jack Campisi, who has served as a consultant to the Oneida Tribe of Indians of Wisconsin and as an expert witness in many land claims cases, analyzes the conflicting claims of these sovereignties during the critical period, in order to establish the political context for Iroquois land loss. He demonstrates not only that New York and the U.S. competed vigorously for the right to usurp Iroquois territory, but also that the independent Iroquois nations guarded their own rights against a faltering Confederacy. They dealt with New York and the U.S. as separate Iroquois nations, making their own foreign policy even when they signed the same treaty documents with others of the six nations. The Iroquois nations had always made their own policies, even when the Confederacy was powerful; in the post-Revolution period the Confederacy was at its nadir and the individual Iroquois nations fended for themselves.

For those who ask if Iroquois lands were taken fairly and legally, Campisi provides case studies that draw cogent conclusions. Specifically, the State of New York in the 1780s and 1790s took millions of Oneida Indian acres by the most blatant and "calculating defrauding," not only toward the Oneida nation, but also toward the new national government. Campisi is only one of the many authors in *Iroquois Land Claims* to refer to the Indian Nonintercourse acts (1790–1834), by which Congress attempted in vain to prevent the states from treating with Indian nations and taking their lands. New York State representatives knew of these acts, and flouted them systematically, providing for the contemporary legal claims of the Iroquois and other eastern Indians. The federal system failed to protect the Oneidas, although by 1795 the national government had gained ascendancy over the state in making Indian policy and conducting land transfers.

The period from 1763–1842—from the ineffective Proclamation Line to the second Treaty of Buffalo Creek—encompasses the era of major Iroquois land loss. Prior to 1763, the Oneidas and Mohawks had given away some of their territories in the form of grants to non-Indian friends and neighbors; however, boundary lines established in the 1760s seriously eroded Iroquois holdings. Set adrift by Britain in 1783 at the close of the American Revolution, the Iroquois were unsuccessful in quelling the currents of the new nation's and New York's land tide. Lands recognized as belonging to each of the Six Nations before the Revolution (see Frontispiece) were now up for grabs.

In 1781 the New York State legislature promised to certain revolutionist soldiers large tracts of land in what was then the center of Iroquoia, what is now central New York State. In 1782 surveyors identified almost two million acres of this military tract, and the state moved to clear the way for its parceling and distribution. In 1786 New York persuaded Massachusetts to agree to relinquish all prior charter claims to land east of what is now Geneva, New York, in return for pre-emptory rights to property west of Geneva. Massachusetts then sold these rights to land speculators: Phelps and Gorham in 1786, Robert Morris and son in 1797. Through payments and promises of payment, these speculators attempted to extinguish Seneca title to the lands, leaving tracts of Indian land secure, in the Morris Reserve, for instance (see Map 3).

In the meantime, the Oneidas, Onondagas, and Cayugas were leasing lands to U.S. citizens, then ceding these and other parcels to New York State in treaties of disputed legality. Mohawk territories were reduced by fur trader Alexander Macomb's purchase of three million Adirondack acres in 1791, and by 1797 Mohawk leaders were abandoning their protests against the sale. During the 1790s and early 1800s, various Iroquois officials complained to the U.S. government—including directly to George Washington—charging that New York was confiscating and selling off Iroquois lands to private companies. The Indians requested federal protection under the 1790 Nonintercourse Act and the Treaty of Canandaigua, to little or no avail.

Further sales to David A. Ogden's land company in 1826 reduced Seneca property, and in 1838 the Ogden Company arranged the Treaty of Buffalo Creek, which almost eradicated Seneca territory. With the help of the Society of Friends, the Senecas managed in 1842 to regain

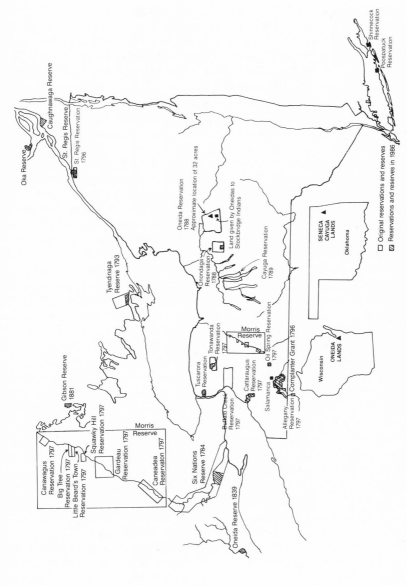

Map 3: Lands reserved to Iroquois, circa 1800, with contemporary Iroquois lands

Oka Reserve

Caughnawaga Reserve

St. Regis Reserve
St. Regis Reservation 1796

Shinnecock Reservation

Poospatuck Reservation

Tyendinaga Reserve 1793

Oneida Reservation 1788
Approximate location of 32 acres

Land given by Oneidas to Stockbridge Indians

Onondaga Reservation 1788

Cayuga Reservation 1789

□ Original reservations and reserves

☑ Reservations and reserves in 1986

SENECA CAYUGA LANDS

Oklahoma

Gibson Reserve 1881

Morris Reserve

Tonawanda Reservation 1797

Morris Reserve

Oil Spring Reservation 1797

Tuscarora Reservation 1797

Cattaraugus Reservation 1797

Salamanca

Allegany Reservation 1797

Cornplanter Grant 1796

Wisconsin

ONEIDA LANDS

Canawagus Reservation 1797

Big Tree Reservation 1797
Little Beard's Town Reservation 1797

Squawky Hill Reservation 1797

Gardeau Reservation 1797

Caneadea Reservaton 1797

Six Nations Reserve 1784

Buffalo Creek Reservation 1797

Oneida Reserve 1839

9

the Cattaraugus and Allegany reservations through a renegotiation of the 1838 treaty; however, there was little land left. In 1783 the Iroquois held half of what is now New York State; by 1842 their property was negligible. The process of land loss included sales, leases, and cessions involving U.S. citizens, companies, New York State and the nation. On the Iroquois side, it should be said, there were many, including chiefs, who favored the constriction of Iroquois lands in return for cash and other forms of wherewithal.

The years following 1842 did not witness the solidification of Iroquois property holdings. During the remainder of the nineteenth century, the Oneidas—having possessed their allotments of land since 1842 as individual owners—leased and lost every parcel of property. Between 1886 and 1888 the Onondagas lost four-fifths of their tribal territory through leases, and in the latter year ceded all but one hundred square miles to New York State. Further diminishments came in the 1950s and 1960s due to the construction of dams, hydroelectric plants, and other non-Indian technological projects. This brief survey reviews the history of Iroquois land loss, and brings us up to date concerning their contemporary territory.

Readers need to know not only who the Iroquois were in the past, and how they lost most of their lands, but also who the Iroquois are today, who are making these claims. Is there a single Iroquois political organization that speaks for all Iroquois? What are the relations between specific Iroquois nations and the Confederacy? Are the six Iroquois nations still politically intact, and if not, what is their relation to one another? On the other side, what are the relations among the federal government, the State of New York, and these various Iroquois sovereignties? Since the state was party to the majority of land transfers for which the Iroquois now seek redress, is there a regular state policy for treating such claims?

Inherent in contemporary Iroquois affairs is a tangle of relations among the following parties: the United States (i.e., the branches of its government), the State of New York, the counties and municipalities within the state, individual citizens of the U.S. in New York, the Iroquois Confederacy, and the nations—more than six now—that make up the Confederacy and that are not part of the Confederacy, both in the United States and in Canada. Laurence M. Hauptman, author of two books and many articles on twentieth-century Iroquois, unravels this tangle, and writes that land issues are the most important elements within all these sets of relations. He identifies the various Iroquois communities and tells how they reached their present configurations.

The contemporary divisions in Iroquoia have their roots in the factional splits that took place during the American Revolution and were exacerbated by Christian missions, removals, losses in political autonomy, and the facts of landlessness. For all their internal differences, however, the Iroquois in New York, Canada, Wisconsin, Oklahoma and elsewhere—numbering around 50,000 in the 1980s—continue to assert their sovereignty, particularly through land claims, and regard the State of New York as an ancient and intransigent foe whose policies tend to deny Iroquois autonomy and prevent successful resolution of land claims.

Hauptman's piece sets the stage for chapters on Cayugas, Senecas, Oneidas and Onondagas, and looks closely at the takeover of Moss Lake territory by Canadian (and other) Mohawks in 1974. Mario Cuomo, then New York Secretary of State, helped negotiate a settlement that suggested a possible approach to future land settlements, but also revealed an absence of state Indian policy. Hauptman reports that to this day state policymakers have failed to recognize the realities of Iroquois political presence, have failed to admit state culpability in past land deals, and have failed to act positively to resolve Iroquois land claims. He suggests that only threats of violence have moved these public servants to sit up and take notice, and not even the legal threat of Indian claims to non-Indian property has moved Governor Cuomo and his aides to effective action, so far.

Chris Lavin's article on responses to the Cayuga land claim serves as an example of the recent history made by Iroquois land claims. What impact have such claims had on local, non-Indian populations? Has the lack of Iroquois consensus been matched in the non-Iroquois state community? What factors have aided or impeded the resolution of the claims? What lessons can be learned from the Cayuga case for the conduct of future land cases?

Based on a decade of his reporting for upstate New York newspapers, Lavin's essay points out the incredulity and resistance with which non-Indians in the contested area have greeted the Cayuga claim over the past decade. The local population resented the notion that Iroquois might live in their midst, and responded angrily to moves made by state, federal, and Indian representatives to bring about a settlement that would set up a Cayuga territory within the claim area. The local non-Indians did not see why they should be affected by events centuries old and legalities of which they were unaware. The competing sovereignties among state, federal, and Iroquois governments tied up any progress in the resolution of claims, and political issues that seemed to have little to do with the Cayugas—county-state tensions, Democrat-Republican wrangling—got in the way; thus federal, state and local "snags" have thwarted the resolution of the Cayuga claim for a decade now, despite what appeared to be an amicable settlement in 1978.

Although Laurence M. Hauptman does not describe an Iroquois land claim per se, his portrait of the anomalous situation in Salamanca, New York, within the Allegany Indian Reservation, where the Seneca Nation leases portions of a municipality to non-Indians—leases that are soon to run out—touches on many of the issues raised in other chapters. His history of the constant threat to Seneca land title matches those of the Oneidas and Cayugas. His picture of Iroquois-white animosities, and the hostility of New York State politicians toward the Iroquois, corroborates the evidence of other pieces in the book. For all the particulars of the Seneca story, it concerns fundamentally an attempt by non-Indians to wrest control of lands from Iroquois by refusing to pay rents, maneuvering to undermine Seneca government, and asserting state jurisdiction over Seneca territory.

The impact of the waning leases of land where the Seneca Nation holds title has produced the same responses among non-Indians—fear of higher taxes, lower property values, and potentially the loss of property—as in land claim cases. Similarly, the non-Indian tenants profess innocence and powerlessness, and ask their governments in Albany and Washington, D.C. to bail them out. The lack of successful communication in the Seneca case bodes ill for future negotiations, if this pattern continues to prevail. Salamanca represents a disaster in the making, maybe a disaster already made.

Allan van Gestel elaborates on the issue of impact on non-Indians; indeed, he argues that the contemporary non-Indian landowner in the contested areas is a "hostage" to the claims—not only to the Indian demands, which he regards as excessive, but also to the unresponsive national and state political systems. Using a perspective he has employed as defense attorney in arguing before the Supreme Court and elsewhere, van Gestel emphasizes that the local landowners deserve better than perpetual litigation and threats to their property implied in the claims.

He suggests that the Iroquois land transfers of the post-Revolution era were normative within the context of their times, and he questions the validity of present Oneida claimants to the mantle of the Oneida nation of two centuries ago. In so doing, he provides arguments against the validity of the claims. He writes that Indian claims based on a unique history and legal status are overblown and threaten the integrity of United States justice. The Indians may have been wronged, but so have others, van Gestel argues. Why should the Iroquois and other Indians be granted special treatment, perhaps at the expense of innocent non-Indians? However valid the Iroquois claims may be, not only in morality but according to the law, van Gestel states that they are unworkable because of the disruptions they may cause to others in the disputed areas. His view that justice in these cases is nearly impossible to attain, turns the reader's concern to non-Indians, rather than to the Iroquois claimants.

When van Gestel made similar appeals before the United States Supreme Court, his opponent was Arlinda F. Locklear, an attorney for the Native American Rights Fund, representing the Oneida Tribe of Indians of Wisconsin. In her essay, she presents a review of the legal claim the Oneidas have made repeatedly over the past two decades, asserting what she sees as the "legal merit of the claims" within the context of U.S. federal law. She notes that the Nonintercourse Act declared illegally conducted state Indian treaties null and void, and she denies the assertion that two centuries after the fact, the Iroquois have lost any right to obtain redress. She writes that the Oneidas have pressed their claims continually over the two centuries, despite discouragement from government officials.

Both Locklear and van Gestel discuss issues common to most Indian (and Iroquois) land claims, but focus their scrutiny on the Oneida cases, which have become the axial forces in the galaxy of eastern land claims. Although the two advocates make mutually opposing contentions, they both agree that the claims would best be resolved out of court, by negotiation rather than litigation. The fact of these cases coming before courts—up to the U.S. Supreme Court—speaks of an unwillingness of some parties (specifically the State of New York and Congress) to recognize their responsibilities in the matter.

An emphasis in most of these chapters has been placed on individual Iroquois nations—Cayugas, Senecas, and Oneidas in particular. Nevertheless, the Iroquois Confederacy, represented by its spokespersons at Onondaga and elsewhere, maintains that all claims should be coordinated through the Grand Council. In his essay, Irving Powless, Jr., one of the Grand Council chiefs, reminds the reader that the real claimants are non-Indians who are essentially squatters—not "hostages"—on the land of the rightful "owners," the Iroquois. He notes the irony in the effort that must be made by the Indian owners against all-powerful claimants who make all the decisions in their own courts, legislatures, and executive offices regarding claims and rights.

For Powless, Iroquois land rights are the support of Iroquois sovereignty, and are in turn grounded in the longstanding sovereignty of the Confederacy, the Houdenosaunee, the People of the Longhouse. The Iroquois assiduously guard their sovereignty, which is constantly threatened, by the application of principles contained in the Great Law, established centuries ago by their Peacemaker and his helper, Hiawatha, both commissioned by the Creator. While defining the role of the Confederacy in pressing claims and rights, Powless states that negotiations can resolve the land issues only if the proper parties use the peaceful, intelligent "mind" that the "Creator has given us." Like the two lawyers, he calls for sincere interchange, rather than courtroom debate, to resolve the Iroquois land claims.

Why are these land claim issues so important to the Iroquois and other Indians? The answer lies in the fact that their sovereignty, cultural identity, and economic stability all rely on a land base. The Iroquois future depends on an expanded and secure land and its resources; hence, to find the claims unimportant is to deem the Iroquois future inconsequential.

The final essay, an epilogue by William A. Starna, is an attempt to gauge the potential for a resolution to the claims, as well as the possible effects of successfully completed claims on the Iroquois nations, their constituents, the non-Indians in the claimed areas, the legal and jurisdictional relations among the affected sovereignties, and other issues germane to the settlement and implementation of claims. Starna assesses the obstacles to a speedy resolution, the necessary ingredients for amicable conclusions, and the forms that a conclusion might take, keeping in mind that any resolution is merely a commencement toward the Iroquois future.

Throughout the essays that compose *Iroquois Land Claims*, an historical as well as a legal consciousness prevails. These land claims issues may be news to non-Indian readers, but they are part of a long and often-told history among the Iroquois; they are part of the Iroquois heritage. The regularity with which the authors return to the events surrounding the period of the American Revolution reflects the frequency with which Iroquois dwell upon these formative events of the past. Certain treaties and pieces of legislation, and the historical events that produced them, are mentioned repeatedly in the essays, and the editors have let these repetitions remain in the texts, so that non-

Indians can become accustomed to encountering the continuous presence of the memory of past events, as the Iroquois do in their daily
political life. If we look at the 1790 Nonintercourse Act or the 1795
Treaty of Canandaigua as things discontinuous to us, if they seem like
arcane acts, we do not share or appreciate the historical consciousness
of the Iroquois, for whom the events of the past are living as long as
their stories are still told and heard. The events of the 1780s and 1790s
and those of the early nineteenth century are aspects of the Iroquois
identity, and the insistence of the Iroquois on retelling those stories is a
means to persist as a people. Equally, by regarding the Nonintercourse
Act as dead, we fail to attain a legal consciousness since the Act and its
successors are still on the books; it still "lives," legally. The same holds
for federal treaties.

When Lew Lehrman was running for the governorship of the
State of New York in 1982, he wrote in an editorial entitled, "Indian
Land Claims Should Be Returned to the Past," "We had all thought
that the Indian wars were over."[2] Like other non-Indians, Mr.
Lehrman expects (and desires) Indians to exist only as elements of the
past. Many non-Indians think that the only *real* Indian is a dead
Indian, an artifact to be dug up, but certainly not a representative of a
sovereign Indian nation, with an effective lawyer in tow, reminding us
not of some hazy immorality committed by our non-Indian ancestors,
but of our own United States laws. Some non-Indians may not want to
hear the Iroquois proclamations of historical persistence and legal
survival as sovereign nations; however, the land claim cases re-tell
Iroquois stories in order to help continue the Iroquois identity.

The historical awareness of the Iroquois people manifests itself in
their patience as well as their persistence. They are willing to wait, not
only because of the rightness they perceive in their cause, but also
because of the long years during which they have pressed their claims.
Twenty years ago, Jacob Thompson, then President of the Oneida
Nation in New York, and the nation's counsel, George Shattuck, were
explaining the bases for land claims, as well as the Oneidas' expectations for eventual success,[3] themes already possessing a long Oneida
history. If one reads their statements, one sees that little in their
approach has changed. Twenty years ago, Thompson and Shattuck
were trying to assure non-Indians that claims would not challenge the
land titles of individual landowners. Twenty years ago, Thompson was
expressing the hope for a considerably, but not inordinately, expanded
Oneida reservation, with capital funds to finance housing, agriculture,
and industry. He said that the Iroquois needed land and money to

redress the wrongs committed by New York State: "We want the state to reappraise its treatment of us by a normal American process,"[4] Thompson said.

Thompson and other Iroquois learned that the way to make effective claims was to make legally sound ones, because without a solid legal foundation, no one would be moral enough to return land or provide funds to right past wrongs. Thompson and the Iroquois also learned that they had to raise public consciousness by continuing to tell their historical, legal story, until enough non-Indians knew the story, regarded it as true and important, and were willing to act upon it. They learned that once the claims won court cases—as they have over the past decade and more—then non-Indian policymakers might be moved to regard the claims seriously. They also learned that legal decisions depended largely on the climate of opinion in which they were made. Thompson was regarded as an eccentric dreamer in 1970 when the Oneida Nation filed its suit. Today he might be regarded more as an activist prophet who has helped change the climate of opinion, so that today federal and state officials no longer scoff at the notion of Indian rights to claims, rights to lands. Today the issues are, "How can these claims be settled out of court?" and "How much land and money will the Indians receive?"[5] Thompson and the Iroquois have learned and practiced patience. "Five or ten years more and we'll have some land back,"[6] Thompson now says. Whatever the merits of his people's claims, only time will tell if he is correct.

NOTES

1. Imre Sutton, ed., *Irredeemable America* (Albuquerque: University of New Mexico Press, 1985).

2. "Indian Land Claims Should Be Returned to the Past," *Syracuse Post-Standard*, October 8, 1982, A-14.

3. George A. Leidal, "Oneidas Seek Court Redress," *Syracuse Herald-American*, July 9, 1967.

4. Ibid.

5. Chris Lavin, byline article, Gannett News Service, April 5, 1986.

6. Ibid.

2

"To Correct Certain Evils"
The Indian Land Claims Cases

WILLIAM T. HAGAN

Strong words

Indian claims are, by and large, the backwash of a great national experiment in dictatorship and racial extermination."[1] Thus, in 1945, spoke the acknowledged dean of authorities on Indian law, Felix Cohen, in the aftermath of the war against Hitler and the genocidal policies he had espoused.

But Felix Cohen also stated that it was "because, at the same time we committed these wrongs we recognized and affirmed a higher standard of dealing than we followed that we have a problem of Indian claims today."[2] This recognition of injustices committed by the United States against the native peoples of North America was a long time coming.

An educated guess is that representatives of the United States purchased about 90 percent of the land in the forty-eight contiguous states by means of treaties or the agreements that replaced them after 1871.[3] That these negotiations were not true bargaining sessions between equals was apparent at the time to the participants, and is easily discernible many years later to the historian prepared to carefully sift the evidence.

The flaws in the process and in the documents conveying to the United States title to Indian land are many, although some are more frequent. The government initiated some of the purchases as a part of negotiations ending hostilities, at times when the Indians were demoralized by defeat and the government in effect dictated the terms. Even if all members of a tribe, or even most of them, had not taken up arms against the United States—the situation of the Creeks in 1814 and the Sac and Fox in 1832—the entire tribe would be forced to agree to a cession on government terms.

Even in the absence of direct military threat, land cessions by Indians seldom were the result of true bargaining by equals. For example, members of a tribe would be attracted to a council by the promise of a distribution of rations, and gifts that might include sugar, tobacco, even firearms and ammunition. The true import of the complicated negotiations (accomplished through interpreters), possibly resulting in a treaty transferring to the United States half of the tribe's land, would not be completely understood by the tribesmen, even those chiefs and headmen actively participating in the process.

Sometimes the blow would be softened by delaying the implementation of the treaty terms, as, for instance, permitting Plains Indians to continue for several years to hunt over land sold to the United States, or as in the case of the Sac and Fox Treaty of 1804, calling upon those tribes to surrender the land involved not until the late 1820s. Indian leaders could be more easily brought to affix their signs to treaties that did not require their people to abandon homelands immediately.

Other tactics that proved effective in obtaining the consent of tribes to land cessions included bribery. Examinations of treaties frequently reveal clauses favoring chiefs, mixed bloods, interpreters, and traders. Chiefs would be wined and dined to prepare them for the negotiations and then rewarded by land, houses, and pensions. Mixed bloods, because of their contacts in both camps, could exert critical influence and were often the recipients of extra allotments of land to ensure their cooperation. White traders who might have done business with a tribe for ten or fifteen years and won the confidence of its members, were in a position to use this trust to hinder or expedite negotiations, and thus might need to be bought off. A trader might be persuaded to cease his opposition by the inclusion of a clause in the treaty calling for the tribe to pay him $25,000 from the proceeds of the sale of its land, to cover debts, years old, which otherwise would have been written off by the trader. Finally, interpreters could make or break a negotiation, because commissioners dispatched to negotiate treaties could almost never speak the languages of the Indians with whom they would be dealing. An interpreter who used his position to advance Indian land cessions might be remembered in the treaty by a handsome grant of land, or a substantial cash payment.[4]

Aside from improprieties in the treaty process, tribes also might suffer from a variety of other cession-related problems. Frequently not all of a tribe's bands or villages would be represented at councils leading to land cessions; nevertheless, they all would be considered by the United States to be bound by the resulting treaty. The more fundamental question raised by Tecumseh and others, about any Indians being able to sell land whose ownership would be shared by all members of a tribe, was simply ignored, as it conflicted with the white person's theories of land ownership.[5]

And there were other problems. Not only might the Indians not completely comprehend the bounds of the area being sold, but actual errors might be made resulting in more land being transferred than intended, or the sale could include territory of neighboring tribes not party to the negotiations. Also, the goods and services that were part of the sale price to be paid the Indians might, on delivery, prove to be inferior in quality. The correspondence of Indian agents contains countless references to shoddy clothing, farm tools that could not take a day's heavy use, and rations of such a poor quality as to be inedible— all delivered to Indians as part of the purchase price of their land.

Tribes that were the victims of such perversions of the bargaining process had little hope of redress. As a sovereign power the United States cannot be sued in its courts without its permission. At least that possibility had been provided in 1855 by the creation of the Federal Court of Claims. A few tribes filed suit against the United States, although none of the cases that had been adjudicated before Congress in 1863 specifically barred Indians from access to the Court of Claims, unless authorized by specific acts of Congress.[6]

The result was a process almost prohibitively expensive for tribes. Non-Indian lawyers would have to be hired for a period that might entail several years' work before a bill could be lobbied through Congress getting the tribe access to the Court of Claims. Then, assuming that unlikely event, the case might be before the courts several additional years. Tribes could not employ legal council for that length of time, and attorneys would be reluctant to invest much time and energy on a purely contingency basis.

Not until 1881 did the first tribe win approval by Congress of its petition for access to the Court of Claims. In the next forty-two years, only thirty-nine cases reached the court with Congress' permission, and only seventeen, less than half, resulted in awards to the Indians.[7] Given this record, attorneys could not view this as a lucrative field to enter. One lawyer who did took over fifty claims cases and won one; others devoted years and thousands of dollars to developing cases only to lose in the end.[8] It is little wonder that tribes had difficulty attracting able legal representation.

The awarding of citizenship to all Indians in 1924, however, led to a great deal more activity in Indian land claims. The tribespeople themselves seem to have been reinvigorated to seek justice, and the national conscience was sufficiently awakened to create a climate in Congress conducive to the passage of the enabling legislation. By 1927 as many claims had been filed with the court as had been authorized by Congress in the forty-two years before the passage of the Indian citizenship act, and by 1946 two hundred claims had been approved for adjudication.[9]

But the mills still ground slowly. In a four-year period in the 1930s, of ninety-six bills introduced in Congress to give tribes a hearing before the Court of Claims, only one became law.[10] And of the two hundred that had reached the court by 1946, only twenty-nine had produced awards and most of the others had been dismissed because of flaws in the jurisdictional acts.[11] The process seemed interminable.

One tribe, the Klamath of Oregon, finally obtained access to the court in 1920, only to have their case dismissed fifteen years later. And this was despite persuasive evidence that the government had paid $108,750 for land worth nearly $3 million. These Indians had to go back to Congress for an amended act that enabled the Court to re-examine the evidence. Finally, in 1937, seventeen years after the original enabling legislation had been passed by Congress, the court rendered a judgment in favor of the Indians.[12]

As the backlog of cases mounted and the demands upon federal agencies for data for the suits multiplied, the General Accounting Office and the Department of Justice were forced to hire scores of new employees and they still were unable to keep pace with the workload.

Meanwhile, there was a growing movement to create a new forum for the adjudication of Indian claims. In the 1920s congressional committees began to address the issue, and toward the end of that decade the Meriam Report, compiled by a special commission addressing the problems of the Indian, included a recommendation for some form of an Indian claims court or commission. By 1945 the movement had the support of those who believed the time had come to render long-overdue justice to the Indians, as well as those who hoped that settlement of the claims would facilitate ending the special relationship the tribes had with the federal government. Termination was in the air, and its proponents saw some long-range gain in settling Indian claims, if the resulting cash awards would free the government of dependent tribes.

It was in this atmosphere that members of Congress shaped the bill that was signed into law in 1946 as the Indian Claims Commission Act. It was a remarkable piece of legislation. One judge acclaimed it "the greatest submission ever made by a sovereign state to moral and legal claims."[13] In signing the bill, President Truman referred to the purchase by the United States of "more than 90 percent of our public domain, paying them [the Indians] approximately 800 million dollars in the process. It would be a miracle," the President continued, "if in the course of these dealings . . . we had not made some mistakes and occasionally failed to live up to the precise terms of our treaties and agreements with some 200 tribes. But we stand ready to submit all such controversies to the judgment of impartial critics," said Truman. "We stand ready to correct any mistakes we have made."[14]

The stage was set for a process that would address the problem for over twenty years. During that period the Indian Claims Commission personnel would undergo the inevitable changes as members died, retired, or were replaced. Procedures were altered and emphases changed, although certain guidelines laid down in the original legislation provided continuity and delimited the areas in which the Commission could operate. For example, claims of wrongs to individual Indians, like Geronimo and the other Apaches who had been imprisoned in Florida, were not within the jurisdiction of this court. In the same fashion, Sioux could not collect for pain and suffering stemming from the 1890 Wounded Knee Massacre.[15] Nor could Indians who had lost land when reservations were broken up and individual farms were allotted, hope for reimbursement at the hands of the Indian Claims Commission. But to many Indians, most grievous of all was the restriction that limited the Commission to financial compensation; no land would be returned to the tribes. The final report of tribespeople assembled in Chicago in 1961 for a conference eloquently stated the relationship of Indians and land:

> Our forefathers could be generous when all the continent was theirs. They could cast away whole empires for a handful of trinkets for their children. But in our day, each remaining acre is a promise that we will still be here tomorrow. Were we paid a thousand times the market value of our lost holdings, still the payment would not suffice. Money never mothered the Indian people, as the land has mothered them, nor have any people become more closely attached to the land, religiously and traditionally.[16]

In determining the financial compensation the Indians were to receive in lieu of land being returned to them, the Indian Claims Commission developed a pattern that most of the cases followed. First there would be testimony designed to establish the claim of the Indians to the area in question. Then the fair market value of the land would be estimated as of the time of the cession. This figure would then be compared with the price per acre actually paid by the government, together with any offsets. The offsets were government expenditures in behalf of the tribe not required by treaty, and might be in the form of rations, tools, or services such as education and medical care.[17]

At all stages of the process, volumes of testimony were presented to the Commission. Historians and anthropologists testified for both sides, and the relative credibility of these expert witness had to be weighed.[18] A particularly thorny issue was the question of occupancy. The government sought to persuade the Commission to limit Indian claims to the areas used by the tribe on a daily basis. Fortunately for the Indians, the Commission chose the more realistic approach that tribes required for their way of life thousands of acres that they visited only at certain times of the year, for example when certain roots or nuts were ready for harvest, or when fish came upstream to certain points. The Commission would not accept, however, a tribe's claim to land that it shared jointly with other groups of Indians; it had to be an exclusive occupancy. In general, Indians have sought restitution of land as a primary goal, and in general the process has avoided such a goal.

In determining the value of the land at the time of the cession, the Commission refused to consider its potential value as regards mineral or timber resources that might be exploited by subsequent generations. Compensation for the Indians of California, for example, did not take into consideration the hundreds of millions of dollars in gold later extracted from the area, and amounted to a minute seventeen cents per acre lost. Nor was interest allowed, from the date of the transaction, on the amount the tribe was underpaid.[19]

A serious problem, never resolved, was what Congress had meant when it used the term "unconscionable consideration" to describe the degree of underpayment that could be remedied by the Indian Claims Commission. Did it have to be less than 50 percent of the market value to be unconscionable, or was only 35 percent unconscionable? On several occasions, the Commission's decisions were overruled on appeal to the Court of Claims, and judges used terms like "very gross" or "shock the conscience" to try to further define "unconscionable." In vain, efforts were made to get Congress to amend the law by substituting "inadequate" for "unconscionable."[20]

During its three decades of operation, the Commission did gradually move in the direction of ruling for the Indians if any significant underpayment of the tribe could be determined. Nor was this difficult in many cases, with the Commission concluding that, for example, the Quapaws had been paid only two cents an acre for land worth eighty-five cents, and the Osage had received thirty-four cents an acre for land valued at $1.50.[21] With reference to a Miami claim, however, the Commission determined that the government's paying seventy-nine cents an acre for land worth $1.25 per acre somehow was not unconscionable, although on appeal, more sensitive judges on the Court of Claims did.[22]

The old legal aphorism, "Justice delayed is justice denied," takes on new meaning in the Indian land claims cases. Access to the courts might have been denied a tribe for a century and a half, and when it did get its claim before the Commission the case might not be resolved for another fifteen years.

A final frustration for the Indians was the provision in the law that any award to the Indians would have to be appropriated by Congress. That body did not refuse in any instance to do so, but it might require more than a single session to take action. And even after it had, one final hurdle remained. Congress would not release the money to the tribe until the Indians had prepared a plan, acceptable to Congress, for spending the money. Left to their own devices, the Indians usually would have preferred a per capita distribution of all, or at least most, of the award.

The government, however, exercised its right as guardian and would withhold all the money until provision was made for some of it to be retained by the tribe for education, economic development, and other purposes deemed worthy by the "Great White Father."

The Kalispels of Oregon, who celebrated in May 1963 the appropriation by Congress of the $3 million the Commission had awarded them, had to wait an additional two and one-half years before they received their money. To get it finally they not only had to submit a distribution plan acceptable to Congress, but take action toward termination, the severance of their special relationship with the federal government. This pressure on the Kalispels (and the Menominees had a similar experience) was a government exploitation of tribal desires to get the money awarded them, a manipulation of the Indians that was really unconscionable.[23]

Congress had set September 30, 1978, as the date on which the Indian Claims Commission would cease to function. Any dockets not disposed of at that time would be transferred to the Court of Claims, and over sixty were. Originally created to function for ten years, the Commission had secured extensions to 1978. It had adjudicated over five hundred claims, the overwhelming majority relating to land, with the Indians winning judgments in over 60 percent of the cases, with awards totaling about $800 million.[24] The Court of Claims once described the Indian Claims Commission as "designed to correct certain evils of long standing and well known to Congress."[25] The result, however, had been far from satisfactory to many Indians, and a few groups refused to accept monetary consideration in lieu of the lands of which they had been defrauded. What the Commission did most successfully was to ease the collective conscience of the American people about the injustices perpetrated countless times by their government since 1790. A member of one of the law firms most active in representing tribes subtitled his article on the Indian Claims Commission, "The Conscience of the Nation In Its Dealings With the Original Americans."[26]

But only those tribes with claims against the federal government had their day in court under the terms of the Indian Claims Commission Act. Those Indians who sought compensation as a result of state action had no recourse under the 1946 law. What the three decades of litigation before the Commission had done, however, was to reaffirm the unique guardian-ward relationship of the federal government and the Indians, recognized by the U.S. Supreme Court as early as 1831 in its celebrated *Cherokee Nation v. Georgia* decision. In the 1970s that angle would be exploited by tribal attorneys pressing claims against states in the East, opening up a whole new area of litigation.

It all began with a Passamaquoddy, John Stevens, who could not discover how his tribe's 23,000-acre reservation in Maine had somehow been reduced to 17,000. Stevens' concern about 6,000 acres would ultimately lead to a lawsuit seeking the return to Maine Indians of over twelve million acres. A first step along this long trail came when Stevens' attention was called by an elderly fellow tribesman to a copy of a 1794 treaty between the Passamaquoddy and Penobscot tribes and Massachusetts, that state's jurisdiction then including what would in 1820 become Maine.[27] This had been the first of a series of treaties by which first Massachusetts and then Maine acquired most of Maine from the Indians.

Several years passed before the Maine Indians were able to get an attorney, and then he was from an agency of the federal government created to provide legal counsel for Indians otherwise unable to afford it. This attorney helped the Passamaquoddy file their first case, which they lost. The tribe then acquired the services of Thomas N. Tureen, from the same agency. In 1971 Tureen took the case with him when he affiliated with the Native American Rights Fund (NARF). This national, nonprofit legal defense association was funded in part by the federal government. This would make possible the expensive and protracted search for justice for the Passamaquoddy and Penobscots.[28]

Attorney Tureen's position was that the Indians were wards of the United States. It then followed that if the treaties by which the Maine Indians had lost their lands did not have the authorization of the federal government required by the 1790 Trade and Intercourse Act, and they did not, that the treaties were therefore invalid. Moreover, Tureen argued, as part of its trust relationship with the tribes, the United States had to take legal action against Maine, and in 1972 he helped the Passamaquoddy petition the Department of the Interior to do so.[29]

The Bureau of Indian Affairs endorsed the idea of a suit, but the Department of the Interior argued that the Maine Indians did not have federal recognition, their dealings having been only with the state. The Justice Department adopted this view and so notified the U.S. District Court in Maine. The Indians then filed a civil suit asking the federal government to sue Maine. Finally in December 1975 a U.S. Court of Appeals upheld the ruling of a district court that the federal government, according to the 1790 Trade and Intercourse Act, had to supervise all negotiations between the states and tribes. Moreover, all tribes, whether federally recognized or not, were covered by the 1790 legislation.[30] This opened the door to challenges of state actions that might have led to the alienation of lands by any Indians.

What gave weight to what would now be the federal government's espousal of the Maine Indians' land claims was the shadow cast over land titles in the disputed area. Until this legal cloud could be dissipated, the real estate business was paralyzed, new bond issues were blocked, and no one was inclined to begin new construction. The economy of whole towns was endangered, and Maine was faced with the loss of possibly two-thirds of its tax base.[31]

Confronted with a series of federal suits against individuals and companies with large land holdings, suits very likely to be successful given the precedents provided by rulings of federal courts, Maine reluctantly agreed to an out-of-court settlement. Under its terms the Passamaquoddy and Penobscots received a $27 million federal trust fund and 300,000 acres of forest land purchased with federal funds.[32]

By the time this suit had been resolved, fourteen others had been filed by tribes in eastern states, including Iroquois whose cases will be discussed by others in this book. A look at suits filed by the Narragansetts of Rhode Island, the Western Pequots of Connecticut, and the Mashpee of Massachusetts will suggest some of the possibilities.

The Narragansetts filed suit in 1975 to regain thirty-nine hundred acres lost to the state of Rhode Island in 1880, in violation, according to the tribe, of the 1790 Trade and Intercourse Act.[33] In 1975 the land in question was part of Charlestown, a little seacoast community whose population jumped from less than 4,000 to nearly 20,000 when the tourist season was at its height. The suit had the anticipated effect. Construction in Charlestown ground to a halt, real estate agents could not function because no buyer could get title insurance, and the local school district had to borrow money at short-term bank rates because it could not find purchasers for long-term bonds.

After three years of legal skirmishing, which cost the realtor who led the opposition to the Indian claim $20,000 in legal fees, a compromise settlement was negotiated. The Indians would drop the suit and receive eighteen hundred acres of land, nine hundred of it from the state and nine hundred from private landowners compensated from a fund of $3.5 million appropriated by Congress. It was the first of the eastern claims to be settled, and a NARF spokesman expressed the hope that it would provide a pattern for other settlements.

The Mashantucket Pequots of Connecticut offer the second example of how eastern tribes have fared with their land claims.[34] They filed suit against local landowners in 1976 for return of eight hundred acres. The Pequots had lost the land in 1855 when a county court ordered them to sell most of the reservation that they had been able to hold on to since colonial days. The Pequot tribe, which numbered only fifty-five people in 1974 when it incorporated under a dynamic young leader, was assisted in its twin drives for federal recognition and an enlarged reservation by an anthropologist employed on a grant from the Indian Rights Association.

The landowners hoped to avoid extended expensive litigation, and successfully lobbied their congressional delegation for federal help. The result was a bill passed by Congress and sent to President Reagan in early 1983, a bill that he vetoed. The President argued, among other things, that the settlement, which called for a federal appropriation of $900,000 to enable the Pequots to buy land, contained insufficient contribution from Connecticut. He also maintained that the settlement had been too generous, that the Pequots should have received less than $20,000 for what amounted to the loss of four-fifths of their reservation.

Faced, however, by a NARF-aided drive to override the veto, President Reagan accepted a bill whose only significant difference from the original was an agreement by the state to provide $200,000 worth of road work for the expanded reservation. Included in the law was recognition of the Pequots by the United States, which made them eligible for a wide range of federal programs, an opportunity that an innovative tribal leadership promptly seized.

Federal recognition also was at the heart of the third case, that involving Wampanoags, more often referred to as the Mashpee Indians of Cape Cod.[35] In 1976 the Mashpees filed suit to recover 11,000 acres. Much of this land the Indians had sold following actions of the state of Massachusetts in 1869 and 1870 declaring the Indians citizens and removing restrictions on the sale of their individual allotments as well as a few thousand acres they still held in common. The Indian suit was directed against a corporation (which was the largest real estate developer on that part of Cape Cod), the town of Mashpee, and one hundred large landowners. Despite this limitation, all land titles in the town were beclouded. Mashpee, which had been the fastest growing town in Massachusetts in the previous decade, began to suffer the economic ills common to an area where land titles have been brought into question.

The Indians indicated a willingness to settle out of court, but with land estimated to be worth $30 million at stake, the corporation and other large landholders decided to fight. In the next three years they would expend over a million dollars while NARF, which took on the Mashpee cause, found itself involved in very complex and expensive litigation.

The case was decided in what was essentially a preliminary court skirmish to determine if the Mashpees could legally be defined as a tribe. If they were, then they could go on to the major point at issue, whether or not the 1790 Trade and Intercourse Act had been violated by Massachusetts permitting the Mashpees to sell their land. A jury, however, after a forty-day trial replete with expert testimony, held that the Mashpees did not in the 1970s constitute a tribe in the legal sense. Therefore they could not claim that their rights had been violated when the Massachusetts legislature in 1870 permitted them to alienate their land. Friends of the Indians criticized the presiding judge for a charge to the jury that placed the burden of proof on the Mashpees, and specified that if jurors had doubts they were to find for the defendants. Nevertheless, a Court of Appeals upheld the verdict and the U.S. Supreme Court declined to review the case.

This decision was the only one in the Indian land claims cases to be rendered by a jury. It undoubtedly was noted by attorneys for the Indians, perhaps persuading them that compromise settlements out of court were preferable to seeking complete restitution, if there were the possibility of losing everything by pursuing it all the way through the courts. As a result, out-of-court settlements can be expected to be the means of resolving many of the suits pending or to be filed in the near future. Other suits will require the Bureau of Indian Affairs to grant official tribal recognition before moving for federal settlement legislation.

The last forty years saw the Indians finally getting their day in court. First the Indian Claims Commission provided western tribes an opportunity to press their claims against the federal government. The Indians living in what had been the original thirteen states, and who had lost land due to state action, could not file suit before the Indian Claims Commission. Nevertheless, these eastern tribes profited greatly from the commission's twenty-year existence. The national publicity accorded the commission inevitably brought attention to the claims of eastern tribes against states. Nor did the testimony before the Commission leave any doubt about the ward-guardian relationship of the tribes and the federal government. When wise attorneys tied this in with the 1790 Trade and Intercourse Act's provision for supervision by federal authorities of any tribe's negotiations with a state government, scores of state actions involving Indian land were brought into question. And unlike the situation when western tribes had to employ attorneys on a contingency basis, in the new series of suits against the states, the federal government, in its guardian role, would help carry the burden of the litigation for the Indians.

The tactic of filing suit against landowners as well as states has proved highly successful in generating pressure for settlement. Among those who have felt the heat are members of state congressional delegations who have been persuaded by their constituents to sponsor bills shifting much of the burden of the settlement to the federal treasury. Thus, a curious situation has emerged in which federal employees press tribal suits against states, but end up by helping negotiate settlements financed in large part by the federal government. Nevertheless, court decisions clearly uphold the right of tribes to federal protection, under the 1790 Trade and Intercourse Act, against state action. In the next ten years, we can expect to see that confirmed several times in New York.

NOTES

1. Lucy Kramer Cohen, ed., *The Legal Conscience: Selected Papers of Felix S. Cohen* (New York: Archon Books, 1970), 265.

2. Ibid., 266.

3. This is the figure used by President Truman when he signed the bill creating the Indian Claims Commission.

4. Evidence of this type of arrangement is apparent in treaties with the Winnebagoes in 1829, 1832, and 1837. See Charles J. Kappler, ed., *Indian Treaties 1778–1883* (New York: Interland Publishing Inc., 1972). Most treaties involving cessions of land probably included special provisions for interpreters and/or mixed bloods, chiefs, and traders.

5. For a discussion of Tecumseh's views on landholding, see R. David Edmunds, *Tecumseh and the Quest for Indian Leadership* (Boston: Little, Brown and Company, 1984), 97–98, 109.

6. Sandra C. Danforth, "Repaying Historical Debts: The Indian Claims Commission," *North Dakota Law Review* 49 (Winter 1973): 360–61.

7. Harvey D. Rosenthal, *Their Day in Court: A History of the Indian Claims Commission* (Ann Arbor, Mich.: Xerox University Microfilms, 1976), 28–30.

8. Ibid., 39.

9. *United States Indian Claims Commission: Final Report* (Washington, D.C.: U. S. Government Printing Office, 1979).

10. Monroe E. Price, *Law and the American Indian* (Indianapolis: Bobbs-Merrill Company, Inc., 1973), 472.

11. *Indian Claims Commission*, 3.

12. Rosenthal, *Their Day in Court*, 35–36.

13. Ibid., 64–65.

14. Ibid., 136.

15. Ibid., 200–01.

16. Quoted in Danforth, 392. Taos Pueblo was the only exception, receiving land around Blue Lake.

17. For a thorough discussion of this issue, see John R. White, "Barmecide Revisited: The Gratuitous Offset in Indian Claims Cases," *Ethnohistory* 25 (Spring, 1978): 179–92.

18. Problems with expert testimony are discussed in the entire issue of *Ethnohistory* 2 (Fall 1955). See also Robert A. Manners, "The Land Claims Cases: Anthropologists in Conflict," *Ethnohistory* 3 (Winter 1956): 72–81; and Nancy Oestreich Lurie, "A Reply to 'The Land Claims Cases: Anthropologists in Conflict,'" *Ethnohistory* 3 (Summer 1956): 256–79.

19. Danforth, "Repaying Historical Debts," 397.

20. Ibid., 395–96.

21. Ralph A. Barney, "Some Legal Problems Under the Indian Claims Commission Act," *The Federal Bar Journal* 20 (Summer 1960): 236–37.

22. Ibid., 237.

23. Robert C. Carriker, "The Kalispel Tribe and the Indian Claims Commission Experience," *The Western Historical Quarterly* 9 (January 1978): 25ff.

24. *Indian Claims Commission: Final Report*, 20–21.

25. Quoted in Rosenthal, *Their Day in Court*, 198.

26. Robert W. Barker, "The Indian Claims Commission—The Conscience of the Nation in Its Dealings with the Original Americans," *The Federal Bar Journal* 20 (Summer 1960): 240–47.

27. *Indian Tribes: A Continuing Quest for Survival* (Washington, DC: United States Commission on Civil Rights, 1981): 107.

28. Ibid., 107–8.

29. Ibid. Jack Campisi, in an April 19, 1986 letter to the author, credits attorneys Marvin Chapman and George Shattuck with identifying the applicability of the 1790 Trade and Intercourse Act to state actions. Moreover, Campisi attributes to Shattuck the strategy of suing counties to circumvent the Eleventh Amendment protection of states. Both Chapman and Shattuck represented the Oneidas.

30. *Indian Tribes*, 108–9. See also, Francis Paul Prucha, *The Great Father*, 2 vols. (Lincoln: University of Nebraska Press, 1984), 2:1172–73.

31. "Maine Municipalities in Turmoil," *New York Times*, October 5, 1976, 14.

32. Prucha, *The Great Father*, 1174. Another group of Maine Indians, the Houlton Band, received $900,000 as part of the settlement.

33. This account of the Narragansett claim is based on: *Indian Tribes*, 111–12; "Winds of Change Ruffle Charlestown, R.I.," *New York Times*, March 8, 1978, A-18; "Settlement of Indian Land Claim in Rhode Island," *The Wall Street Journal*, September 13, 1978, 40; "Narragansett Settlement," *Indian Truth* 223 (December 1978): 3.

34. This account of the Mashantucket Pequot claim is based on: "Pequot Recognition," *Indian Truth* 247 (October 1982): 3; "Lobbying to Overturn the Pequot Land Claim Veto," *Indian Truth* 251 (June 1983): 3; "Pequots and Friends Celebrate Their Land Claim Victory," *Indian Truth* 254 (December 1983): 6; "650 Acres Regained by Indians," *New York Times*, September 2, 1984, 55.

35. This account of the Mashpees is based on: James M. Kulikowski, "Mashpee Revisited," *American Indian Journal* 6 (November 1980): 18–20; "Report from Mashpee," *American Indian Journal* 4 (October 1978): 2–16; *Indian Tribes*, 112–37; "Indians Lose in Court in Fight to Save Land," *New York Times*, January 7, 1978, 1.

3

Aboriginal Title
and Traditional Iroquois Land Use
An Anthropological Perspective

WILLIAM A. STARNA

TRADITIONAL IROQUOIS LAND USE PATTERNS

At the time of European contact, early in the seventeenth century, five tribes collectively known as the Iroquois were resident in what is today upstate New York (see Map 4). All of these tribes, and many of those surrounding them, practiced a system of swidden or slash-and-burn horticulture. This form of farming is characterized by "(1) partial or complete clearance of forest vegetation by cutting and burning; (2) temporary cultivation of crops in the cleared areas; (3) abandonment of the plot to fallow for a longer period than it was cultivated, to allow for forest regeneration."[1] In their practice of horticulture, three crops were of primary importance to the Iroquois: corn, beans, and squash—the familiar "Three Sisters." Of these domesticates, corn was the most important and popular.[2] Although there are no comparable figures for the Iroquois, Heidenreich estimates that for each Huron person, approximately 65 percent of the daily caloric intake and 43 percent of the daily bulk intake was from corn.[3] However, there was probably somewhat less of an emphasis placed on corn in the Iroquois diet due to the fact that hunting played a larger dietary role for the Iroquois than for the Huron.[4]

Hunting provided the major dietary component following domesticated plants and was a year-round endeavor. Although a large variety of mammals, avian fauna, and other animals were exploited throughout the year by Iroquois populations,[5] there was a seasonal emphasis on deer. A number of works indicate that white-tailed deer *(Odocoileus virginianus)*—the principal source for meat (venison) and

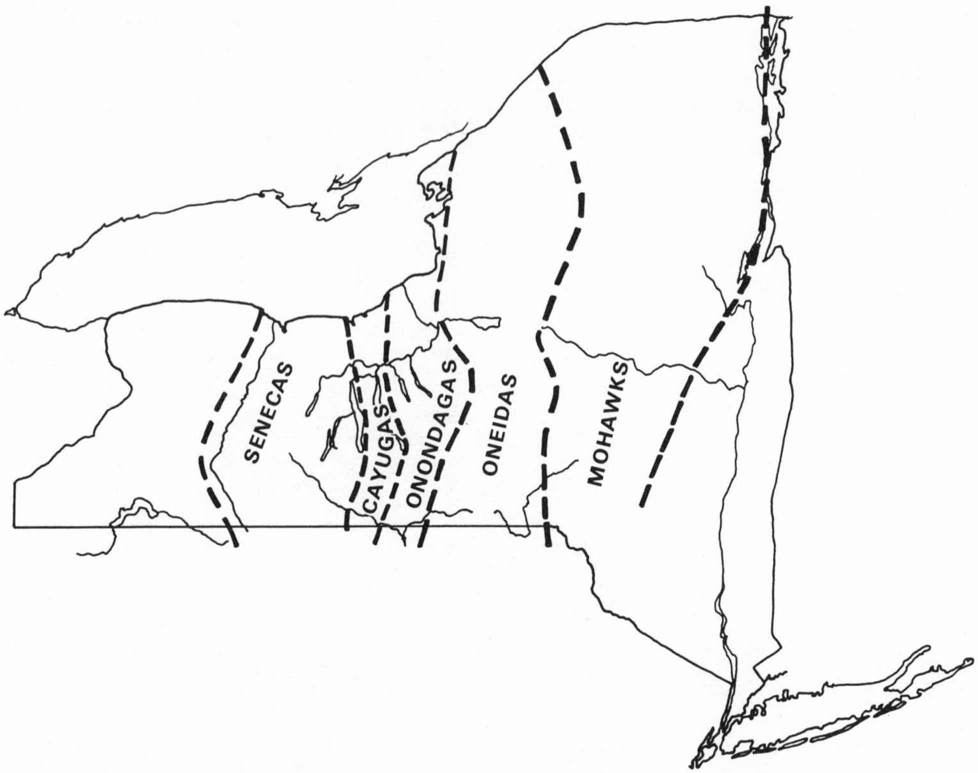

Map 4: Five-nation Iroquois, approximate aboriginal territory, circa 1600

hides—were hunted in late fall and early winter.[6] There also appears to have been a late winter deer hunt, probably during the month of March.[7] Deer hunting not only provided the main supply of meat for the Iroquois but it also furnished raw materials to be used in the manufacture of clothing, footware, shelters, and various technological items. Deer hides and other animal skins were also traded through extensive exchange networks in the Northeast and Ontario.[8] Such trade extended well into the eighteenth century, involving both Indians and Europeans.[9]

Fishing held a prominent place in the subsistence behavior of the Northern Iroquois[10] and contributed a significant, seasonal source of protein to the diet. A considerable range of fish species was available to and exploited by Indian populations.[11] In addition, documentary evidence suggests that fish were also a trade item. In the journal of Harmen Meyndertsz van den Bogaert, written during the winter of 1634–35 while he was traveling from Fort Orange into the Mohawk Valley, Oneida women were observed trading Atlantic salmon (*Salmo salar*) with the Mohawk.[12] These anadromous fish are known to have ascended the Oswego and Oneida Rivers and numerous other tributaries to the St. Lawrence River and Lake Ontario. They were not found in the Mohawk River.

In addition to farming, hunting, and fishing, the Iroquois also exploited wild plant resources. These included seasonally available berries, nuts, and other foods. However, gathered foods such as these were probably a minor part of the overall Iroquois diet.[13]

The population of each Iroquois tribe lived in villages in proximity to their cultivated fields. The typical village consisted of a cluster of traditional Iroquois dwellings called longhouses often surrounded by a palisade. Sizes of villages varied, ranging from small hamlets of several houses, less than one acre in extent, to large, densely populated communities of thirty, forty, or more dwellings occupying six or more acres. Populations within communities varied, of course, ranging from one or two hundred individuals to several hundred, some villages approaching two thousand inhabitants.[14] Village locations shifted periodically throughout the settlement area of any one Iroquois tribe. The necessity and timing of such movements were dependent upon several factors, some more significant than others. Soil productivity may have been the most important determinant. That is, a fall in crop production related to the exhaustion of arable lands would be a reason for a village moving to a new location to take advantage of either previously uncultivated land or land that had lain fallow. Other possi-

village location based on soil and defense

ble causes include the depletion of local sources of firewood, con-
flagrations, the deterioration of houses and surrounding palisades,
chronic warfare, the accumulation of refuse, insect infestation of fields,
the scarcity of game, and others.[15] It appears, however, that choices
dictating village locations were predicated primarily upon the concerns
of soil productivity, and defensibility.[16]

The number of villages occupied by each of the Iroquois tribes
varied for reasons tied to population size and distribution, resource
availability, quality and quantity of arable lands, warfare, sociopolitical
constraints, and ideological concerns. For example, during the protohistoric and historic period, reported numbers of Mohawk villages
range from two or three to as high as eight.[17] Similar shifts in numbers
of villages during these periods are apparent among the other Iroquois
tribes as well.[18]

Given the labor-intensive requirements and spatial-temporal constraints of horticulture, Iroquois populations remained in or around
their villages for a considerable part of the year. Nonetheless, the
scheduling of hunting and fishing activities operated to disperse a
majority of the population into the deep woods on a seasonal basis.
Fenton[19] notes that "after the harvest, hunting parties of men and a few
women abandoned the villages, leaving the old people, some pregnant
women, and children, and walked several days into the forest where
they set up camp to hunt deer and bear, dry the meat, and pack it
home at midwinter." At times, parties of men remained in the woods
for weeks.[20]

TERRITORIALITY

Requirements and constraints influencing choices for village locations, resource distribution and availability, and the conditions set by
the populations themselves, all functioned, to varying degrees, in
establishing tribal territories and their attendant boundaries. Territory
is defined here as "an area occupied more or less exclusively by an
individual or group by means of repulsion through overt defense or
some form of communication."[21] Communication refers to the use of
symbols, signs, or signals to convey information—in this case, information regarding territory and boundaries. For instance, it can be used

Map 5: Oneida aboriginal territory, circa 1600, with present-day counties

by a group in claiming boundaries, or it can be an indicator of the acknowledgment of these boundaries by adjacent or otherwise non-member groups. A case in point concerns the Oneida Indians (see Map 5) and the 1784 Treaty of Fort Stanwix. On September 4, 1784. Governor Clinton of New York addressed the Oneida chiefs and warriors requesting that they provide him with the "Metes and Bounds of their territory.[22] The Oneida, in turn, described and communicated in detail both their east and west boundaries to the governor, clearly identifying their tribal territory.[23]

Initially, the establishment of tribal territories can be approached from the point of view of operating ecological variables. For the purposes of this chapter, a model focusing on "economic defendability" is considered.[24] According to this model, "Territoriality is expected to occur when critical resources are sufficiently abundant and predictable in space and time, so that costs of exclusive use and defense of an area are outweighed by the benefits gained from resource control."[25] The issue of resource predictability is a critical one, since those that are predictable in their overall availability have greater economic defendability.

The abundance and density of resources are also factors in defining economic defendability. In the model, resource density refers to *effective density*, and not absolute abundance or even carrying capacity. For example, a given area may have a higher biomass of a particular small mammal than of large game; however, the human population would instead direct its efforts toward exploiting the large game and with greater efficiency. Thus, the large game would be at a greater effective density than that of the small mammals.[26]

Clearly, the human population is involved in making choices regarding not only the exploitation of game, e.g., game preferences, but also as they reflect considerations associated with horticulture, choices that may or may not be fully understood or appreciated by the outside observer. The understanding of the environment by the observer—the historian, anthropologist, or wildlife specialist—is likely to be different from that of the native. Traditionally, the analyses of archaeological sites and their location in terms of subsistence have been predicated on the assumption that we, the researchers, have an essentially complete knowledge of environmental details and that this was also the case for the sites' inhabitants. This is not always true.[27]

Following logically from this model is the issue of competition over resources as a factor in the establishment and maintenance of bounded territories. Although Trigger[28] has denied there was competition among Iroquoians in terms of arable land and hunting territories, especially prior to contact, the reverse may have been true. For example, Gramly[29] has argued that conflict and the need for defense among protohistoric horticulturalists in the Northeast arose in response to competition for deer hides, a source of clothing, meat, and other items. If this was the case, hunting territories must have been defined, bounded areas, established and defended by a particular population while recognized by others. This would assure that resource requirements of a given group would be met. Such concern over availability of resources would have also extended to fishing.

Competition for arable lands is a somewhat more difficult question. Although there was apparently no shortage of farmland in New York State from any manner of objective judgement, major alluvial valleys containing the most productive soils were limited. Further-more, from an emic perspective, that is, one based on the world view of the Iroquois, all cultivated land may have been perceived as being in short supply and a valuable, finite resource. At the same time, given the high labor costs, time, and energy investment required of hor-ticulture, field areas may have been seen not only as a limited resource, but one demanding defense.

[margin note: horticulture is finite resource]

Following the arrival of the Europeans and the almost immediate and pervasive involvement of the Iroquois in the fur trade, it is likely that aboriginal settlement and land use areas, i.e., hunting territories, were even more precisely defined and vigorously defended. Competi-tion over the available but fast-dwindling fur resources would have been increased greatly, further justifying the establishment of tribal boundaries.[30]

Finally, tribal territories may have functioned as a means of ethnic boundary maintenance. Territorial contiguity is one of the markers of a tribe,[31] a "cultunit" as defined by Naroll,[32] and/or an ethnic unit.[33] As such, it assists in the identification of the group in terms of its self-perception, group identity, and levels of inclusiveness and exclusiveness in terms of membership. Thus, the establishment and maintenance of tribal boundaries would have operated as one of several structural elements employed to define the group.

ABORIGINAL TITLE

[handwritten note: Aboriginal title → land discovery and use]

Aboriginal title, as a legal theory, is derived partly from "com-mon law feudal concept"[34] and partly from seventeenth-century Spanish theology and evolving international law as attributed to Fran-cisco de Vitoria.[35] It is generally defined as equitable title based upon the actual, exclusive, and continuous use and occupancy of a definable area of land for a long time period, usually phrased as "from time immemorial."[36]

American legal history points to the fact that, following the doctrine of discovery, actual title was vested in the European govern-ment whose agents or officials discovered the land. That is, the sov-ereign, the European discoverer, held full title to all aboriginal lands, while at the same time recognizing a right of occupancy by the

[handwritten note: europeans argue it is theirs]

Indians. Thus, the Supreme Court has found that European sovereigns held "ultimate dominion" in the land "subject only to the Indian right of occupancy."[37]

Following the formation of the United States, it was concluded by the court that "only the United States could extinguish the tribal right of occupancy, and the tribes had no independent power to sell and convey their aboriginal homelands . . . without approval of the sovereign."[38]

The principles of aboriginal title as they have evolved legally have recently been summarized in *Oneida Indian Nation v. County of Oneida* (414 U.S. 661 [1974]):

> It very early became accepted doctrine in this Court that although fee title to the lands occupied by Indians when the colonists arrived became vested in the sovereign—first the discovering European nation and later the original States and the United States—a right of occupancy in the Indian tribes was nevertheless recognized. That right, sometimes called Indian title and good against all but the sovereign, could be terminated only by sovereign act . . . Indian title, recognized to be only a right of occupancy, was extinguishable only by the United States.[39]

A large number of land claims cases brought before courts in the United States have dealt with the issue of aboriginal title and the ways in which aboriginal title must be proved.[40] Cohen[41] summarizes these proofs as follows:

> In order to prove aboriginal possession, a tribe must prove actual, rather than constructive, possession of the land in question. The occupation shown must have been continuous and exclusive unless it was during a period of forcible, involuntary dispossession. Land used seasonally for recurring hunting or similar purposes is subject to aboriginal claims, but lands that were simultaneously travelled over or hunted by many tribes are not subject to original Indian title. Thus, tribal occupancy of the claimed area generally must be shown to have been exclusive of other Indian groups. Proof that two or more tribes jointly and amicably occupied the land to the exclusion of other tribal groups, however, will demonstrate original Indian title jointly in such tribes. Although proof of original Indian title must show a substantial period of exclusive occupancy the fact that the occupancy commenced after discovery

or after the assertion of territorial claims by European powers does not defeat the Indian title.

TERRITORIAL CONCEPTS

From the outset, it must be stressed that there is a distinction to be drawn when considering concepts of land use, possession, occupancy, and territoriality in terms of the perceptions of Anglo-Saxons (Europeans) and Indians (Native Americans). For Europeans of the modern era, land (i.e., real estate or territory) is allocated through strict economic modes of transfer; for example, conveyances such as sale, lease, assignment, mortgage, deed, and contract. Warfare as a form of acquisition is not considered here. It is also noted that the forms of land transfer listed above require the establishment of clear, inflexible and demarked boundaries.

Also explicit in the European concept of land use is the recognition of ownership. In short, land is a commodity that is parceled out through conveyances, for a specified value in money or its equivalent, and then regarded as "owned" or property by an individual, groups of individuals, or some other sociopolitical or economic unit. Essentially, it is property that can be purchased, sold, or otherwise transferred.

Among horticulturalists like the northern Iroquoians, land is not regarded as real estate, or in any sense real property. It cannot be bought or sold, nor is it regarded as being owned by anyone, whether an individual, groups of individuals, or otherwise. It is not property, personal or public. In general, land tenure among horticulturalists and other small-scale societies, both egalitarian and ranked, is seen as the geographical expression of social structure.[42] Land is thus allocated as an extension of kinship through the social structure in what is termed "usufructuary privilege."[43] Usufruct in anthropology is defined as "use-right."[44] Simply stated, individuals or groups of individuals have rights to use or extract resources from and within a given territory, although there is no direct ownership of the territory. Instead, land is held communally, with benefits and burdens shared by all in the society.[45]

In horticultural societies where there is tribal organization, the economy is embedded in institutions such as the family, the lineage,

usufruct

and the clan, again functioning as an expression or extension of the kinship and social structure. In most instances, the family constitutes the fundamental economic unit exercising its usufructuary privileges in the production of goods. However, above the family are larger corporate groups, and ultimately the tribe, that discharge a proprietary or controlling function over territory and thus resources. "Proprietary," in this sense, pertains to rights of access in terms of both territory and resources, not ownership as recognized by Europeans. Instead, rights to land and its resources, controlled by the corporate group, are dictated and defined through membership in that group.

The governance of rights of access to territory is acknowledged not only by the members of the controlling corporate group, but, importantly, by adjacent populations not affiliated with the group. For example, control of the rights of access to the territory and thus the resources of the Mohawk, Oneida, Onondaga, and other Iroquois tribes was recognized by surrounding populations. At the same time, each of these groups was cognizant of the boundaries of those tribes that surrounded them.

That territoriality and a concept of boundaries existed in the manner described among northern Iroquoians is demonstrated clearly in Bruce Trigger's *The Children of Aataentsic*, an ethnohistory of the Huron. In his discussions of Cartier's voyages in 1534, 1535, and 1541, Trigger[46] describes well the conflict between European and Indian concepts of territory. In Gaspé Harbor, Cartier had erected a cross bearing the coat of arms of his king. Donnacona, head man of the Stadaconans, a group of St. Lawrence Iroquoians, reacted angrily to the fact that the French were presuming to use land that was not theirs without first acquiring the right to do so. In another instance, Cartier's sailors constructed a small fort on the St. Charles River, this being a still greater infringement on land belonging to Donnacona's people. Another serious provocation to the Indians resulted from Cartier's building of the settlement he named Charlesbourg-Royal. This was done without asking permission or acquiring use of the land from the Stadaconans. In a final example,[47] Cartier decided to travel farther inland through the territory of the Stadaconans to that of the Hochelagans. Donnacona's territorial rights were again infringed upon since Cartier had not requested permission to pass through one group's territory in order to get to another's.

The boundaries mentioned above are by no means equivalent to those generally established by Europeans in their delineation or definition of territory or property. To Europeans, territorial boundaries

$10^{-6} \rightarrow$ micro (μ)

$10^{-3} \rightarrow$ milli (m)

$10^{3} \rightarrow$ kilo (k)

$10^{6} \rightarrow$ mega (M)

$10^{9} \rightarrow$ giga (G)

$10^{12} \rightarrow$ tera (T)

$10^{-15} \rightarrow$ femto (f)

recognized or claimed by Indians may have appeared vague and imprecise. However, this does not obviate the existence of boundaries and territories. For the most part, the "vagueness" perceived by Europeans was a result of the difference in view expressed by them and the Indians.

To the Indian, land is a part of the total environment in which they live, which includes not only the physical domain, but also the supernatural. It is the resources provided by the land that are of importance, not land per se. Developing from this environmental perspective are concepts of territorial boundaries.

As described by Lewis Henry Morgan in his *League of the Iroquois*,[48] boundaries between the various Iroquois tribes were delineated by and associated with various environmental phenomena. For example, when boundaries are discussed they are invariably expressed in terms of waterways, i.e., rivers, lakes, and streams. Fenton[49] points to Morgan and other historical evidence in his descriptions of Iroquois tribal boundaries that are also defined by waterways and watersheds. The point here is that among the Iroquois and other horticultural groups, boundaries recognized by the population are generally delineated by localities such as streams, ridges, and valleys. These are ecologically specific designations relating to environmental zones. For the Indian, such locales might be expressed as "the area where (such-and-such river) flows," or "the area where (such-and-such lake) where we fish flows," or "the area where (such-and-such a forest-type) grows," etc. Given these kinds of descriptors or designators, it follows that borders cannot have sharp edges or in fact be fence or line-like boundaries. Instead, there will be some blurring due to the morphology of the ecologically specific areas. In addition to separating hunting territories, boundaries established for the various Iroquois tribes assured the social individuality and political autonomy of each group.[50]

Land use in terms of the exploitation of resources in the production of goods among horticulturalists varies. Therefore, perceptions of land and land use by the Indian, control of rights of access and allocation of such rights by the tribe as a corporate group, and the exercising of usufructuary privileges, will also vary. For example, arable, cultivated land—Iroquois gardens, if you will—were managed differently from fishing or hunting territories. The control of horticultural production was in the hands of the women. They formed work parties that were directed by a senior matron operating on the principle of mutual aid.[51] Parcels of land within the cornfields were designated as being for the use of the tribe or clan, although individuals were allowed to cultivate crops as long as they carried out their tasks for the various corporate groups.[52] Cultivated fields were rather circumscribed areas, of necessity being close to the villages.

Fishing was the responsibility of men. Areas where fish were taken were often near the villages, although extensive and highly productive fisheries were frequently at a distance, certainly well beyond those areas designated as cultivated fields. For example, the Oneida were known to have fished the areas around Oneida Lake and also the Oneida and Oswego Rivers where they caught salmon.[53] Oneida fishing parties would have had to travel anywhere from five to fifteen miles or farther to reach these fishing grounds. The Mohawk, with their villages situated in the middle Mohawk Valley, often journeyed to the Otsego Lake region, some twenty-five miles distant, to fish.[54]

Hunting, and its emphasis on white-tailed deer, was of major importance to all of the Iroquois tribes. Next to domesticated crops, it provided the largest contribution to the subsistence base. In addition to being the critical subsistence item, deer were the symbol of men's labor and the emblem of the chiefs.[55] Thus, as an essential and predictable resource,[56] white-tailed deer, along with other animals,[57] would have been exploited from a region defined as the "hunting territory."

For Northern Iroquoians, hunting territories would have included primarily those regions at a distance from the villages that were controlled by the tribe. The size of the hunting territory would be regulated by a number of variables including human population size; environmental carrying capacity; variety, abundance, predictability, and density of required resources; and the dynamics of surrounding populations.

Accordingly, bounding aboriginal territory can be approached in a number of ways. Initially, any definition or identification of territory must take into account both the "settlement area" of the population in question, and the "land use area." The settlement area includes the zone immediately around the villages of the tribe—the fields, fishing sites, summer camps, and, of course, the villages themselves. Since villages were moved periodically, the settlement area is a zone of shifting location and boundaries, and includes isolated dwellings or hamlets outside the village complex. Outside of the settlement area is the second zone, the land use area, which produced most of the meat, furs, and other non-horticultural consumables. There probably did not exist a clear demarcation between these areas, nor was one area more highly prized or valued than the other. Both were necessary and integral to Iroquois adaptations and subsistence strategies. This view is roughly analogous to Linton's[58] "home range" and "extended range" concept, while at the same time, it fits, to a degree, the site catchment area or approach used in archaeological studies.[59]

DEER AND HUNTING TERRITORIES

The following is an example of one way in which aboriginal territory can be defined using some of the concepts and data sets discussed to this point. It involves an assessment of the requirements of a human population for white-tailed deer and the dynamics of a given deer herd.

White-tailed deer are universally regarded as a critical resource for northern Iroquoian populations. This is because they are clearly the major source of meat protein and also provide the raw material from which clothing, footwear, and other technological items are man-ufactured. Gramly[60] has argued that human population size and its requirements for clothing, hunting territory, and availability of deer are closely linked. He also furnishes some details regarding these factors. For example, he notes that for the Huron, every individual would need 3.4 deer skins per year in order to be adequately clothed. Working from this figure, a formula can be developed that leads to an estimate of required hunting territory, thus aboriginal territory.

In this illustration, a hypothetical tribe of Indians in New York State has a population of one thousand individuals. If each person required 3.4 deer skins for clothing, then the total demand to be met for a single year would be thirty-four hundred hides or deer. Starna and Relethford[61] have recently analyzed deer herd dynamics and compiled deer density statistics for New York State. Using their figures, which are regarded to be appropriate for the late prehistoric period, the mean deer density for the state is 3.21 deer per square kilometer. Assuming a culling rate or kill rate of 31 percent of a herd derived from the Huron data,[62] hunting territory can be derived. Thus, the yearly demand of thirty-four hundred deer for one thousand people, using the 31 percent culling rate, results in a total deer population of approximately eleven thousand. Applying the density figure of 3.21 deer per square kilometer to this produces a required hunting area of about thirty-four hundred square kilometers or 1360 square miles. This area would also represent the aboriginal territory. Specific boundaries and their locations would have to be determined through an analysis of materials on adjacent populations as well as the one in question.

[handwritten margin note: 1360 mi² ↓ aboriginal territory]

CONCLUSION

The information and concepts discussed in this paper can be brought to bear to establish the boundaries or configurations of land claims related to the issue of aboriginal title. That is, to one degree or another, the "proofs" of aboriginal title as outlined by Cohen[63] and others[64] can be approached using the same or similar sets of data as presented here. I hasten to add that none of this methodology is new. It has generally been identified in the literature as "ecological theory" or an "ecological model," and was applied extensively in land claims brought before the Indian Claims Commission in the 1950s.[65]

This ecological model employs a complex of factors that functions to establish territorial boundaries for the purposes of any specific group. The purposes are group-specific, and also ecologically specific, given the fact that each discrete Indian population was adapted to, and functioned within, a known and well-defined environmental zone. Thus, for the Jicarilla Apaches,[66] such factors included the explication of hunting patterns, preferred game, the agricultural system, plant habitats, settlements, trade, social networks, and subsistence ecology. In isolating and defining these factors for use in interpreting and delineating boundaries and territories, historical, archaeological, geographical, ethnological, environmental, biological, and other lines of evidence can and have been used with success.[67]

Delineating the boundaries of a particular Indian tribe for the purposes of an aboriginal claim is a difficult but not insoluble problem. It involves the gathering, evaluating, and synthesizing of data from many different sources that were compiled for many different reasons. At the same time, there is the requirement of translating these data into a form that is understandable and meaningful to the court. This latter task may be the most formidable of all.

NOTES

1. Clark M. Sykes, "Swidden Horticulture and Iroquoian Settlement," *Archaeology of Eastern North America* 8 (1980):45; D. R. Harris, "Swidden Systems and Settlement," in *Man, Settlement, and Urbanism*, ed. P. J. Ucko, R. Tringham, and G. W. Dimbleby (London: Duckworth, 1972), 246.

2. F. W. Waugh, *Iroquois Food and Food Preparation* (Ottawa: National Museums of Canada, 1916); Geological Survey Memoir 86, Anthropological Series 12; Arthur C. Parker, "Iroquois Uses of Maize and Other Food Plants," *New York State Museum Bulletin* 144 (482) (1910): 5–113.

3. Conrad Heidenreich, *Huronia: A History and Geography of the Huron Indians, 1600–1650* (Toronto: McClelland and Stewart, 1971), 163.

4. William N. Fenton, "Northern Iroquoian Culture Patterns," in *Handbook of North American Indians, the Northeast* 15, Bruce G. Trigger, ed. (Washington, D.C.: Smithsonian Institution, 1978), 298.

5. Donald K. Grayson, "The Riverhaven No. 2 Vertebrate Fauna: Comments on Methods in Faunal Analysis and on Aspects of the Subsistence Potential of New York," *Man in the Northeast* (1974) 8:23–40.

6. Cf. Elisabeth Tooker, *An Ethnography of the Huron Indians, 1615–1649* (Washington, DC: Bureau of American Ethnology, 1964), Bulletin 190, 65; Heidenreich, *Huronia* 205; Michael R. Gramly, "Deerskins and Hunting Territories: Competition for a Scarce Resource of the Northeastern Woodlands," *American Antiquity* 42, 4 (1977): 601–5; Fenton, "Northern Iroquois Culture Patterns," 300–301; Samuel Kirkland, *The Journals of Samuel Kirkland*, ed. W. Pilkington (Clinton, N. Y.: Hamilton College, 1980), 180.

7. Heidenreich, *Huronia*, 205; Bruce G. Trigger, *The Children of Aataentsic: A History of the Huron People to 1660*, 2 vols. (Montreal: McGill-Queen's University Press, 1976), 39; Kirkland, *Journals of Samuel Kirkland*, 104.

8. Bruce G. Trigger, "Settlement as an Aspect of Iroquoian Adaptation at the Time of Contact," *American Anthropologist* 65, no. 1 (1963): 86–101; Donald Lenig, "Of Dutchmen, Beaver Hats and Iroquois," in *Current Perspectives in Northeastern Archaeology: Essays in Honor of William A. Ritchie*, ed. R. E. Funk and C. F. Hayes III (Rochester: New York State Archaeological Association, 1977), Researches and Transactions 17, no. 1, 71–84; Heidenreich, *Huronia*.

9. Edmund B. O'Callaghan, ed., *Documents Relative to the Colonial History of the State of New York* (Albany: Weed, Parsons, 1853–1887), 6:709.

10. Cf. Trigger, *Children of Aataentsic*; Heidenreich, *Huronia*; Fenton, "Northern Iroquois Culture Patterns"; William N. Fenton, "Fish Drives among the Cornplanter Senecas," *Pennsylvania Archaeologist* 12, no. 3 (1942): 48–52.

11. Cf. William A. Ritchie, *The Archaeology of New York State* (New York: Natural History Press, 1969); William A. Ritchie and Robert E. Funk, *Aboriginal Settlement Patterns in the Northeast* (Albany: New York State Museum and Science Service, 1973), Memoir 20; William A. Starna and Robert E. Funk, "Floral and Faunal Resource Potential for Prehistoric Human Groups in the Upper Susquehanna Valley of New York State," in *Upper Susquehanna Prehistory*, Robert E. Funk, ed. (Albany: New York State Museum and Science Service, in press); William A. Starna, "Late Archaic Lifeways in the Middle Mohawk Valley: A Framework for Further Study," Ph.D. dissertation, State University of New York, Albany (Ann Arbor: University Micro-

46   WILLIAM A. STARNA

films, 1976); J. R. Greeley, "Fishes of the Watershed with Annotated List," in *A Biological Survey of the Mohawk-Hudson Watershed*, ed. C. W. Greene (Albany: New York State Conservation Department, 1934), Supplemental to the Twenty-fourth Annual Report.

12. F. J. Jameson, ed., "Narrative of a Journey into the Mohawk and Oneida Country, 1634–1635," in *Narratives of New Netherland 1609–1664* (New York: Charles Scribner's Sons, 1909), 135–162; Charles T. Gehring and William A. Starna, "A Journey into Mohawk and Oneida Country: The Journal of Harmen Meyndertsz van den Bogaert," ms. in author's possession.

13. Cf. Heidenreich, *Huronia*, 164.

14. William N. Fenton, "Problems Arising from the Historic Northeastern Position of the Iroquois," in *Essays in Historical Anthropology of North America* (Washington, DC: Smithsonian Institution, 1940), Miscellaneous Collections 100, pp. 159–252; Thomas S. Abler, "Longhouse and Palisade: Northern Iroquoian Villages of the Seventeenth Century," *Ontario History* 62 (1970): 17–40; Heidenreich, *Huronia*; William D. Finlayson, *The 1975 and 1978 Rescue Excavations at the Draper Site: Introduction and Settlement Patterns* (Ottawa: National Museum of Man, 1985), Mercury Series, Archaeological Survey of Canada Paper 130; William A. Starna, "Mohawk Iroquois Populations: A Revision," *Ethnohistory* 24, no. 4 (1980): 371–82.

15. William A. Starna, George R. Hamell, and William L. Butts, "Northern Iroquoian Horticulture and Insect Infestation: A Cause for Village Removal," *Ethnohistory* 31, no. 3 (1984): 197–207; Heidenreich, *Huronia*; Abler, "Longhouse and Palisade."

16. Cf. Stanley C. Bond, Jr., "The Relationship between Soils and Settlement Patterns in the Mohawk Valley," in *The Mohawk Valley Project: 1982 Field Season Report*, ed. D. R. Snow (Albany: State University of New York, 1985), The Institute for Northeastern Anthropology, 17–40.

17. Starna 1980, "Mohawk Iroquois Populations"; Fenton 1940, "Problems Arising"; (Rev.) Thomas Grassmann, *The Mohawk Indians and Their Valley, Being a Chronological Documentary Record to the End of 1693* (Schenectady: Eric Hugo Photography and Printing, 1969); Lenig, "Of Dutchmen."

18. Cf. Fenton 1940, "Problems Arising"; Mary Ann Palmer Niemczycki, *The Origin and Development of the Seneca and Cayuga Tribes of New York State* (Rochester: Rochester Museum and Science Center, 1984), Research Records no. 17; Peter P. Pratt, *Archaeology of the Oneida Iroquois* 1 (George's Mills, N. H.: Man in the Northeast, 1976), Occasional Publications in Northeastern Anthropology, no. 1; James A. Tuck, *Onondaga Iroquois Prehistory* (Syracuse: Syracuse University Press, 1971).

19. Fenton 1978, "Northern Iroquoian Culture Patterns," 298.

20. Cf. Trigger 1976, *Children of Aataentsic*.

21. Rada Dyson-Hudson and Eric Alden Smith, "Human Territoriality: An Ecological Reassessment," *American Anthropologist* 80 (1978): 22; cf. Torsten Malmberg, *Human Territoriality* (New York: Mouton, 1980), 9–11.

22. Franklin B. Hough, *Proceedings of the Commissioners of Indian Affairs Appointed by Law for the Extinguishment of Indian Titles in the State of New York*, 2 vols. (Albany: Joel Munsell, 1861), 1:41.

23. Ibid.

24. Dyson-Hudson and Smith, "Human Territoriality."

25. Ibid., 21.

26. Ibid., 25.

27. Mitchell T. Mulholland and William A. Starna, "Temperate Forest Subsistence and Settlement: A Reassessment," in *Proceedings of the Conference on Northeastern Archaeology*, James A. Moore, ed. (Amherst: University of Massachusetts, 1980), Research Reports no. 19, 149–53.

28. Bruce G. Trigger, *The Huron: Farmers of the North* (New York: Holt, Rinehart and Winston, 1969); Trigger 1976, *Children of Aataentsic*.

29. Gramly, "Deerskins and Hunting Territories."

30. Cf. George T. Hunt, *The Wars of the Iroquois: A Study in Intertribal Trade Relations* (Madison: University of Wisconsin Press, 1940); George S. Snyderman, "Behind the Tree of Peace: A Sociological Analysis of Iroquois Warfare," *Pennsylvania Archaeologist* 18, nos. 3 and 4 (1948): 3–93; Trigger 1976, *Children of Aataentsic*.

31. Lewis H. Morgan, *Ancient Society, or Researches in the Lines of Human Progress from Savagery through Barbarism to Civilization* (New York: Henry Holt, 1877); Franz Boas, *General Anthropology* (New York: Heath, 1938); E. Adamson Hoebel, *Anthropology: The Study of Man* (New York: McGraw-Hill, 1958); Morton H. Fried, *The Notion of Tribe* (Menlo Park, Ca.: Cummings Publishing Company, 1975).

32. Raoul Naroll, "On Ethnic Unit Classification," *Current Anthropology* 5, no. 4 (1964): 283–312.

33. Cf. Ronald Cohen, "Ethnicity: Problem and Focus in Anthropology," *Annual Review of Anthropology* 7 (1978): 379–403; Ronald A. Remick, *Theory of Ethnicity* (New York: University Press of America, 1983).

34. Felix S. Cohen, "Original Indian Title," *Minnesota Law Review* 32 (1947): 43.

35. Cf. ibid., 28–59; Gordon I. Bennett, "Aboriginal Title in the Common Law: A Stony Path through Feudal Doctrine," *Buffalo Law Review* 27 (1978): 617–35; James Y. Henderson, "Unraveling the Riddles of Aboriginal Title," *American Indian Law Review* 5 (1977): 75–137; Howard R. Berman, "The Concept of Aboriginal Rights in the Early Legal History of the United States," *Buffalo Law Review* 27 (1978): 637–67; Ralph Erickson, "Aboriginal Land Rights in the United States and Canada," *North Dakota Law Review* 60 (1984): 107–39; Nell Jessup Newton, "At the Whim of the Sovereign: Aboriginal Title Reconsidered," *Hastings Law Journal* 31 (1980): 1215–85.

36. Michael J. Kaplan, "Issues in Land Claims: Aboriginal Title," in *Irredeemable America*, Imre Sutton, ed. (Albuquerque: University of New Mexico Press, 1985), 71–86; Erickson, "Aboriginal Land Rights"; Felix S. Cohen; *Handbook of Federal Indian Law* (Charlottesville, Va.: Michie, 1982), 487.

37. 21 U.S. (8 Wheat.) 574 (1823), cited in Cohen 1982, 487.

38. Ibid.

39. Ibid., 488.

40. Cf. *Confederated Tribes of Warm Springs v. United States*, 177 Ct. Cl. 184 (1966); *Swinomish Tribe v. United States*, 26 Ind. Cl. Comm. 371 (1971); *United States ex rel. Hualpai Indians v. Santa Fe Pac. R. R.*, 314 U.S. 339, 345 (1941); *Pawnee Tribe of Oklahoma v. United States*, 1 Ind. Cl. Comm. 245, 262 (1950); *Coos Bay Indian Tribe v. United States*, 87 Ct. Cl. 143, 152, *cert. denied* 306 U.S. 653 (1938).

41. Cohen 1982, p. 492.

42. Manning Nash, *Primitive and Peasant Economic Systems* (Scranton, Pa.: Chandler Publishing Company, 1966).

43. Marshall Sahlins, *Tribesmen* (Englewood Cliffs, N.J.: Prentice-Hall, 1968), 76.

44. Cf. Marshall Sahlins, *Stone Age Economics* (New York: Aldine-Atherton, 1972), 93.

48   WILLIAM A. STARNA

45. Blake A. Watson, "State Acquisition of Interests in Indian Land: An Overview," *American Indian Law Review* 10 (1984): 221–22; Kaplan, "Issues in Land Claims."
46. Trigger, *Children of Aataentsic* 182, 192, 203–4.
47. Ibid., 187.
48. Lewis H. Morgan, *League of the Iroquois* (New York: Corinth, 1962).
49. Fenton 1940, "Problems Arising."
50. Morgan 1962, 47.
51. Cf. Fenton, 1978, "Northern Iroquoian Culture Patterns"; John A. Noon, *Law and Government of the Grand River Iroquois* (New York: Viking Fund, 1949), Publication in Anthropology 12; Parker, "Iroquois Uses of Maize."
52. Ibid.
53. Fenton 1940, "Problems Arising"; Jameson, "Narrative of a Journey"; Gehring and Starna, "A Journey into Mohawk and Oneida Country."
54. William N. Fenton and Elisabeth Tooker, "Mohawk," in *Handbook of North American Indians, the Northeast* 15, Bruce G. Trigger, ed. (Washington, D.C.: Smithsonian Institution, 1978), 466–80.
55. Fenton 1978, "Northern Iroquoian Culture Patterns," 301.
56. William A. Starna and John H. Relethford, "Deer Densities and Population Dynamics: A Cautionary Note," *American Antiquity* 50, no. 4 (1985): 825–32.
57. Cf. Grayson, "Methods in Faunal Analysis."
58. Ralph Linton, *The Study of Man* (New York: Appleton-Century, 1936).
59. Cf. C. Vita-Finzi and E. S. Higgs, "Prehistoric Economy in the Mount Carmel Area of Palestine: Site Catchment Analysis," *Proceedings of the Prehistoric Society* 36 (1970): 1–37; Kent V. Flannery, ed., *The Early Mesoamerican Village* (New York: Academic Press, 1976); Christopher S. Peebles, "The Determinants of Settlement Size and Location in the Moundville Phase," in *Mississippian Settlement Patterns*, Bruce Smith, ed. (New York: Academic Press, 1978), 369–414.
60. Gramly, "Deerskins and Hunting Territories."
61. Starna and Relethford, "Deer Densities."
62. Ibid., 830.
63. Cohen 1982, 492.
64. Cf. Imre Sutton, *Indian Land Tenure* (New York: Clearwater Publishing, 1975); Erickson, "Aboriginal Land Rights."
65. Cf. Imre Sutton, ed., *Irredeemable America* (Albuquerque: University of New Mexico Press, 1985), 137–39; and the following articles therein: Imre Sutton, "Configurations of Land Claims: Toward a Model," 111–32; Ralph L. Beals, "The Anthropologist as Expert Witness: Illustrations from the California Indian Land Claims Case," 139–55; Omer C. Stewart, "The Shoshone Claims Case," 187–206; David J. Wishart, "The Pawnee Claims Case, 1947–1964," 157–86.
66. Sutton 1985, 113; Lynn Price, "Proving Aboriginal Title via Expert Testimony: Lessons from the Indian Claims Commission," *American Indian Journal* 7, no. 2 (1981): 16–24.
67. Sutton 1985, esp. 111–32.

4

From Stanwix to Canandaigua
National Policy, States' Rights and Indian Land

JACK CAMPISI

INTRODUCTION

The signing of the preliminary treaty of peace in 1782 ended hostilities between the United States and Great Britain, but it left unsettled the status of the Indian tribes who had sided with the Crown. To remedy this, the Continental Congress, in October of 1783, took steps to conclude treaties of peace with the still hostile tribes in New York and the Ohio Valley. These efforts, which took ten years to consummate, went far to define the relationship between the new republic and its constituent states, as well as the status of the tribes within the boundaries of the two entities.

If there was a single issue in the period from the formation of the Second Continental Congress to the termination of war with England likely to inflame the oratory, divide the states into bickering adversaries, and raise the hackles of frontiersmen, it was the issue of who owned the western land—more particularly, the land in the Ohio Valley. Several states claimed title to that land by virtue of colonial charters, although the boundaries of their claims were vague and overlapping. By contrast, New York based its claim on a treaty made in 1701 by the Crown with the five Iroquois tribes.[1] The Continental Congress claimed title by virtue of the preliminary treaty of peace wherein Britain ceded its title pretensions. It was this issue that delayed the signing of the Articles of Confederation, and nearly destroyed the fledgling union. Those lands were of course occupied by tribes that also asserted title, and many of these tribes were still in a state of war with the United States.

Before the landless states would approve the Articles, they demanded that those states with land claims outside their accepted boundaries surrender those claims to the national government. The relinquishment of these claims still left several states with large areas of land occupied by Indian tribes within their respective boundaries. The question that arises is what, if any, were the limitations on the authority of a state to extinguish these claims? The answer is crucial to an understanding of the Indian policy as it developed during and immediately after the revolutionary war, and as it was modified after 1789.

What the states and the national government possessed was a right of preemption, the underlying title to Indian land, which derived from the discovery of those lands according to the doctrine of discovery. By the same doctrine of discovery, the sovereign alone could extinguish the tribe's right of occupancy. This right to purchase the tribe's usufruct was essentially a property right that could be, and was, sold by the government. But the power to determine when and under what conditions Indian title would be extinguished rested solely with the sovereign. In short, only when the general government exercised its power to extinguish Indian title could the holder of the right of preemption take possession of the land.

Congressional leaders recognized early that the issues of war and peace and Indian title were intertwined. When establishing the Articles, the Continental Congress sought to deal with these concerns. In Article IX, Clause 1, it reserved to itself ". . . the sole and exclusive right and power of determining on peace and war . . ." and ". . . entering into treaties and alliances . . ."

THE FORMULATION OF A NATIONAL INDIAN POLICY

This understanding of the relationship of peace and land was reinforced by the Committee on Indian Affairs, which in October 1783 issued a report stating in detail the realities that faced the Continental Congress in its impending negotiations with the tribes: that Indian affairs and settlement of the West were "inseparably connected"; that while the tribes were disposed to peace, they were not willing to give up land; and that if another war were to start the United States could drive the Indians out, but could not prevent them from returning without great cost. The committee went on to argue that to drive the Indians out of the United States would be to push them within the jurisdiction of British Canada, ". . . which by so great an accession of strength would become formidable in case of any future rupture, and in peace, by keeping alive the resentment of the Indians for the loss of their country, would secure to its own subjects the entire benefit of the fur trade."[2] The committee recommended a middle ground, one that would satisfy the national requirements for a source of revenue, allow the tribes to retain large areas, and result in the separation of the Indian tribes from the American communities. The committee recommended ". . . that lines of property should be ascertained and established between the United States and them, which will be convenient to the respective tribes, and commensurate to the public wants, because the faith of the United States stands pledged to grant portions of the uncultivated lands as a bounty to their army."[3] Thus while the United States waived its right of conquest, it expected the hostile tribes to make atonement for the expenses and losses incurred by the United States during the war by accepting the proposed boundaries.[4]

Having said that, the committee recommended that a series of treaties be held to receive ". . . them into the favor and protection of the United States . . .," adjust the boundaries ". . . separating and dividing the settlements of the citizens from the Indian villages and hunting grounds, and thereby extinguishing as far as possible all occasion for future animosities, disquiet and contention."[5]

Exercising its treaty-making power, the Congress appointed three commissioners in 1784 to negotiate peace with the hostile tribe on terms dictated by Congress. Early in the summer of that year the three commissioners—Arthur Lee, Richard Butler, and Oliver Wolcott—informed Governor Clinton of New York, and the leaders of the four hostile Iroquois tribes—the Seneca, Onondaga, Cayuga, and Mohawk—of their intention to hold a council that fall at Fort Stanwix to bring the war to an end. They also warned the state and the Iroquois tribes that any treaty made with the state involving land transactions would be void. New York ignored the warning, insulted the commissioners, defied their request for troops to protect them while at Fort Stanwix, and in general proceeded against the national interests. Writing to the commissioners appointed by the Congress, Governor Clinton made clear his position that the state alone was sovereign within its borders with respect to the Iroquois.

The Indians of the six Nations, whom I have requested to convene at Fort Schuyler [Fort Stanwix], have advised me that they will be accompanied by Deputies from other Nations possessing the Territory within the Jurisdiction of the United States; I shall have no Objection to your improving this Incident to the advantage of the United States, expecting however and positively stipulating that no Agreement be entered into with Indians, residing within the Jurisdiction of this State (and with whom only I mean to treat) prejudicial to its Right.[6]

Jacob Reed, writing to Washington, expressed the sense of the Continental Congress's indignation at New York's actions:

What think you of the State of New York undertaking to hold a treaty of its own authority with the six Nations in defiance of our Resolves and the Clause of the Confederation restricting the individual States. The Governor is actually now at Albany for the purpose. Such a step will render all our endeavours abortive and be attended with worse consequences with respect to the Indians than almost any other state could take—tis said to be under an expressed law of the State. If this Conduct is to be pursued our Commissioners are rendered useless.[7]

New York's bellicose posture can be attributed to a number of factors. First and foremost was the fact that the state had the weakest of claims to the land west of the Property Line of 1768. To add to the state's problems, that part of their claim within the present boundaries of New York was disputed by Massachusetts. If the claim of Massachusetts, based as it was on a royal charter, was sustained over the more nebulous claim asserted by New York based on the Treaty of 1701, much of the coveted land would be lost. This opinion was relayed to the governor by the New York delegates to the Continental Congress. They told him: "It appears to us that the Delegates in general have not an over high opinion of the Validity of our Western Claim, and we are persuaded that should the Massachusetts People once get a footing in that Country our State in that case is to expect little aid from Congress."[8] If congressional negotiators were allowed to deal with the Iroquois tribes, New York would lose much of its assumed authority in the area.

The state officials knew that if they did not act swiftly to establish sovereignty over the Iroquois tribes, they would lose any opportunity

to take their lands. They had been warned by their delegate to the
Continental Congress, James Duane, that ". . . if the Tribes are to be
considered as independent Nations, detached from the State, and
absolutely unconnected with it, the Claim of Congress would be
incontrovertible."9 The claim in question was the power to determine
when Indian land rights could be purchased by the state. To affix the
tribes to the state, and strengthen its land claims, New York embarked
on a policy to make the tribes "Members of the State."10 Governor
Clinton moved quickly to secure the state's interests. In April 1784 he
sent a message to the Mohawks, Onondagas, Cayugas, and Senecas
inviting them to a meeting to adjust all differences between them and
the state and the Oneidas and Tuscaroras.11 After an exchange of
letters, a meeting was set for late August at Fort Stanwix.

The state's treaty council accomplished little. One of its objectives
was to convince the Oneidas to sell their land to the state and move to
land owned by the Seneca, a suggestion that even the New York
commissioners found so unpalatable that they refused to bring it to the
attention of the Oneidas. However, the Oneidas had been made aware
of the governor's intention by their minister, Samuel Kirkland,12 so
when the governor met with the Oneidas on the fourth of September,
all he could do was deny the allegation. "Brothers," he told them, "We
have been informed that some designing Persons have endeavoured to
persuade You that We mean to take away your lands. This is not true;
You must not believe it. We have no Claim on your Lands: its just
extent will ever remain secured to You. . . ."13 All the state desired of
the Oneidas, the governor said, was to know the extent of their
domain. The Oneidas obliged by describing a strip of land extending
fifty or so miles from the Unadilla River to the Owego River in the
west and from the Pennsylvania border on the south to Lake Ontario
and the St. Lawrence River in the north.14

Having failed to secure any concessions from the Oneidas, the
governor and the other New York commissioners moved on to their
meetings with the other Iroquois tribes led by Joseph Brant. They
were no more successful, the governor being unable to get either land
cessions or recognition of the state's sovereignty. Worst of all, he was
unable to prevent the tribes from meeting with the United States
commissioners. The council ended on the tenth of September without
achieving a single objective of the state. The governor, apprehensive
over the upcoming council between the tribes and the United States,
left a representative behind to observe, and if the parties took any
actions detrimental to the interests of the state, he was to use his ". . .

best Endeavours to counteract and frustrate"[15] the United States commissioners.

The national commissioners opened the treaty negotiations on October 3, 1784, again cautioning the tribes that no state had the right to buy Indian land without congressional permission.[16] The proceedings were then delayed a few days while the commissioners awaited the representative of the Six Nations of Canada, Aaron Hill. Hill arrived on October 8 and four days later made his greetings and apologies to the commissioners. On the seventeenth the work of the council began with a speech by Hill in which, after repeating that the purpose of the council was to settle all differences between the four hostile tribes and the United States, he stated their position:

> You also acquainted us that it remained entirely with us whether there should be peace or not, and that it was your wish to establish a lasting peace. I see clearly the purport of your speech and beg your attention to the words of the Warriors for there are no Sachems among us.
> The words of the Warriors are strong. They are persons who have travelled through the world and have borne all the difficulties of the war. It is in their power to make a lasting peace. You told that it was entirely on us to make a lasting peace—but we apprehend that it is equally dependent upon both parties. I speak in the name of the Six Nations and not only in their name but also in the name of all the tribes.[17]

The following day Cornplanter offered, on behalf of the Senecas, a land cession that excluded the Ohio Valley and most of the Seneca lands.

On October 20 the commissioners answered the two speeches. They said they were surprised to find that Hill spoke for all the tribes to the west and south, since "We summoned the Six nations only to this Treaty."[18] The commissioners then rebuked them for their attitude, telling them that they had waged war without provocation, and that their belief that they were a free people was incorrect.

> "Again you are mistaken in supposing that having been excluded from the treaty between the United States and the King of England you are become a free and independent nation and may make what terms you please. It is not so. You are a subdued people. You have been overcome in a war which you entered into

with us, not only without provocation but in violation of the most sacred obligations.[19]

The commissioners then dictated a series of harsh terms to the four hostile tribes. The treaty opened with the following statement: "The United States of America will give peace to the Senecas, Mohawks, Onondagas, and Cayugas, and receive them into their protection upon the following conditions." Those conditions included providing hostages to insure that all prisoners held by the tribes would be returned, the surrender of all land west of a north-south line drawn from Niagara to the Pennsylvania border, and the yielding of Fort Oswego. In return, the United States guaranteed to the four hostile tribes their remaining lands in New York. As to the Oneidas and Tuscaroras, they ". . . shall be secured in the possession of the lands on which they are settled." The commissioners gave as their explanation that "It does not become the United States to forget those nations who preserved their faith to them and adhered to their cause, those, therefore must be secured in the full and free enjoyment of those possessions."[20] It is clear that the United States dealt with independent tribes and not a league or confederacy, and that it differentiated between those who had remained loyal to the united colonies and those who had been hostile. Without other recourse, the chiefs signed the treaty and returned to their homes to face hostile receptions. This treaty was followed in the next year by treaties at Hopewell and Forts Finney and McIntosh. By these treaties the United States sought to end the war with the Ohio tribes, and secure land cessions.

The question must be asked: Besides peace, what did the United States desire from these negotiations, if indeed they may be called that? First, the United States had secured title, or more precisely the right of preemption, to the Ohio Valley by the Treaty of Paris. In order to sell the land and settle it, the Continental Congress needed to extinguish Indian title, including any claims held by the Iroquois tribes of New York. Second, the commissioners wanted to punish the hostile tribes, particularly the Senecas. Thus they forced the Senecas to surrender most of their land within New York to the United States. This was land claimed by Massachusetts and New York. Third, as improbable as it might seem, the United States wanted to insure peace by confirming to the tribes their remaining lands. Fourth, the United States was anxious to protect its frontier from the British in Canada by securing land for forts and roads along lakes Erie and Ontario. Thus, national policy at the end of the war consisted, on the one hand, of treating the tribes as conquered enemies to whom terms could be dictated with impunity, while, on the other hand, assuring the tribes that the Continental Congress would control the avarice of the states.

One may inquire as to the basis for congressional authority to prevent states from purchasing Indian land. The general power of Congress to control relations with Indian tribes derived from Clause 4 of Article IX of the Articles of Confederation, which reads, in part: "The united states in congress assembled shall also have the sole and exclusive right and power of . . . regulating the trade and managing all affairs with Indians not members of any state, provided that the legislative right of any state within its own limits be not infringed or violated."

There are two phrases in this clause that require some explication: "not members of any state," and "the legislative right of any state within its own limits." If the Iroquois tribes were within the limits of New York, how could the United States prevent the state from buying Indian land? The answer to this question hinges on the meaning of the word "members." Madison, writing to Monroe in November of 1784, provides the best explanation of the phrases.

Richmond Novr. 27, 1784

Dear Sir

Your favor of the 15th inst: came to my hand by thursday's post. Mine by the last post acknowledged your preceding one. The umbrage given to the Comsrs. of the U.S. by the negociations of N.Y. with the Indians was not altogether unknown to me, though I am less acquainted with the circumstances of it than your letter supposes. The idea which I at present have of the affair leads me to say that as far as N.Y. may claim a right of treating with Indians for the purchase of lands within her limits, she has the confederation on her side; as far as she may have exerted that right in contravention of the Genl. Treaty, or even unconfidentially with the Commissrs. of Congs. she has violated both duty & decorum. The federal articles give Congs. the exclusive right of managing all affairs with the Indians not members of any State, under a proviso, that the Legislative authority, of the State within its own limits be not violated. By Indian[s] not members of a State, must be meant those, I conceive who do not live within the body of the Society, or whose Persons or property form no objects of its laws. In the case of Indians of this description the only restraint on Congress is imposed by the Legislative authority of the State. If this proviso be taken in its full latitude, it must destroy the authority of Congress altogether, since no act of Congs. within the limits of a State can be conceived which will not in some way or other encroach upon the authority [of the] States. In order to give some meaning to both parts of the sentence, as a known rule of interpretation requires, we must restrain this proviso to some particular view of the parties. What was this view? My answer is that it was to save to the States their right of preemption of lands from the Indians.[21]

Thus a tribe could be within the boundaries of a state, yet not part of it. In this instance, while the state possessed the legislative right (the right of preemption), it could not exercise that right without permission from the Congress.

In the context of the established complimentary principles of the right of discovery, which belonged to the sovereign, and the right of undisturbed use, which belonged to the tribe, the clause would seem to preserve the states' right of preemption without bestowing the power to extinguish. This power resided with the sovereign, in this case the Continental Congress. Preemption was (and is) only a proprietary interest.

Before abandoning its policy of coercion, the United States made one more effort to substantiate its claim to the Ohio Valley. In the fall of 1788, it negotiated another set of treaties with the Iroquois and Ohio Valley tribes at Fort Harmar. Although treaties were eventually signed, they did not resolve the national difficulty.

NEW YORK STATE INDIAN POLICY

The failure of the Iroquois to accept the sovereignty of New York, the refusal of the Oneidas to sell their land, and the actions of the United States commissioners at Fort Stanwix served to intensify New York's efforts to secure title to the western lands. Ignoring the promises it had made to the Oneidas, the state moved in 1785 to force them into a land cession. It called the Oneidas to a meeting at Fort Herkimer in June 1785, and pressured them to sell a tract of land along the New York-Pennsylvania border. The Oneidas informed the state that they had resolved not to sell any land, but to keep it for future generations.

58   JACK CAMPISI

They did, however, offer to lease a portion, which the New York commissioners rejected as an insult. The commissioners then warned the Oneidas that they would not protect them from squatters, and they would hold the Oneidas responsible for any disorder. The Oneidas responded, saying that the state had much unsettled land and that this land was vital to the tribe's survival.[22]

The Oneidas met in private and returned to the council the following day with an offer to sell a strip of land along the Susquehanna River. The governor accepted, but said that because the land was half of what he desired he could not give them all the money he had brought. Good Peter replied that they were selling the land to maintain New York's friendship and not for profit, and that this was the last sale they would make. The following year the Oneidas relinquished the counties of Chenango, Broome, and Tioga for the sum of $11,500 in goods and cash.[23]

When Massachusetts found out that New York had purchased land west of the Property Line of 1768, land that she claimed by royal charter, she took immediate steps to redress the loss. She called upon the Continental Congress to establish a court to hear the matter. But New York stalemated any action by refusing to agree upon the judges. In the meantime, the states worked out a compromise whereby Massachusetts' right of extinguishment was recognized in the area claimed by the Seneca, and New York's right of extinguishment was recognized over the rest of the land. In addition, New York's right of governance was recognized over the entire area once Indian title had been surrendered. The two states signed the accord at Hartford, Connecticut, on December 16, 1785.

With Massachusetts' claim effectively eliminated, New York set about negotiating treaties with the Oneida, Onondaga, and Cayuga to gain control over their territories. In 1788 and 1789 the state took by fraud and deceit over seven million acres of land, the largest amount from the Oneidas. Their case is illustrative of the state's methods. In January of 1788 a speculator named John Livingston, representing a group of investors called the New York Genesee Company, approached some Oneidas with an offer to lease all of the land for 999 years, the rent was to be $1,000 a year. The tribe did not accept the offer. The state legislature refused to approve the lease and directed the land commissioners to hold a council with the Oneidas.

The council began on August 28, 1788, and the first days were spent negotiating with the Onondagas, who subsequently surrendered most of their land. After some delay the governor took up the negotiations with the Oneidas, who reminded him that just three years previous he had assured them that he ". . . should not want to buy any of our land, no not forever."[24] The governor responded that he was not there to buy land. He told them:

> Brothers! Be not deceived in supposing that it was our intention to kindle a Council Fire at this Time in order to Purchase Lands from you for our People. We have already more Lands than we have people to settle on them. If we had wanted Lands for our People to settle on, we would have told you so and requested you to have sold us some and would have paid you a reasonable Price for them.[25]

The purpose of the council, the governor told them, was to protect them and their land from unscrupulous whites. To accomplish this the governor proposed that they cede their land to New York, and receive in exchange an annual payment.[26] The Oneidas responded by saying that while they welcomed the interest of the state, it had to bear some of the responsibility for these "cunning and intriguing men," since the state had the power to stop them.

The New York commissioners in their communications with the Oneidas had led them to believe that they had lost all their land to the New York Genesee Company, and that the commissioners were there to restore the title. The Oneidas expressed confusion over this since they had never signed any instruments to that effect, but Governor Clinton just waved that aside. Nor did he tell the Oneidas that the state had repudiated the Livingston deal. Thus the Oneidas agreed to the lease arrangement with the state because it seemed the only way they could get back their land. The state received some five million acres for $2,000 in cash, $2,000 in clothing, $1,000 in provisions, and $600 in annual rental. So complete was the deception that Good Peter thanked the governor for his efforts.

> We now return you our Thanks, Brother Chief, that you have brought to a happy close the Business of this Treaty. My Nation are now restored to a Possession of their Property which they were in danger of having lost. Had not my Father the French Gentleman discovered it we should have drowned; had it not come to your Ears, we with all our Property would have been buried very deep in Ruin; therefore we do heartily congratulate you this Day

upon having accomplished the Treaty and thereby secured to us so
much of our Property which would otherwise have been lost.[27]

As if to salt the wound the governor in his closing remarks told the
Oneidas that they would again meet in twenty-one years to discuss the
lease arrangements. In 1792 Good Peter reported Governor Clinton's
remarks to Timothy Pickering: "After this, the governor of New York
said to us;—you have now leased all your territory, exclusive of the
reservation, as long as the grass shall grow & the rivers run. He did not
say 'I buy your country' Nor did we say—"We sell it to you.' "[28]

Thus by the end of the 1780s New York State had achieved much
of what it desired in the way of land cessions from the Iroquois. It had
lost title to the Seneca land, but had secured the rest by a policy that
involved the calculated defrauding of the tribes, and an insolent dis-
regard for national policy and confederal law. The national government, too, had achieved some of its objectives, although it was far from
a total success. It had forced the hostile tribes to sign peace treaties and
to relinquish their claims in the Ohio Valley. But in doing so it had
increased the likelihood of war in the region it wished to pacify. It had
asserted its sovereignty over the tribes in New York, but had not
honored its agreements to protect them from the avarice of New York.
As to the New York Iroquois, those to the east of the dividing line
agreed upon at Hartford had just grievances against New York, while
the Seneca to the west were angry with the national government for
their treatment at Fort Stanwix. It was clear by the time that Washington took office that a new approach to the Indians in New York was
in order.

NATIONAL POLICY 1790–1794

The policy of forcing land concessions had failed and the threat of
concerted hostilities was real and immediate, particularly in the Ohio
Valley. To prevent the Senecas and the other Iroquois tribes living in
their territory from joining the Ohio tribes, Washington appointed
Timothy Pickering as a special commissioner to the Iroquois. Through
the critical years from 1790 to 1795, Pickering held a number of
councils with the Senecas and others to assuage their anger and

maintain their neutrality. While the principal source of trouble was the treaty of Fort Stanwix, which had deprived the Seneca of most of their land in New York, this loss of land to the United States was only a part of the threat faced by the tribes. As previously described, New York, under the leadership of George Clinton, had ignored the prohibition on land purchases, and by deceit, fraud, and threat, forced large cessions from the Oneidas, Onondagas, and Cayugas.[29] Alarmed at the possibility of involving the tribes in a general war caused by the actions of states or individuals, the United States Congress passed the first of a series of laws called the Indian Trade and Intercourse Acts, in 1790 (1 Stat. 137). Generally speaking, these acts prohibited states or individuals from purchasing Indian land without national approval.

But neither the act and its revision in 1793, nor the promises of Pickering and Washington were enough to placate the Senecas. By 1794 it seemed certain that they would join the tribes in the Ohio Valley. The danger became more immediate during the winter of 1793, when the governor of Pennsylvania took steps to survey the area around Presque Isle, on Lake Erie. Although Pennsylvania had purchased the land at the Treaty of Fort Stanwix, with the approbation of the Continental Congress, its decision to develop the area in 1793 was inopportune. In the spring of 1794 General Israel Chapin warned Washington of the danger and suggested a council to calm the Senecas.[30] By this time Pickering had become well acquainted with the causes of Seneca hostility. Directed to meet with the tribes and to settle all outstanding differences, Pickering left for Canandaigua at the end of August. The council, which was attended by all the tribes except the Mohawk, lasted a bit more than two months.

At the outset, I should make clear that the United States sent invitations to the leaders of the various villages in the Seneca territory, not to the tribes as such, or to the Confederacy. While this reflected the political reality, it brought together leaders who were hostile to each other. Despite the rhetoric, this was not a treaty negotiated by the Six Nations Confederacy; it was essentially a Seneca show to which the others were invited, in part as a courtesy and in part as a necessity.

When the United States proposed the treaty there was a strong likelihood that the Senecas and their allies would join the western tribes, but soon after the council began, news came of General Wayne's victory at Fallen Timbers. With the threat removed, why did the United States continue with the treaty? There are, I believe, two reasons. In the first place, Pickering thoroughly understood the predicament of the Seneca and other Iroquois tribes, as well as the greed of

New York. He was genuinely concerned with establishing peaceful relations with the tribes. To do this he had to restore to the Senecas the land they had lost in 1784. He had also to affirm the power of the United States to protect them from the state.[31]

There was a second reason. The treaties of Fort Stanwix and Fort Harmar had failed to clear Iroquois title to the Ohio Valley. Pickering was charged with removing any remaining cloud over American title to the Territory.

There are seven articles in the Treaty of Canandaigua. The first affirmed peace and friendship between the United States and the Six Nations. In Article 2 the United States confirmed to the Oneida, Onondaga, and Cayuga the lands reserved to them in the various treaties made with the State of New York. Article 3 returned to the Senecas most of the land taken by the United States in the Treaty of Fort Stanwix. In Article 4, the four tribes returned the favor, but in language that is opaque. The article reads:

> The United States having thus described and acknowledged what lands belong to the Oneidas, Onondagas, Cayugas, and Senecas, and engaged never to claim the same, nor to disturb them, or any of the Six Nations, or their Indian friends residing thereon, and united with them, in the free use and enjoyment thereof: now the Six Nations and each of them, hereby engage never to claim any other lands within the boundaries of the United States, nor disturb the people of the United States in the free use of enjoyment thereof.[32]

Article 5 dealt with the cession of some land by the Senecas along Lake Erie, while Article 6 provided for $4,500 to be paid in perpetuity. Finally, Article 7 established a means to adjust any difference between the United States and the tribal signatories.

Article 2 was included at the behest of the tribes as an extra assurance that the U.S. would protect their lands from the state. Because of their suspicion of the federal and state governments, they spelled out quite clearly what lands were of concern. By contrast, Article 4 is deliberately vague. Pickering explained the reason behind this in a letter to Secretary of War Knox a few days before the signing of the treaty.

> I supposed the day before yesterday that the treaty was closing very satisfactorily: the Chiefs not objecting to explicit relinquish-

ments of all the lands belonging to Pennsylvania, including Presqu'Isle, but yesterday they uncovered the mystery that had veiled their proceedings:—they were desirious of a fresh confirmation of their lands; but were unwilling to relinquish, or give up or use any words of that import, respecting the lands ceded by former treaties to the United States. When I pressed them for the reason of their objection, they would answer, that the lands having been ceded by former treaties, there was no need of saying anything about them. Do you then, said I, acknowledge yourself bound by those cessions, including those made by the Delawares and Wyandots (which they mentioned) as far as the Musk[i]gum and Cayahoga?—To this they gave no answer. As you decline saying that you give them up, do you mean to claim them hereafter?—No. Where then is the difficulty?—A war-Chief of the Tuscaroras present, and who lives within seven or eight miles of Niagara, solved the difficulty. "They are afraid of offending the British." This was not denied.—Cornplanter, Captain Billy, and two or three others were present last evening at this conversation. Afterwards, Captain Billy, who is a war chief of the Senekas, acknowledged the fears of the Sachems of offending the British and said he had often reproached them with it, saying they pretended to be a free people. The Farmer's Brother also told Genl. Chapin last evening, that these fears made all the difficulty in our present negociations. The War Chiefs above named, finally said they had no objection to engage that they would never claim any land out of their acknowledged boundaries; and of course no part of Pennsylvania or the Triangle including Presqu'Isle: and added, "If the Sachems also say Yes, we shall soon close the treaty."[33]

The day after the treaty Pickering wrote to Knox telling him:

The fear of offending the British on one hand and the Western Indians on the other, induced the chiefs to persist in their opposition to an explicit cession of land; tho' finally they said they were willing to declare that they would never claim any of the land which we were solicitous to have relinquished. On this ground the treaty has assumed its present form.[34]

The treaty was a personal diplomatic triumph for Pickering. It achieved the principal object of ten years of negotiation: the cession by the Iroquois tribes of any interest they might have had in the Ohio

64   JACK CAMPISI

Valley. The Senecas received back much of the territory they had lost, thus resolving the major point of discord between them and the United States. For the other tribes, the results were more illusory, for the United States did not live up to its trust obligations. The state of New York pursued its policy of land purchases in contravention of the federal law and this treaty.

The treaty also marked a shift in the relationship between the Iroquois and the United States. After Canandaigua, the tribes were never in a position to threaten the nation. The change that had occurred was a transition from independent indigenous nations, to what Justice Marshall was to call, some forty years later, domestic dependent nations.

The decade from Stanwix to Canandaigua began with the arrogant view that all Congress had to do to settle the Indian land problem was to force a series of treaties on the tribes. It ended with a more pragmatic policy of dealing with the individual tribes in a manner designed to calm their fears while gaining their land. With respect to the states, national policy remained unchanged, if poorly enforced. The United States retained the sole power of extinguishment. It could do no less if it were to retain its full sense of sovereignty.

NOTES

1. Edmund B. O'Callaghan, ed., *Documents Relative to the Colonial History of the State of New York*, 15 vols. (Albany: Weed, Parsons, 1853–1887), 4:908–11.
2. Washington C. Ford et al., eds., *Journals of the Continental Congress, 1774–1789*, 34 vols. (Washington, DC: United States Government Printing Office, 1904–1937), 25:682.
3. Ibid.
4. Ibid., 683.
5. Ibid., 684.
6. Franklin B. Hough, ed., *Proceedings of the Commissioners of Indian Affairs, Appointed by Law for the Extinguishment of Indian Titles in the State of New York*, 2 vols. (Albany: Joel Munsell, 1861), 1:21.
7. Edmund C. Burnett, ed., *Letters of Members of the Continental Congress*, 8 vols. (Washington, DC: United States Government Printing Office, 1921–1936), 7:583–84.
8. Ibid., 487.
9. Hough, *Proceedings*, 22n.
10. Ibid.
11. Ibid., 9–11.

12. Ibid., 35.

13. Ibid., 41.

14. Ibid., pp. 45–47.

15. Ibid., 63.

16. Anthony Wayne, *Papers* (Philadelphia: Historical Society of Pennsylvania, 1778–1796), vol. 13.

17. Ibid., vol. 24.

18. Ibid., vol. 32.

19. Ibid., vol. 34.

20. Neville Craig, ed., *The Olden Times*, 2 vols. (Pittsburgh: Wright & Charlton, 1847–1848), 26.

21. Robert A. Rutland et al., eds., *Papers of James Madison* (Chicago: University of Chicago Press, 1962), 8:156–57.

22. Hough, *Proceedings*, 97.

23. Ibid.

24. Ibid., 220.

25. Ibid., 224.

26. Ibid., 225.

27. Ibid., 235.

28. Timothy Pickering, *Papers* (Boston: Massachusetts Historical Society, 1793–1795), vol. 60.

29. Hough, *Proceedings*.

30. Henry O'Reilly, *Papers* (New York: New York Historical Society, 1787–1795), vol. 10.

31. Edward H. Phillips, "Timothy Pickering at His Best—Indian Commissioner, 1790–1794," *Essex Institute, Historical Collections* 102 (1966): 163–202.

32. In *American State Papers: Documents, Legislative and Executive, of the Congress of the United States, from the First Session to the Third Session of the Thirteenth Congress, Inclusive* 4 (Washington, DC: Gales and Seaton, 1832), 545.

33. Pickering, *Papers*.

34. Ibid.

5

Iroquois Land Issues
At Odds With the "Family of New York"

LAURENCE M. HAUPTMAN

Land issues are without question the backdrop to contemporary Iroquois–New York State relations. They influence attitudes as well as strategies on both sides, they color as well as poison the air, and most importantly, they prevent real progress in so many other areas affecting the state's relationship to the Indians. Land issues shape how the contemporary Iroquois view the outside world; they also determine many of the official decisions made in Albany relative to Indian communities. The state of New York and the Iroquois come into conflict in other important areas, such as the custody of wampum housed in the New York State Museum, taxation issues, hunting and fishing rights, the sanctity of Indian burial sites, and jurisdiction; however, the key issue in understanding the present uneasy relationship between the Iroquois and New York State is the land issue. The Indians' memory of land lost, even as recently as two decades ago, produces constant distrust of outsiders, marks Albany as the "enemy's capital," and negates certain positive responses made by some progressive state officials and their agencies. It also contributes to internal tribal differences and fractionated Indian political behavior about the strategies to use in Indian-state negotiations.

To many of the Iroquois, treaties with the United States government put them above the legislative actions of any one state. They trace the source of their sovereignty to the period 1784–1794 and define their world as far different and distinct from other Indian nations. This is based upon four historical factors: the long-established practice of colonial governments and their rulers in England, France, and Holland to negotiate with tribal representatives of the Iroquois Confederacy in

council; and the three major treaties consummated after the American
Revolution—Fort Stanwix (1784), Jay (1794), and Canandaigua (1794).
To the Iroquois, these treaties guaranteed individual national and/or
collective Iroquois sovereign status, as well as free passage and unre-
stricted trade for Indians across the international boundary between
the United States and Canada, a border seen by these Indians as non-
existent and artificially created by whites.[1] Nevertheless, in 1948 and
1950, the United States Congress awarded New York State criminal
and civil jurisdiction over Indian affairs. Despite the passage of these
important acts, which became the model for Public Law 280 applied in
other states, the Iroquois have steadfastly rejected the idea, however
real in American law, that they are subject to the laws of a state,
especially one that had earlier dispossessed them.[2] Moreover, the
Iroquois also have had the persistent belief that outsiders' ability to tax
them, still a real issue, is the first step to the alienation of the Indians
from their land. Their elders also take exception to any reference to
them as "New York Indians."[3]

The Iroquois in New York, Oklahoma, Wisconsin, and Canada
have been viewed as distinct from each other in their culture, history,
and institutions ever since the late eighteenth and first half of the
nineteenth centuries. Indeed, they are six separate nations historically—Mohawk, Oneida, Onondaga, Cayuga, Tuscarora, and Seneca—who occupy fifteen separate settlements today. Each of these
Indian nations has beliefs in its individual tribal sovereignty and many,
though not all, have a collective belief in a body called a league. At the
present, two Iroquois leagues continue to function, one centered at
Onondaga near Syracuse, New York, and the other at the Six Nations
Reserve near Brantford, Ontario. Despite this second supralevel affir-
mation of Iroquois sovereignty, governmental officials in Albany as
well as Washington, D.C. and Ottawa historically have recognized
Iroquois sovereignty only in the existence of individual tribal or band
governments, in certain tribal judicial authorities, such as the Peace-
makers' Court of the Seneca Nation, and in the acceptance of some
features of Indian customary law. The continual rejection by the
United States and Canada of the idea of collective Six Nations Confederacy sovereignty has frequently motivated many of these Iroquois
League supporters to protest against policy makers and their policies.

Since the American Revolution, much of the Iroquois focus, as
individual nations or as a collective body, has been to protect their
shrinking land base, especially from New York State. Consequently,
most Iroquois in New York see themselves as citizens of their own

Indian nations; do not choose to participate or vote in local, county, state, or American national elections; and rarely lobby or even visit the state capital. In the high-powered lobbying and political world of Albany, this conscious Indian separation is an anomaly, and it reduces the Indians' ability to effect change in areas where the state is willing to accede, namely those unrelated to Indian land rights.[4]

The present generation of leadership in each of the Iroquois communities reached political maturity during a period of severe trauma as a result of land loss from the late 1940s to the mid-1960s.[5] This fact is especially important in understanding Indian perceptions of state and federal officials as well as their renewed push for land rights from the mid-1960s on. The Iroquois, in the twenty-year period after World War II, lost significant acreage in five of their reservation communities, beginning with a dam project at Onondaga in the late 1940s. The St. Lawrence Seaway project in the 1950s led to the expropriation of approximately thirteen hundred acres of Caughnawaga Mohawk land near Montreal as well as 130 acres of St. Regis (Akwesasne) Mohawk land near Massena; it also weakened economic self-sufficiency by destroying the Indian fishing and cattle industries along the St. Lawrence River, in part because of increased industrialization and resulting pollution of the air and waters. The Kinzua Dam, which opened only twenty years ago, pushed by Pennsylvania interests and the Army Corps of Engineers, flooded the entire Cornplanter Tract, the last Indian lands in Pennsylvania, and over nine thousand acres of Seneca Nation lands. The New York State Power Authority's Niagara Power Project, completed in 1961, condemned one-eighth or 560 acres of the Tuscarora Indian Reservation near Lewiston, New York, in a plan for a massive reservoir conceived of by master builder Robert Moses.

In the process of condemnation, expropriation, and removal, the Iroquois Indians' psyche was also affected. Destroying the Old Cold Spring Longhouse and taking the Cornplanter heirs away from a source of their medicine and spirituality, the Allegheny River, and placing them in more crowded communities in two ranch-style housing developments with far different spatial relationships, produced nightmares and lifelong tragic memories. These travesties occurred at a time when Indian land needs were becoming acute on the reservations.

One important sidelight not generally recognized was that Cayugas, outsiders without land rights on the Cattaraugus Indian Reservation, and Oneidas, outsiders without land rights at the Onondaga Indian Reservation, were in some ways more affected by state and federal policies than the nations directly involved in dealing with government officials. Every time there is a land crisis on these two reservations, as in the Kinzua and Onondaga dam crises, land pressures intensify and Indians with no reservation land rights such as the Cayugas and Oneidas are increasingly seen as outsiders or as "Indians who came to dinner and stayed two hundred years." Hence, it is no coincidence that these two landless Indian nations in New York are at the forefront of Indian claims litigation.

Today, the main issues affecting Iroquois–New York State relations are the claims of various Indian nations to sizeable tracts of land. These claims assertions are not new, despite popular belief, but have been maintained by Iroquois people for nearly two hundred years. Land claims have been the subject of countless council meetings, and their settlement was the stuff of family hopes during times of economic and political despair. Moreover, the Iroquois have, over the years, inculcated in their children the righteousness of their land claims and a belief in the eventual favorable conclusion of this agonizing process. Despite their meaning to the Iroquois, these claims were purposely ignored and discounted by the non-Indian world.[6]

The claims of the Cayugas, Mohawks, and Oneidas affect the present and future of much of the central and northern regions of New York State. The Oneidas in their pursuit of their two-centuries-old claim have been most successful in overturning American legal precedents, winning two favorable decisions in the United States Supreme Court; yet, despite their success in litigation, they have not yet received any land or financial compensation from New York.

Much of the Indian legal arguments in the land claims cases center around New York State violations of the Indian Trade and Intercourse Acts of 1790 and 1793. The 1790 act regulated trade with the Indians and prohibited the unauthorized purchase of land on all land sales not approved by the federal government. The 1793 act tightened federal control over Indian policy by adding a section requiring the presence and approval of a federal commissioner when the states intended to extinguish Indian land rights. From this act onward, as Jack Campisi has correctly observed, the process of ratification of so-called state treaties, i.e., land transactions, was "the same as with any federal treaty."[7]

In November, 1970, before a special hearing of Chairman Reilly's New York State Subcommittee on Indian Affairs, George Shattuck, at that time the attorney for the Oneidas, explained how these Indians were systematically dispossessed by state violations of the Trade and

Intercourse Acts. Although the state recognized the need for a federal commissioner's presence at land negotiations and purchase in 1798, no federal commissioner was present at the 1795 Oneida-New York State "treaty" or at twenty-four of the twenty-six "treaties" made after 1798. According to Shattuck, "If you simply dismissed the Oneida argument as a 'clever legal technicality to go back 200 years,' you would ignore these Indians' longstanding pleas for justice."[8] Shattuck then described how the Indians had been locked out from state and federal courts. Without special enabling legislation allowing for the suit, the Indians would be ignored again. Shattuck argued:

> So the State has done a very great job, they take away the land fraudulently from people who couldn't even sign their full names, then they conveniently make the law that says, 'We are sorry we have got your land, but you are not a person or a corporation or an entity which can bring a lawsuit to get it back, and furthermore the State has sovereign immunity and you can't sue us anyway.' So they were just locked out, they were just locked out, they had no recourse.[9]

Shattuck then insisted that the federal remedy was not satisfactory either since the Oneidas could only bring an action before the Indian Claims Commission against the United States for breach of fiduciary responsibility in allowing the state illegally to take Indian lands. Shattuck also pointed out that a potential Oneida victory in the federal Indian Claims Commission would also not allow interest on the 175 years of damages that the Oneidas claimed.[10]

After the failure to convince the federal or state governments of the seriousness of the claim, Shattuck in 1970 filed a test case in federal court. He sued Oneida and Madison Counties, challenging the validity of the Oneida-New York State "treaty" of 1795 and seeking trespass damages for a two-year period, 1968 and 1969. By suing the two counties and not New York directly, Shattuck attempted to circumvent the previous federal legal restrictions against such an action. Hence, the case revolved around whether the federal courts had jurisdiction in this matter.

William L. Burke, the attorney for the two counties, supported by the New York State attorney general's office, argued that the federal courts had no jurisdiction in the matter. Burke, joined by Assistant Attorney General of New York State Jeremiah Jochnowitz, also emphasized the legal theory of laches, namely that the Indians had not brought "timely suit" but had waited 175 years to do so. Subsequently, the United States District Court for the Northern District of New York and the United States Court of Appeals for the Second Circuit dismissed the action, deciding that the Oneidas' complaint had indeed not raised a question under federal law as Burke and Jochnowitz had argued in their first contention.[11]

Oneida hopes, nevertheless, were soon raised when the United States Supreme Court agreed to hear the case. In his arguments in November, 1973 before the high court, Shattuck reiterated the long-held Oneida position that the 1795 New York State treaty was executed in violation of the Constitution, three federal treaties, and the Trade and Intercourse Acts. Using archeological, historical, and linguistic expert findings, Shattuck insisted that the Oneidas bringing suits were federally recognized successors in interest to the Oneidas of the 1790s and those of the pre-contact period. The Oneidas were not, as Shattuck observed, complaining of mere technical failures to comply with the letter of the law. In his exhibits, Shattuck clearly showed that federal officials responded to Oneida queries by denying the merit of the claims and discouraging legal action; wrongly advised them after 1920 that they had no federal tribal status in New York; advised them that Congress would retroactively ratify any illegal land sales even if they won in court; and indicated, even before the jurisdiction bills of 1948 and 1950, that the Oneidas were under state jurisdiction, which precluded any federal action of redress. Since the Indian nations were also barred from New York State courts, the Oneidas were in effect denied a legal forum. Thus, Shattuck argued, as their guardian, the United States had a constitutional, treaty, and congressional responsibility to provide the Oneidas with their day in court by allowing them to sue in federal courts.[12]

The Supreme Court rendered its decision on January 21, 1974. In a unanimous decision with eight justices participating, the court sustained the Oneidas' position and remanded the case back to the lower federal courts. In this landmark decision, by holding that the Trade and Intercourse Acts were applicable to the original thirteen states including New York, the Supreme Court opened up the federal courts to the Oneidas as well as to other Indians seeking to get back land in these states. No longer would they be stymied by jurisdictional barriers placed in their path. According to Justice Byron White's written opinion of the court: "The rudimentary propositions that Indian title is a matter of federal law and can be extinguished only with federal consent apply in all of the States, including the original 13." White added that controversy arises under the laws of the United States sufficient to invoke the jurisdiction of federal courts, and reversed the earlier federal court determinations, remanding the case for further proceedings to the federal District Court for the Northern District of New York.[13]

Since the Supreme Court ruling of 1974, the Oneidas have squabbled amongst themselves and with other Iroquois about the direction of the claim. Separate feuding groups have brought actions and counteractions that have drained energies and delayed a final settlement of any legal doings. They have been divided over who should be parties to the claim, who should lead the action, what is the role of the Six Nations' Confederacy council at Onondaga in the suit, whether land or money or both are the goals, and even who are the rightful heirs in interest to the thirty-two acres of remaining Oneida lands in New York. Although there is internal discord, the Oneidas as a whole continue to believe that they were wronged by the state of New York.[14]

Despite these continuing divisions, the Oneidas, on March 4, 1985, won another legal battle in the United States Supreme Court. In a five-to-four decision, in a test case argued by Arlinda Locklear, an attorney for the Oneidas, involving fewer than nine hundred acres of the extensive Oneida tribal land claim, the court held that Oneida and Madison Counties were liable for damages—fair rental value for two years, 1968 and 1969—for unlawful seizure of Indian ancestral lands. Associate Justice Lewis F. Powell, Jr., who wrote the majority opinion, insisted that the Indians' common-law right to sue is firmly established and that Congress did not intend to impose a deadline on the filing of such suits. Since the counties had firmly maintained that the Indians had not made a timely effort to sue and thus had forfeited their legal rights, the decision nullified the major non-Indian argument and opened the door for further Oneida litigation involving their lost lands. The court also suggested that, because of the tremendous economic implications of the case, Congress should help settle the New York Indian claims as it had done in Connecticut, Maine, and Rhode Island.[15] Despite this decision, no formal negotiations took place between New York State officials and the Oneidas until September 1986.

New York State officials were stunned by both of these decisions. For years they had minimized or denied the issues, even though they had admitted in an earlier court and in legislative reports that the state title to former Indian-held lands was clouded.[16] It is clear that state officials had underestimated the Indians' ability to bring suit and now are faced with overwhelming political opposition to settlement on the Indians' terms by state agencies, county legislatures, farm groups, wine growers, school districts, church groups, as well as many individual landholders in the claims area.[17]

When a Cayuga Indian land settlement bill restoring a 5,400-acre Indian land base was defeated by less than two dozen votes in the House of Representatives, the Indians, angered by this setback, brought legal suit for 64,000 acres of land. This litigation, along with six million acres of land tied up in the Oneida suit and 12,000–14,000 acres in the Mohawk action, put economic pressure on the state by making it difficult at best for corporations, counties, individuals, institutions, and municipalities to secure bank loans, federal grants, and home mortgages. It also intensified already existing anti-Indian feelings and led, in 1982, to the so-called "Ancient Indian Land Claims Bill," introduced by Representative Gary Lee and Senators Alfonse D'Amato and Strom Thurmond. This bill called for a federal monetary formula and the extinguishment of all Indian land claims six months after passage; however, the bill died in committee.[18] Today, state officials claim that Cayuga negotiations are still in effect, with federal, state, country, and Cayuga representatives at the table; however, in reality, no meetings of the principals are being held and no new piece of federal legislation has yet been introduced or even drafted.

Besides these three land claims, New York State–Iroquois land relations are and have been seriously affected by the problem of the Salamanca leases.[19] Although this is not a land claims issue, Albany bureaucrats and legislators, and southwestern New York politicians and their constituents attempt to tie this lease issue to other problems that the state has with the Iroquois.[20] The City of Salamanca and its environs are almost entirely on the Allegany Indian Reservation of the Seneca Nation of Indians. Founded with the coming of the railroad in the mid-nineteenth century, this city is composed of thousands of non-Indians who live and work on land leased from the Senecas. Salamanca's residents have ninety-nine-year leases with the Seneca Nation formally confirmed by Congress in the years from 1875 to 1892. Most of these approximately 3,000 leases run out in 1991.

For the last decade, the lease negotiations have made little progress because of Seneca memories of past bigotry and current racial tensions in Salamanca; the persistent attempts by non-Indian residents of the city to get Washington or Albany to dispossess, allot, or buy out the Senecas' land interest; and the volatile world of Seneca Nation politics. In 1902, Congressman Edward B. Vreeland from Salamanca expressed his motives for urging allotment legislation on the Senecas: "I represent 8,000 people who live upon these reservations; who hold ninety-nine-year leases from these Indians, and want to get a title to their lands."[21] In November 1985, at a congressional hearing initiated by Congressman Stanley Lundine focusing on the Salamanca-Seneca lease stalemate, the city's attorney indicated to members of the House Committee on Interior and Insular Affairs that Congress' original intent in giving ninety-nine-year leases was to give what he claimed was "tantamount title" to the non-Indian citizens of Salamanca. He then urged Congress to "buy the City from the Seneca Nation of Indians."[22] Although in the past (through 1969) New York State policy makers of Indian affairs directly intervened on behalf of the southwestern New York interests and not the Senecas, state Indian policy makers have shied clear of direct involvement, insisting that it is a federal matter.[23] Nevertheless, southwestern New Yorkers have made their concerns known in Albany.[24]

New York State officials, both openly and by inference, confirm today the importance of land issues, fear the implications of Indian claims litigation such as that brought by the Oneidas, and bemoan the constant unresolvability of the Seneca-Salamanca lease disputes. The ever-present issues of land, especially the Oneida and Cayuga claims, led a prime mover of state Indian policy in the Department of State to deny there is even an American Indian policy emanating out of Albany, for fear that a outsider might affect the tense negotiations.[25] They also led the powerful Democratic majority leader of the New York State Assembly to label his current relationship with the Seneca Nations as "adversarial," and another powerful Republican state senator to describe the Seneca-Salamanca lease dispute as his "albatross" that just won't go away.[26] Important to note, land issues also affect agency responses to American Indian concerns, including the delivery of health and educational services to the Iroquois.[27] Moreover, unresolved land issues affect municipalities', counties', and the state's ability to sell bonds. The most recent New York State prospectus for a $3.5 billion bond offer devoted two pages to potential state and county liability in the event of successful Indian litigation and/or settlement in the Oneida, Cayuga, and Mohawk claims cases.[28]

Land issues influence the state's relationship with the Iroquois in many other ways. Although a formalized "Indian office" has been suggested on numerous occasions, many American Indians themselves have been critical of the idea, in part because the state has not settled outstanding issues, most significantly those involving land.[29] Because of the litigational nature of Indian-state relations, key figures in state Indian policies are non-Indian attorneys, who have been long familiar with Indian land issues: Robert Batson, Gerald C. Crotty and Mario M. Cuomo. Batson heads the "desk," as it is called, at the Department of State, working to devise statewide strategies and solve the day-to-day land and jurisdictional problems brought to it by other agencies. Referred to by legislators and staffers for the governor as the state's "Indian expert," despite the presence of an Indian with seventeen years of administrative experience in policy matters in Buffalo, Batson serves as a major policy maker on land issues and works closely with the governor's office, the Department of Law and the New York State Legislature.[30] As the designated "expert" since his legal work on the Moss Lake agreement of 1977–1978, Batson's job is to separate out extraneous issues from the real issues of land claims. He represents the governor at discussions with federal officials in Washington and at national meetings on state Indian affairs, is a personal envoy of the Governor at land negotiations to settle Indian claims, and cooperates with the Department of Law, the Governor's Counsel and agency counsels in legal controversies affecting New York State-Indian relations. He also is in direct communication with Howard Rowley of Rochester Gas and Electric Company who serves as a mediator in conflict areas, ranging from the sales tax issue to Iroquois land claims.[31]

Another key to New York State-Indian negotiations is Gerald C. Crotty, who now serves as Governor Mario Cuomo's Secretary/Chief of Staff. Mr. Crotty, a thirty-five-year-old "whiz kid" in New York State government, is from a Buffalo-based politically connected family. His father was head of the Erie County Democratic Party and ran for attorney general of New York State in the 1950s. His brother Peter is counsel to the State Facilities Development Corporation, while another brother Paul is Finance Commissioner of New York City. Since 1979, Gerald C. Crotty has quickly moved up the administrative ladder from Assistant Counsel to Counsel to, presently, number two man in the governor's office. Previous to coming to Albany, he worked with the New York City law firm of Hawkins, Delafield and Wood where he focused on municipal and constitutional law, securities law, and municipal and public finance. His earlier work included defending the state of Maine against American Indian land claims. During his work on the Maine Indian land claims case, Crotty insists that he read every legal decision involving Indian land tenure and drew up the argument for the Maine Mortgage Bank that "the State did not have to give any lands back to the Indians." In 1979, when he was brought into New York State government as Assistant Counsel to Governor Hugh Carey, Crotty turned some of his attention to New York land claims issues, especially those of the Cayuga Indians, as well as to the mediation of the siege between rival Mohawk groups at the St. Regis (Akwesasne) Reservation. Crotty considers his work at mediating the Mohawk confrontation and achieving a peaceful settlement "one of the greatest senses of accomplishment" he has had in working in state government. "Mediation is the key. Saving lives is more important than issues, law or history. We'll negotiate with anyone if they are capable of doing some damage." In the end, "We managed to convince the 'traditionals' that the only way to solve the crisis was to have one of their chiefs run for office."[32]

In contrast, Crotty is frustrated and on the defensive when he talks about the outstanding Indian land issues in the state. Having given assurances to Representative Morris Udall, Chairman of the House Committee on Interior and Insular Affairs, that there was wide support for a Cayuga settlement bill, the Carey administration found that state's congressional delegation bolting after the bill reached the floor of the House of Representatives. Because of the lobbying of New York Representative Gary Lee, the bill was subsequently defeated in 1982. Crotty's explanations about why there has been little if any movement since 1982 are revealing. He insists that the new Cuomo administration had to adjust slowly to the new responsibilities of leadership, that the Indian land claims issues are immensely complicated, that there are "still legislators with Indian-hating attitudes," and that the Indians cannot agree among themselves and/or are unwilling to compromise. On one hand, he suggests that it is "possible to buy a land settlement from the Reagan White House" since "we are willing to give land" to a future settlement; on the other hand, he maintains that New York State is not only worried about the four outstanding land issues but that "there's the potential for other land claims being filed in the future—Shinnecock, Seneca, etc.," which prevents a quick land claims settlement. In order to improve the administration of Indian affairs, Crotty insists that an Indian office/division be created in the Department of State and that Batson be made its director. Although there are other personnel in the governor's office who have had experience in dealing with Indian issues, such as Dr. Henrik Dullea and Jeff Cohen, Crotty and the governor himself have had the longest involvement in this area.[33]

Governor Mario M. Cuomo has had a decade of experience in

negotiating with the Iroquois since the Moss Lake crisis of the mid-1970s, and is at the top of the hierarchical pyramid of decision making with respect to American Indians. As a mediator from his early days in resolving the Forest Hills housing crisis in the early 1970s, he brings both an awareness of the importance of conflict resolution and a key understanding of ethnicity. Because of his personal style of leadership, which is far different from his predecessor in the governor's office, Cuomo is more directly involved in policies and decision making.[34]

Cuomo's involvement in this area began in August, 1976, when he was appointed as Governor Carey's special representative at the Moss Lake (Ganienkeh) crisis negotiations. At the time, Cuomo was Secretary of State. Because of a two-year stand-off situation and the inability of Ogden Reid, then Commissioner of the New York State Department of Environmental Conservation, to resolve this crisis, Cuomo entered the negotiations, joining Howard Rowley and Scott Buckheit of the American Arbitration Association in efforts at mediation.[35]

Moss Lake was a major event in contemporary state-Indian relations. The incident started in May, 1974, when a group of Mohawks, mostly Caughnawagas, took over an abandoned Girl Scout camp at Moss Lake in the Adirondacks. This occupation had been preceded by an earlier temporary seizure of property by Mohawks led by Standing Arrow near Fort Hunter in 1957 and 1958.[36] Claiming aboriginal occupancy of the land in 1974, even though the particular tract was in historic Oneida-claimed territory and in the Adirondack State Park, these Mohawks managed to bring the entire state Indian machinery to a halt. The 612-acre site at Moss Lake had been purchased in August 1973 by New York State, which had plans to clear the land of all structures in order to restore it to a wilderness state. The New York State Department of Environmental Conservation (DEC), which had jurisdiction over the site, and then Governor Malcolm Wilson, feared an armed confrontation during a gubernatorial election year and did not immediately try to remove the Indians; however, DEC Commissioner James Biggane urged Attorney General Louis Lefkowitz to initiate legal proceedings. Initial state actions for summary judgment against the Indians were dismissed. Moreover, a group of non-Indian residents of the area on their own commenced ejectment proceedings against the Indians and were granted a judgment in September, 1975; nevertheless, the court decision was deferred pending the outcome of negotiations between state officials and Indians at Moss Lake.[37] To complicate matters further, the federally and state-recognized Mohawk Tribal Council at the St. Regis (Akwesasne) Reservation condemned the Indians' takeover and called for the assertion of state jurisdiction to remove the Indians from Moss Lake.[38]

In May 1977, New York State officials and the Indians at Moss Lake reached a settlement. The Indians were given use, not land title, of two parcels of state lands in Clinton County, one at Miner Lake in the Town of Altona and the other at the Macomb Reforestation Area. In order to avoid the restrictions of the Indian Trade and Intercourse Act of 1790, the Turtle Island Trust was created with Maytag Foundation money in order to facilitate the transfer of state lands. Other complications arose, namely, questions related to an access road, the Indians' delay in vacating Moss Lake, and the lack of state officials' consultation with Clinton County legislators before the settlement was inked and announced to the media. It is significant to note that although numerous private individuals and state officials were involved in this process from 1974 to 1978, Secretary of State Cuomo is largely credited with the settlement and preventing what Governor Carey feared and called "an Attica in the Adirondacks."[39]

The Moss Lake crisis clearly shows how land is the backdrop to Iroquois–New York State relations. First, Mohawk land claims promoted the takeover. Second, the Moss Lake incident occurred five months after the first favorable Oneida decision in the United States Supreme Court. Third, conflicting land claims of Oneidas, Mohawks, the Iroquois Confederacy, and New York State delayed settlement. Fourth, the standoff was finally resolved when state officials realized that the Indians would settle *only* for land and were less concerned about other outstanding issues.[40] The crisis also had far-reaching results and mostly not positive ones. It helped destroy the position of Director of Indian Services, and with it, by 1977, the Interdepartmental Committee on Indian Affairs; it led to the emergence of Cuomo, Batson and Rowley in Indian policy mediation and formulation; it intensified Indian-Indian conflict in New York State; it delayed state negotiations with those Indian groups seeking more peaceful methods of land acquisition; it resulted in two shootings, including the wounding of a nine-year-old girl; and it brought Governor Carey and the New York State legislative leadership into a political war.[41]

Cuomo's role at Moss Lake reflects on what has and has not occurred in Indian affairs since the mid-1970s. From his earliest involvement in the crisis, beginning in August 1976, he realized the importance of a separate Division of Native American Affairs for coordination purposes and for conflict resolution objectives.[42] Yet, his basic focus was only to look at the immediate in order to mitigate the potential for armed conflict and bloodshed. At first, he listened diligently to the Indians' position but refused to give an explicit commitment of the state's position. He originally deferred to the Indians in terms of the style of the negotiations, where the discussions were held, and accepting the frequent changes of Indian negotiators at the table.[43]

In order to keep peace, Cuomo bypassed, thereby insulting, the recognized Mohawk Indian tribal council in favor of those with rifles and those who claimed official tribal leadership standing in the negotiating process. Moreover, one Seneca Indian activist from Cattaraugus Reservation, who had been previously repudiated by the Seneca traditional Council of Chiefs at the Tonawanda Reservation, ended up at the Moss Lake negotiating table.[44] Cuomo also went against 192 years of state Indian policies by negotiating with the Six Nations Confederacy Council at Onondaga, a body that had never been formally given political recognition by the state of New York.[45] When negotiations did not proceed as swiftly as Cuomo envisioned, the then secretary of state shifted his style to a hard-line approach, insisting that the state would pursue legal ejectment proceedings against the Indians, avoiding deference to Indian symbolism and refusing to call the Mohawks by their Indian names, and withholding information about public support of the Mohawk position from the Indians.[46]

The Moss Lake agreement of 1977 reflects state opinion of the Iroquois and their land claims up to the present day. Secretary Cuomo carefully spelled out the parameters of the Moss Lake agreement to the chiefs of the Mohawk Nation and to the chiefs of the Six Nations of the Iroquois Confederacy by insisting that the accord "will not have any legal effect upon any of the legal claims or rights of the Six Nations Confederacy or the Mohawk Nation under any of the treaties made by the Six Nations." Cuomo added that there "is nothing about this resolution that is legally binding in any way on the Six Nations, the Mohawk Nation, the People of Ganienkeh, or the State of New York." Significantly, the future governor concluded: "Naturally, the State does not concede that the claims of the Six Nations are valid, but the State is committed to resolving all such matters in a legal and peaceful way."[47]

In 1980, Robert B. Goldmann prepared a study for the Ford Foundation on conflict resolution in which Mario Cuomo's efforts and style were lauded in two separate chapters. In one of the chapters, prepared by Richard Kwartler, Cuomo's and Howard Rowley's roles at

Moss Lake receive attention. In a most revealing passage, Kwartler quotes Cuomo about the final Moss Lake settlement:

> The Mohawk settlement has moved us toward a realization that the way to resolve these things is not by letting them go to court because if the Indian goes to court and wins then the court will say that the land belongs to the Indians. *If the land belongs to the Indians, the court will not actually deliver the land to the Indians because the legislative process will then intervene to say that's an absurd result*—for example, to give the whole City of Saratoga to the Indians. We must find a different process—conflict resolution without litigation, a process of negotiation.[48]

Thus, it is quite evident that proper legal redress and justice for American Indians takes a back seat, in Cuomo's mind, to what he considers the hard-boiled "realities" of the political process. It is also clear that truth and historical and legal realities took a back seat to state policy makers' efforts at assuaging a small group of American Indians who were potentially dangerous, threatening, and capable of generating negative publicity for the state and its leadership. In fairness to state officials, memories of Attica (and Wounded Knee) were indelibly marked in their minds as they went to the negotiating table. Having minimized Indian matters for so long, state officials were also extremely ignorant of the Indian world with which they were coming into contact.

Today, Ganienkeh, near Altona, New York, is virtually abandoned, with its original "leaders" scattered as far away as California.[49] The failed community is a testimony to a bankrupt state Indian policy that looks to "immediate fixes" rather than to permanent improvement, such as a major land claims settlement. Although the threat of violence did force the governor's office to support some needed legislation for American Indians, which may or may not have passed without the Moss Lake takeover, state officials' actions did not help foster trust in the long run, since they further alienated several Indian councils, delayed and weakened efforts at other Indian land settlements, and gave further impetus to a negative type of Indian politics based on media exploitation. As various Iroquois communities face important land issues that require good will and informed sensitivity, the record and attitude of New York State officials does not bode well for negotiating success.

82   LAURENCE M. HAUPTMAN

NOTES

1. Laurence M. Hauptman, *The Iroquois and the New Deal* (Syracuse: Syracuse University Press, 1981), chapter 1.
2. For a full discussion of the origins of jurisdictional transfer, see Laurence M. Hauptman, *The Iroquois Struggle for Survival* (Syracuse: Syracuse University Press, 1986), 31–64.
3. See Hauptman, *The Iroquois and the New Deal*, 6–7; and Hauptman, *The Iroquois Struggle for Survival*, 45–64.
4. Interviews of Assemblymen Maurice Hinchey, Feb. 25, 1986; Melvin Zimmer, March 11, 1986; and Daniel Walsh, March 13, 1986; and State Senators Jess Present, March 12, 1986; and James Donovan, April 17, 1986; Executive Deputy Commissioner (Labor) John Hudacs, March 10, 1986; Regent Laura Chodos, February 24, 1986; Leo Soucy (former Assistant Commissioner of Education), March 4, 1986; Adrian Cook, February 24, 1986; Dr. Hazel V. Dean-John, March 19, 1986; and Fernando DiMaggio (former legislative staffer for the Assembly Committee on Indian Affairs), April 17, 1986.
5. For the history of contemporary Iroquois land loss, see Hauptman, *The Iroquois Struggle for Survival*, 85–178. See also Barbara Graymont, ed., *Fighting Tuscarora: The Autobiography of Chief Clinton Rickard* (Syracuse: Syracuse University Press, 1973), 138–152.
6. Hauptman, *The Iroquois Struggle for Survival*, chapter 10.
7. Campisi, "The Trade and Intercourse Acts: Land Claims on the Eastern Seaboard," in *Irredeemable America*, Imre Sutton, ed. (Albuquerque: University of New Mexico Press, 1985), 338.
8. New York State Legislature, Assembly Subcommittee on Indian Affairs of the Standing Committee on Governmental Operations, *Public Hearings*, Nov. 18, 1970 (Albany, 1970), 41.
9. Ibid., 41–42.
10. See Hauptman, *The Iroquois Struggle for Survival*, chapter 10.
11. Ibid.
12. Ibid.
13. 94 S. Ct. 772.
14. Laurence M. Hauptman, Oneida Indian field notes, 1977–1986.
15. U.S. Sup. Ct. 83–1065; 83-1240-opinion.
16. New York State, *Legislative Document No. 15: Report of the Joint Legislative Committee on Indian Affairs, 1959* (Albany, 1959), 4; Exhibit III: Memorandum of Law and Fact, 16–17, undated, contained in petition of February 9, 1968, attached to letter of Joseph Califano to Jacob Thompson, February 28, 1968, Lyndon Johnson MSS., White House Central Files, Box 3, IN/A–Z LBJ Library, Austin, Texas.
17. The anti-settlement correspondence is immense. See, for example, Frederick R. Clark (chairman of PASNY) to Robert J. Morgado, March 6, 1978; Hugh Carey to Louis Lefkowitz, February 4, 1978; Albert B. Lewis (Superintendent of Insurance) to Hugh Carey, September 18, 1978, Hugh Carey Records, Subject Files, Reel 104, New York State Archives, Albany; Peter Borzilleri (New York State Wine Grape Growers, Inc.) to Hugh Carey, May 15, 1979; Michael DelGuidice to Peter Borzilleri, May 29, 1979; Richard McGuire (New York Farm Bureau) to Hugh Carey, May 27, 1980; Gary Lee to Hugh Carey, February 21, 1979, November 20, 1980; Marilyn Schiff

to Ward DeWitt; Madison County Legislature Resolution Requesting Ratification of the "Allegedly Invalid Treaties and the September 8, 1981 Extinguishment of the Aboriginal Titles to the Land Being Claimed by Native Americans," September 8, 1981; Sean Walsh to Governor Hugh Carey, June 17, 1980, Governor Hugh Carey Records, Subject Files, Reel 65, New York State Archives, Albany.

18. United States Congress, House of Representatives, Committee on Interior and Insular Affairs, *Hearings on H.R. 6631: Settlement of the Cayuga Indian Nation Land Claims in the State of New York*, March 3, 1980, 96th Cong., 2nd sess. (Washington, D.C., 1980); United States Congress, Senate, Select Committee on Indian Affairs, *Hearings on S. 2084: Ancient Indian Land Claims*, 97th Cong., 2nd sess. (Washington, D.C. 1982). For the Iroquois protest against the Ancient Indian Land Claims Settlement Act, see Barry Snyder (President of the Seneca Nation of Indians) to Governor Hugh L. Carey, March 8, 1982; Chief Corbett Sundown (Chairman, Council of Chiefs, Tonawanda Band of Senecas), February 23, 1982; Grand Council of the Houdenosaunee, The Six Nations Iroquois Confederacy Onondaga Nation to President Ronald Reagan, February 14, 1982, Governor Hugh Carey Records, Subject Files, Microfilm Reel 65, New York State Archives, Albany.

19. For a full discussion of the history of the issue, see Laurence M. Hauptman, "The Historical Background to the Present Day Seneca Nation-Salamanca Lease Controversy: The First Hundred Years, 1851–1951," Rockefeller Institute of Government, *Working Paper No. 20* (Fall, 1985), chapter 8 in this book.

20. Interview of Assemblyman Daniel Walsh. Lou Grumet to Mario Cuomo, September 15, 1976, Moss Lake Indian Negotiations, New York State Department of State Records, Series 726, New York State Archives, Albany; Robert C. Batson to Ward DeWitt, July 28, 1981, Governor Hugh Carey Records, 2nd term, Subject Files, Microfilm Reel 65, New York State Archives, Albany.

21. United States Congress, House, *Congressional Record*, 57th Congress, 2nd sess, 1902, 36, pt. 1: 337.

22. Salamanca City Attorney David Franz Testimony, House of Representatives, Committee on Interior and Insular Affairs, Hearings on the Salamanca leases, November 7, 1985, Washington, D.C.

23. Prepared statement of Robert Batson, Associate Counsel, New York State Department of State, House of Representatives, Committee on Interior and Insular Affairs, Hearings on the Salamanca leases, November 7, 1985, Washington, D.C.

24. Mayor Ronald Yehl (Salamanca) to Governor Hugh Carey, October 13, 1981, Governor Hugh Carey Records, Subject Files, Microfilm Reel 65, New York State Archives, Albany, Interviews of Assemblyman Daniel Walsh and State Senator Jess Present.

25. Interview of Robert Batson, January 16, 1986, Albany.

26. Interviews of Assemblyman Daniel Walsh and State Senator Jess Present.

27. Robert P. Whelan (NYS Commissioner of Health) to Louis J. Lefkowitz (NYS Attorny General), March 18, 1977; Subject Files of the 1st Deputy Commissioner, New York State Department of Health Records, Box 16, acc. #13, 307-82A, New York State Archives, Albany. Formal Opinions of the Attorney General, 1976 (Albany, 1976), 54–55. Lou Grumet to Mario Cuomo, September 15 and 24, 1976, Moss Lake Indian Negotiations, New York State Department of State Records, Series 726, New York State Archives, Albany. Anna Lewis to Mr. Caruso, et al., October 1, 1970, Records of the Native American Indian Education Unit, New York State Department of Education Records, "Regents Research Files," Box 1, Series 729, New

York State Archives, Albany. Interview of Dr. Hazel V. Dean-John (Native American Indian Education Unit), April 8, 1986, Albany.

28. New York State Comptroller, Department of Audit and Control, "New Issue, Official Statement, $3,500,000,000 State of New York 1986 Tax and Revenue Anticipation Notes," April 11, 1986, 48–49.

29. Laurence M. Hauptman, Iroquois field notes, 1976–1986.

30. Interviews of Assemblymen Melvin Zimmer and Maurice Hinchey; State Senator Jess Present; Dr. Henrik Dullea; Jeff Cohen; and Dr. Hazel V. Dean-John.

31. Interviews of Robert Batson, January 16 and March 6, 1986, Albany. Robert Batson to Lou Grumet, July 22, August 10, 1977; Batson to Mario Cuomo, August 14, October 23, December 4, December 11, 1978, Moss Lake Indian Negotiations, New York State Department of State Records, Series 726, New York State Archives, Albany. Robert J. Morgado to Caroline Drake, September 19, 1980; Michael Finnerty to Joe Quetone, August 19, 1982. Robert Batson to Files, February 13, 1979; Batson to Thomas Frey, January 11, 1979; Batson to Nikolaus Satelmajer, May 20, 1980; Batson to Ward DeWitt, July 28, 1981; Batson to Evan L. Webster, January 20, 1981, Governor Hugh Carey Records, Subject Files, Microfilm Reel 65, New York State Archives, Albany. Statement of Robert Batson, Associate Counsel, New York State Department of State, Seneca Nation-Salamanca lease hearings, United States House of Representatives, Committee on Interior and Insular Affairs, November 7, 1985. Interview of Howard Rowley, March 17, 1986, Rochester. Steve Carlic, "The Negotiator: Howard Rowley Brings Casual Approach to Some Critical Talks," *Syracuse Post-Standard*, February 24, 1986.

32. Marc Humbert, "Governor's New Chief of Staff Set to Take Charge of Nuts and Bolts," *Albany Times-Union*, September 18, 1985. *New York Red Book, 1984–1985* (Albany, 1985), 434. Interviews of Gerald C. Crotty, July 9, 1986, Albany; and Gerald Benjamin (Republican County Legislator, Ulster County), April 7, 1986, Albany.

33. Ibid.

34. Mario Cuomo, *Forest Hills Diary: The Crisis of Low Income Housing* (New York: Random House, 1974); interviews of Gerald Benjamin, April 7, 1986 and Alan Chartock, March 25, 1986, Albany. Benjamin is an expert on the New York State governorship, having written and/or compiled three books on Nelson Rockefeller and one on Hugh Carey; Chartock, a syndicated columnist, director of radio station WAMC, professor of political science and communication at SUNY/New Paltz and SUNY/Albany, interviews Governor Cuomo each week on Albany radio and is currently writing a book on Cuomo.

35. Interviews of Louis Grumet, March 24, 1986, Albany; Howard Rowley, March 17, 1986, Rochester; and Martin Wasser, April 11, 1986, New York City. Grumet was the special assistant to Secretary of State Cuomo and is now Executive Director of the New York State School Boards Association. Martin Wasser was the senior counsel for the New York State Department of Environmental Conservation from 1975 to 1977. Both Grumet and Wasser were directly involved in the Moss Lake negotiations.

36. For the earlier occupation, see Hauptman, *The Iroquois Struggle for Survival*, 148–50. Although the Moss Lake occupation (1974–1977) has been written about previously, no one has taken advantage of the extensive (three boxes) correspondence in Moss Lake Indian Negotiations, New York State Department of State Records, Series #726, New York State Archives, Albany; or the Governor Hugh Carey Records, Subject Files, Reel 104, New York State Archives, Albany. For a synoptic analysis that

failed to take full advantage of these materials, see Gail H. Landsman, "Ganienkeh: Symbol and Politics in an Indian-White Land Dispute" (Ph.D. dissertation, Catholic University of America, Washington, D.C., 1982).

37. Mario Cuomo to "The File," November 4, 1976; Robert Batson to Secretary Cuomo, August 14, 1978, Moss Lake Indian Negotiations, Series #726, New York State Archives, Albany.

38. Mohawk (Akwesasne) Tribal Council to Governor Malcolm Wilson, November 25, 1974; Mario Cuomo to Mohawk Chiefs Rudolph Hart, Charles Terrance and Leonard Garrow, February 7, 1977, Moss Lake Indian Negotiations, New York State Department Records, Series #726, New York State Archives, Albany; Mohawk (Akwesasne) Tribal Council to Governor Carey, March 14, 1977; Carey to Mohawk (Akwesasne) Tribal Council, April 14, 1977, Governor Hugh Carey Records, Subject Files, Microfilm Reel 104, New York State Archives, Albany.

39. Robert Batson to Mario Cuomo, August 14, 1978. In order to attempt to defuse the political damage for not consulting beforehand with county legislators about the Moss Lake settlement, Cuomo later addressed the Clinton County Legislature. Importantly, today county legislators are consulted about the status of the Cayuga land claims and are brought into the process. This change was a direct result of the political faux pas at Moss Lake. Interview of Howard Rowley.

40. Interviews of Louis Grumet, Martin Wasser and Howard Rowley. Rowley, for one, kept bringing other issues besides land into the discussions while Cuomo, almost immediately, realized that "the land idea is basic." Louis Grumet to Mario Cuomo, October 22, 1976. For Rowley's role, see Grumet to Cuomo, September 9, 24, 1976 and September 6, 1977, Moss Lake Indian Negotiations, New York State Department of State Records, Series 726, New York State Archives, Albany. It is also clear that not all of the state negotiators at Moss Lake were knowledgeable about the people with whom they were negotiating or about Iroquois-state historical and legal relationships. There also were major personality clashes among the state officials and less-than-objective analyses of Indian leadership and American Indians working in New York State government at the time.

41. See note 38. For other divisions in the Indian world intensified by Moss Lake, see Lincoln White to Dr. Thomas Sheldon, January 27, 1975, Records of the Native American Indian Unit, Box 1, New York State Department of Education, New York State Archives, Albany. State Senator James Donovan was a leading critic of Governor Carey's and Secretary Cuomo's handling of Moss Lake. Interview of James Donovan. James Donovan to Governor Hugh Carey, April 17, 1975, Governor Hugh Carey Records, Subject Files, Microfilm Reel 104, New York State Archives, Albany. Donovan to Attorney General Louis Lefkowitz, July 6, 1977; Secretary of State Cuomo to Senator Donovan, July 25, 1977, Moss Lake Indian Negotiations, New York State Department of State Records, Series #726, New York State Archives, Albany. Interview of Fred DiMaggio; Elma Paterson, p.c., May 28, 1986.

42. Cuomo postscript to Memorandum from Lou Grumet to Secretary Cuomo, November 15, 1976.

43. Mario Cuomo to Louis Grumet, October 11, 1976; Cuomo to "The File," November 4, 1976, Moss Lake Indian Negotiations, New York State Department of State Records, Series #726, New York State Archives, Albany.

45. Lou Grumet to Secretary Cuomo, December 8, 1976; also see note 46. Grumet to Cuomo, December 8, 1976; interviews of Louis Grumet and Martin Wasser. Secretary of State to Lou Grumet, January 17, 1977, Moss Lake Indian Negotiations,

New York State Department of State Records, Series #726, New York State Archives, Albany.

47.   Mario Cuomo to the Chiefs of the Mohawk Nation and to the Chiefs of the Grand Council of the Six Nations of the Iroquois Confederacy, July 27, 1977, Moss Lake Indian Negotiations, New York State Department of State Records, Series #726, New York State Archives, Albany.

48.   Richard Kwartler, "'This Is Our Land': *The Mohawk Indians v. The State of New York*," in *Roundtable Justice: Case Studies in Conflict Resolution. Reports to the Ford Foundation*, ed. Robert B. Goldmann (Boulder, Colorado: Westview Press, 1980), 11 (emphasis added).

49.   Laurence M. Hauptman, Mohawk field notes, 1975–1986. For Cuomo's exaggerated goals for Ganienkeh, see Mario Cuomo to James Donovan, July 25, 1977.

6

Responses to the Cayuga Land Claim

CHRIS LAVIN

Not long after the U.S. Supreme Court ruled in 1974 that the Oneida Indian Nation of New York could sue in federal court to reclaim lands taken by New York State, it became apparent that that decision could have a wide-ranging impact on other parts of New York State. Other members of the Iroquois Confederacy—the six nation alliance of Indians that dates back to the fifteenth or sixteenth centuries—had eighteenth and nineteenth century land dealings with New York State that raise issues similar to those brought to the court by the Oneidas.

Oneida as precedent [margin note, handwritten]

One of those other nations is the Cayuga Indian Nation of New York. Now based where they live as guests on the Seneca Indians' Cattaraugus Reservation near Gowanda, the Cayuga Nation is a small group, numbering about 500 members who trace their ancestry back to Indians who once inhabited lands in what is now considered part of the Finger Lakes region of central and western New York.

Cayuga leaders have always been quick to recount the continual efforts made throughout Cayuga history to reclaim the land that was lost when their reservation lands were taken in the late 1700s and early 1800s. But it wasn't until the 1974 Oneida decision that the Cayugas' story of "illegal" land deals had much impact in the region of their ancestral lands. Most non-Indian residents of the region would say they didn't know the Indian nations that previously inhabited their region still existed. When the issue was raised, even fewer believed the Indians had any justifiable claim to land the Indians' ancestors had left generations before.

But the Cayugas laid claim to the land (see Map 6), first informally and later with a lawsuit. And when the impact of the claim was felt, the non-Indian public's response was sudden, dramatic, and

87

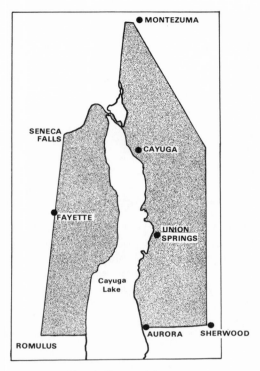

Map 6: Cayuga claim area

ranged from some quiet words of support for the Indians to loud threats of violence.

The as-yet unfinished story of the Cayuga Indian land claim—a legal claim now almost a decade old—is a study in the difficulty in establishing Indian legal rights and meeting obligations that have lingered for more than 200 years; it is also a story that reveals the bitterness and political bickering that have characterized the amorphous relationship that has existed continually among leaders of New York State, the U.S. federal government and the governments of the six Iroquois nations since the earliest days of U.S. colonial history.

Though this chapter is not intended to be an all-inclusive look at the legal complexities of the Cayuga claim, a brief sketch of the Cayugas' colonial history is necessary to understand why, when settlement efforts were made in the Cayuga claim, the issue became embroiled in a thicket of local, state, and federal politics that has made progress toward resolution difficult.

The Cayugas were one of the original member nations of the Iroquois Confederacy or Six Nations Confederacy. Although it was based in what today is upstate New York, the confederacy's influence was felt throughout the eastern region and into the plains. The first colonizers found the confederacy to be a formidable organization whose strength and strategic location gave it power out of proportion to its numbers.

As European colonizers arrived, each was careful to court Iroquois favor. When the American Revolution broke out, the confederacy officially declared its neutrality, but individual nations supported different colonial sides. The Cayugas joined the Mohawks, Onondagas and Senecas in fighting for England, while the Oneidas and Tuscaroras fought with the colonial army.

The end of the Revolution left the Cayugas without their British allies and facing a new nation of Americans who viewed the Cayugas as enemies. The post-Revolution Cayuga history consists of a constant struggle against a tide of land-hungry colonists pushing westward. Though the federal government did try to protect the Indian interests, the state of New York, which wielded much power under the weak Articles of Confederation, continued supporting efforts to obtain Indian lands.

Treaties participated in by the state and the Cayugas in 1789, 1795, and 1807 took all the Cayuga lands. Part of the Cayuga nation eventually moved to Oklahoma; another Cayuga group went to Canada, while others stayed in New York, living as guests of the Seneca Indians on the Senecas' Cattaraugus reservation of the city of Buffalo.

Almost immediately after losing their final lands, the Cayugas began protesting about the treaties that took the land. In court papers filed during the current Cayuga claim, the Cayugas chronicle what they say have been continual efforts to protest those treaties. Among the myriad legal points, they charge that the state had violated federal law by conducting negotiations and consummating land transactions without the involvement of federal inspectors, whose presence federal law intended to protect Indian interests. Further, they charged the land deals were never ratified by Congress and were thus not binding.

Since those land transactions, the desire and necessity of winning back some of their native lands has, in a way, become part of the modern-day Cayuga culture. Pauline Seneca, an eighty-three-year-old

Cayuga Indian, is a lifelong resident of the Senecas' Cattaraugus reservation and for years taught at the Thomas Indian School there. But despite her long ties to the Seneca community, she, like all the Cayugas living in and around the Cattaraugus reservation, remains a second-class Indian citizen—outcast because her nation lacks the thing that gives status to Indian nations—land.

"I'm eighty-three-years old now, and for all eighty-three years I've been going to Cayuga meetings about land," Seneca recounted in a 1985 interview. "This claim meeting and that claim meeting. We've never given up. But I don't think I'll live to see us get our land back."

There was a time, not so long ago, when it appeared that Cayugas like Pauline Seneca might survive to see a homeland established. In the late 1970s, Jimmy Carter was president. The Oneida suit had been fought all the way to the Supreme Court and the justices had ruled that, in fact, the federal Trade and Intercourse Act, long thought not to apply to the original thirteen colonies, could be used as the basis for eastern Indian claims to land taken centuries before. The Carter administration's approach to these legal claims was clear—negotiate rather than litigate. And, if the state and local governments involved in claim areas were reluctant to talk, then Carter's Justice Department threatened to fulfill the federal government's trust responsibility to the Indians by suing on behalf of the Indians for return of the lands illegally taken by state or local governments. The threat of the full weight of the U.S. government behind such Indian claims was a compelling one and negotiations began in several eastern Indian claims. During Carter's administration, the Penobscot and Passamaquoddy Indians of Maine reached a settlement that included millions of dollars and thousands of acres of land. That settlement included participation by federal, state and local governments, Passamaquoddy and Penobscot representatives and major landholders in the area, including major paper companies who supplied much of the forest land returned to the Indian people.

The actors in the Cayuga claim are an equally diverse group. The Cayugas had hired a Washington, D.C. attorney, Arthur Gajarsa, as their representative. Eventually a team composed of officials from the federal departments of Interior, Agriculture, and the Office of Management and Budget, as well as Congressman William Walsh, the Republican who represented the claim area, and New York State representatives, were put together to begin trying to fashion a settlement in the Cayuga case. Though some non-Indian residents of the claim area would later charge that this task force had been formed in secret and operated quickly to "ram something through Congress for the Indians," the public record shows the existence of the task force and its deliberations were publicized regularly in newspapers throughout the claim area. If there was a sense of urgency in the settlement procedures, it probably stemmed from a combination of factors. First, Gajarsa, the Cayugas' attorney, held that the Cayugas would have to either settle the case or file suit before a Congress-imposed statute of limitations on such claims ran out at the end of 1977. That statute of limitations combined with a fear expressed by some, but not all, businessmen, bankers and elected officials that a Cayuga lawsuit would cloud all land titles in the claim area and would bring to a virtual halt all land transactions. If a suit was to be avoided, there was a sense among many that a settlement had to be fashioned quickly.

But fear of real estate tie-ups was not local residents' first reaction to talk of the Cayuga claim. Before the claim was taken seriously by local residents, there was an initial reaction of incredulity. For example, some executives of title insurance companies said they would continue to grant title insurance despite a claim, that, if treated like most claims against title, would have kept any insurance company from getting involved. Paul D. Moonan, Sr., president of Monroe Title and Abstract Company, one of the region's biggest title insurance companies, was quoted in the Rochester *Times-Union* at the time as seeing little risk involved in his offer. He said he believed the Cayugas have "no moral or legal justification" for their claim.

Moonan's view was apparently shared by elected officials in the area, both federal and local. On June 9, 1977, Congressman Walsh was quoted in the Rochester *Democrat and Chronicle* as saying that the claim is unrealistic. "It's hard for me to understand how the federal government can take the position that a treaty signed 170 years ago and held valid all that time, all of a sudden no longer is legal," Walsh said. He speculated at the time it might be possible to set aside the claims through legislation. Similarly, Paul Lattimore, a landowner in the claim area and mayor of Auburn, the largest city in Cayuga County, publicly stated that he didn't fear a lawsuit because he believed the Cayugas were just after money, not land.

But less than a month after Walsh expressed doubts about the seriousness of the Cayuga claim, he was in Congress pushing for a bill that would extend the statute of limitations on the Indian claims from

1977 to 1981 to allow time for negotiations. By July, the threat of a Justice Department suit on behalf of the Cayugas was clear. Interior Department Solicitor Leo M. Krulitz had been quoted as saying that the federal role in the Cayuga claim would be similar to the advocacy role it was playing in the Passamaquoddy and Penobscot claim in Maine.

By late August, 1977, Walsh was leading the call for formation of a joint state-federal task force to negotiate an out-of-court settlement to avoid a lawsuit and to calm the worries of landowners in the claim area. By August, 1977, more than two thousand residents of the area had paid $1 each to become a member of the Cayuga-Seneca Property Owners Association, a group formed to take a role in fighting the land claims. Walsh attempted to calm the fears of local residents, asking them to sit back and wait while the state and federal governments tried to settle the claim.

By March 1978, a Carter task force had been named and task force members—including Gail Acterman, an attorney with the Department of Interior—met that month with property owners in the claim area to explain that the task force would try to have a settlement bill ready quickly for consideration by Congress. Negotiations, however, went more slowly than expected and Walsh or his representative on the task force—Arthur Jutton—made regular reports to constituents about progress in the negotiations. Walsh or his spokesman continually repeated the Congressman's position that a settlement would probably include money and land.

A settlement wasn't finalized before the end of 1978 and Walsh, a long-time Congressman at that point, had chosen not to seek re-election in the fall of that year. That decision changed the cast of characters on the task force and, some would argue later, resulted in the eventual scuttling of this settlement effort.

Replacing Walsh in January 1979, was Republican Gary Lee, a former state Assemblyman from Dryden, who had won election to Walsh's vacated post. Like Walsh, Lee, as Congressman for the claim area, would play a central role in the task force that was seeking to negotiate the Cayuga settlement. And almost immediately, Lee appeared to take up where Walsh had left off, speaking publicly in favor of the negotiation process and against litigation that could tie up property titles for years. Lee kept Arthur Jutton, Walsh's representative on the task force, in that job and the task force talks continued.

Though specific details of the task force deliberations were supposed to be confidential, leaks did occur during the talks and were widely reported by the media. In March 1979, for example, an official in the New York State Park Service told reporters that the Hector Land Use Area, a block of federal land in southern Seneca County, was being considered as part of the settlement. Other reporters in following months included comments from task force members that "all publicly held lands" in Cayuga and Seneca counties were being considered in fashioning a settlement.

By August 1979, the Cayuga land claim task force had fashioned a final proposal. Details of the settlement bill were first reported on August 18, 1979 by the *Finger Lakes Times*, a small daily paper that circulates widely through the claim area and had received a tip from a "federal source" as to the details of the settlement. On August 21, U.S. Interior Department officials formally announced the details of a memorandum of understanding that had been signed by federal, state, and Indian leaders. That agreement would have given the Cayugas, 1,852-acre Sampson State Park in southern Seneca County; 3,629-acre federal Hector Land Use Area, also in southern Seneca County; an $8 million trust fund held by the Secretary of the Interior. Up to $2.5 million of the original amount could be used to purchase more land to be added to the new reservation area, possibly to buy land to join the non contiguous Sampson and Hector land areas.

Prior to the announcement of the settlement, public reaction to the negotiations had been relatively muted. No one knew for certain what the settlement would be and, despite repeated comments to the contrary by Indians and non-Indians on the task force, many local residents still believed a strictly monetary settlement would be reached. However, almost immediately after the details of the memorandum were announced, sides were quickly drawn for and against the settlement. The battle lines were clear.

Residents of southern Seneca County—where the new reservation was to be located—were outraged. They accused the federal and state officials of working in secret and vowed to fight the settlement bill in Congress. The Seneca County Liberation Organization was created by Wisner Kinne, an Ovid farmer, to build opposition to the establishment of a reservation anywhere in Seneca County.

Other residents of the region, however, saw the memorandum differently. The Cayuga-Seneca Landowners Association leadership—headed by attorney Walter Foulke of Union Springs, Cayuga County—found itself opposed to the goals of the Seneca County Liberation Organization. In their view, the memorandum proposal would eliminate the possibility of a lengthy lawsuit and clouded title, and would result neither in the loss of any private lands nor in the loss of public land in the more populous northern ends of Seneca and Cayuga counties.

The degree and depth of disagreement among local residents over the settlement proposal was most dramatically apparent at a public meeting the task force held at Eisenhower College in Seneca Falls on September 11, 1979. More than fifteen hundred people attended. It was the largest public hearing anyone could remember in this largely rural area. Supporters of the settlement were identified by green tags handed out at the beginning of the hearing by the Cayuga-Seneca Property Owners Association. Opponents of the settlement—mainly residents of southern Seneca County—launched virulent attacks against task force members and Cayuga chiefs who also attended the meeting. Several opponents criticized the task force for working secretly and denying the local residents "due process of law." The settlement, leaders charged, would erode the tax base of the southern end of the county and ruin any hopes of economic revival. Others dragged out racist accusations of "surprise Indian attacks" to describe the task force process. "I thought when Clinton and his troops marched through here in the 1700s that the Indian problem was taken care of," Waterloo Supervisor LaVerne Sessler commented at the time. "Obviously, it's not." In a historical comment that became a common theme over the ensuing year, another woman said, "The Cayugas were allies of the British; they lost the war . . . and the land."

In the months following the public hearing, the public battle waged on. As a bill was prepared to bring the memorandum of understanding before Congress, the Seneca County Liberation Organization began raising money to wage a court fight of its own against the settlement. Members of the group flooded local newspapers with letters opposing the claim. The group's president, Wisner Kinne, pledged $5,000 for a court fight and began writing regular newspaper columns. "Act now," Kinne would exhort in his column. "Don't let the Indians surprise you. Surprise has always been their tactic in war." His columns in an Ovid weekly newspaper implied that the American Indian movement had communist ties, and predicted that Indian land claims across the country could destroy the federal government. The campaign seemed to pay political dividends as one by one local town and village boards throughout the county voted resolutions opposing the settlement; the Seneca County Board of Supervisors also voted to oppose it. The municipal boards and county leaders also pledged a willingness to use taxpayers' money to fund a legal challenge of the settlement.

The man in the hot seat—caught between a Cayuga County constituency generally in favor and a Seneca County one opposed—was freshman Congressman Gary Lee. Lee had supported the negotiation process from his first days in office, but in the face of such turmoil over the settlement proposal, his support appeared to wane. At a hearing before the House Interior Committee on March 3, 1980, Lee appeared to continue to support the settlement. "I feel we must proceed with amendment and passage of the settlement," Lee told the committee. "Only one alternative to passage of this bill remains at this point, to go to court. That remains a totally unacceptable alternative under any circumstances." But behind the scenes, Lee's efforts to amend the settlement bill began to reflect the position of residents of southern Seneca County. Though his representative was part of the two-year negotiations of the memorandum of understanding, Lee now became more adamant about amendments that had not been major issues during the previous two years of negotiations. Lee now wanted a cap put on the amount of land the Indians could purchase and wanted a requirement added to force the Indians to make payments in lieu of taxes to local governments. He also wanted any settlement to be approved by the New York State Legislature, a move that would leave the task force the formidable—some said impossible—job of winning the approval of the Republican-dominated state senate.

Lee's amendments were not acceptable to the Cayugas and other task force members and, when Congressman Morris Udall submitted the bill to Congress, it didn't contain all the changes Lee had wanted. When the bill came to the floor of the House of Representatives—just weeks after Lee had supported the settlement at a committee meeting—Lee spoke against the bill. Without the support of the local Congressman, the House—in keeping with House tradition on such local-issue bills opposed by the local Congressman—defeated the bill 201 to 187.

On November 19, 1980, the Cayugas filed suit in the U.S. District Court in Syracuse seeking return of 64,015 acres of land, ejection of about 7,000 property owners from the land, and $350 million in trepass damages. The lawsuit everyone wanted to avoid was on; the lawyers' fee meters were running and haven't stopped since. By 1986, legal fees paid by localities in defending against the Cayuga claim approached the $1 million range and the case still did not pass the pre-trial hearing stage.

After the defeat of the settlement bill, Lee's position changed more dramatically, in part because Lee became increasingly suspicious about the motives of Interior Department officials who had served on the task force. After the settlement bill's defeat, Lee's office received a copy of a letter sent from then U.S. Attorney General Griffin Bell to officials in the Department of Interior saying the Justice Department wouldn't press the land claim suit for the Cayugas. That letter, Lee argued, drastically changed the situation in the Cayuga case and should have been shared with task force members during negotiation of the settlement memorandum. After learning of the "Bell letter," which his office referred to as a "smoking gun," Lee abandoned efforts to fashion a new negotiated settlement and began pursuing efforts to have Congress unilaterally end the Cayuga claim by ratifying the original treaties.

Lee's ratification effort was supported by New York Senator Alfonse D'Amato, a Republican, and the same Seneca County officials who opposed the original settlement bill, but was easily blocked by the opposition of Udall, chairman of the House Interior Committee and long an advocate of fair treatment of Indian tribes. Lee was successful, however, in negating much of the feared impact of a land claim on titles by convincing the federal home and farm loan programs to continue granting mortgages in the claim area. Local banks, for the most part, followed suit, but now required title insurance for all mortgage transfers in the claim area. Title insurance companies continued to serve the area, despite the Indian claims.

While Lee tried to marshall support for his ratification bill, residents of Seneca and Cayuga counties began defending themselves in court. Seneca County hired famed Boston attorney James St. Clair—President Richard Nixon's attorney during the Watergate scandal—to represent its landowners. Cayuga County also retained Allan van Gestel, who had defended landowners in the earlier Oneida Indian claim.

The slow, deliberate pace of court proceedings muffled much of the more dramatic public outcry about the claim that occurred while settlement talks progressed, but local residents' view of the Cayugas' position remained the same. On July 30, 1982, when the Cayuga claim made its first substantive appearance in federal court, landowners from Seneca County were there along with many other Seneca County Liberation Organization members to lend their $200-an-hour attorneys some moral support as they argued to have the claim dismissed. One landowner summarized the Cayuga position as he saw it then: "They're trying to say 'cause 200 years ago some Indians got stuck, I can't have my land. That's just not right. What's done is done."

Those dismissal arguments—like similar arguments in the earlier Oneida claim—were argued before Federal District Court Judge Neal

McCurn. And in this preliminary Cayuga hearing, as with the Oneidas before, McCurn refused to dismiss the claim. The Cayuga case has continued inching its way through a court that has been openly reluctant to bring the case to a full jury trial. McCurn has been quite unusually open for a federal judge in telling reporters, lawyers, and politicians that claims this old should not be tried in court, but should be settled by Congress.

While the court case has moved slowly, there was a political change that rejuvenated settlement efforts. Following the 1980 census, New York's loss of population required that politicians redraw the boundaries of the state's Congressional districts to reflect the state's reduced number of congressmen. When that redistricting was completed, Gary Lee's district had been carved up by other, more senior congressmen, and Lee was forced into an unsuccessful primary battle against Republican incumbent George Wortley. With Lee gone, the Cayuga claim area was now within the expanded district of veteran Republican Congressman Frank Horton, who rejected Lee's unsuccessful efforts to have congress ratify the treaties and quickly revived efforts to seek a negotiated settlement.

Horton appointed long-time New York Indian negotiator Howard Rowley of Rochester to head new settlement efforts, and in May 1983 Rowley convened a meeting of a new task force. Rowley had extensive experience in mediating past conflicts between Iroquois nations and New York State, as well as similar problems throughout the United States. His new Cayuga task force included not only federal, state and Cayuga representatives, but for the first time included representatives of Cayuga and Seneca counties, groups that had complained about lack of representation in the earlier settlement effort.

At the outset, Rowley had several points in his favor with the new negotiations. With the Cayuga suit progressing, it was now apparent that the claims would neither die nor be killed by Congress and legal bills for the counties involved were beginning to mount, an expense these less-than-affluent counties would be glad to bring to an end if possible. Also, the Oneida claim, which had achieved success before the U.S. Supreme Court was scheduled to have a final decision from that court. If that decision, like the previous ones, went in the Oneidas' favor, the similar Cayuga legal position would be further bolstered.

Rowley, an executive with Rochester Gas and Electric Company, appeared to meet with early success. Task force members—even those from southern Seneca County—spoke with hope about reaching a negotiated settlement acceptable to all. Some of the most adamant opposition to the earlier settlement proposal had been muzzled by the fact that their main complaint—lack of representation on the task force—had been met by Rowley and Horton in forming a new settlement team.

So in June 1984, an announcement by Rowley of a new settlement package was met with little of the public rancor the 1979 announcement had brought, even though the new package was substantially larger than the one offered in 1979. In 1984, the Cayugas were offered: the state-owned Howland Game Management Reserve, a 3,200-acre parcel along the Seneca River in Cayuga County; a 2,850-acre parcel along the shore of Lake Ontario in Sterling, Cayuga County, property owned by Rochester Gas and Electric Company; about 2,000 acres of public and private land adjacent to but not including the developed portions of Sampson State Park in Seneca County. In addition, the Cayugas were to receive "well in excess" of the $8 million they were offered in the earlier settlement, but a specific amount was never announced.

The public reaction to this proposal was muted, and public officials were generally supportive. Some of the Seneca County officials who had vehemently opposed the earlier settlement—like Romulus Town Supervisor Raymond Zajac—now talked of the benefits that could accrue to the county through supporting the establishment of a reservation. Zajac, in fact, drew up a sort of shopping list of economic development and in-lieu-of tax payments the county wanted from New York State in order to support the new proposal. Though some residents remained opposed, on principle, to any settlement with the Indians, others who had opposed the earlier settlement seemed to temper their stance as time went on. "Things have changed," Wisner Kinne, the head of the Seneca County Liberation Organization told the Rochester *Times-Union* when Rowley's new proposal was announced. "We're not terrified anymore. The federal government isn't threatening to cram this down our throats the way they did last time." The Cayugas, too, seemed happy with the proposal. The chiefs announced that they would accept the land parcels and expressed optimism for the first time in years that the litigation could end.

That was 1984 and Rowley's effort appeared to be headed for a successful conclusion, but it hasn't been a speedy end. In the years since those land parcels were announced, Rowley has worked behind the scenes to get final approval from New York State officials and federal Department of Interior officials for the land and financial package that could be valued at more than $30 million. Rowley has had to deal with the opposition from national environmental groups that have forced him to consider alternatives to the Howland Island land. Also, because Horton refused to sponsor any settlement not supported by the Seneca and Cayuga county governments, Rowley has had to spend time assuring that votes could be won in both Seneca County and Cayuga County boards of supervisors to support the settlement.

And lastly, Rowley and Horton have been unable to get final approval from President Reagan's administration for the settlement package. Several points make that administration support difficult to come by at this time. The fiscal constraints of the Gramm-Rudman federal budget deficit reduction efforts give any spending tough scrutiny these days. And there are political impediments as well. Horton, though a veteran Republican, often votes with Democrats in the Democrat-controlled House. Horton's votes in 1985 and 1986 against Reagan's efforts to give military aid to the Contras fighting the Sandinista regime in Nicaragua may have lost him any leverage in the White House. And, because Democratic New York Governor Mario Cuomo, rumored to be a presidential contender in 1988, is involved in the issue, there may be reluctance among Washington's Republican leaders to do anything that would help Cuomo, particularly because Cuomo was up for re-election in 1986.

If Rowley's attempt to fashion a negotiated settlement eventually succeeds, the tortured history of the Cayuga land claim talks could hold several lessons in settling not only other Indian land claims in the state, but also in settling disputes between non-Indians and Indians in New York.

The early attempt to settle the Cayuga claim may have been performed too quickly. While the original Cayuga task force was open about when and where they were meeting, their refusal to discuss openly the specific land parcels being considered, coupled with the relative speed of their negotiations, left the memorandum of understanding vulnerable to attack from residents and local politicians of the area where the new reservation would be established. In addition to the racist and xenophobic concerns expressed by opponents of the earlier plan, there were some legitimate concerns about the changing nature of their community, the possible erosion of the tax base, and questions over law enforcement on the new reservation. Though the Cayuga chiefs attempted to calm residents' fears, the closed nature of the negotiations and the lack of local representation in the original settlement talks undermined any trust that might have been brought about between the local residents and the Cayuga Nation, which would be southern Seneca County's new neighbor.

With such a charged atmosphere, it would take unusual political leadership to bring about a final out-of-court settlement. With fresh-man Congressman Gary Lee, at the forefront of the settlement issue was a newcomer to Washington and to the land claim issue itself. It is possible that he was not yet of the political stature to carry the settlement bill in the face of such local opposition. It could also be argued that even if Lee had not reversed his position and opposed the first settlement, lawsuits brought by local municipalities or residents of the area attacking the settlement could have tied up the process in any event. Regardless of the perceived merits of such a legal action, the willingness of the people to put their financial support behind such a move suggests that a congressionally imposed settlement would not be easy or quick, nor would it result in an environment in which a fragile Cayuga community could easily begin settlement and development efforts.

Since the early failure, state, federal, and local governments have proceeded on new settlement talks with the understanding that there must be agreement among at least the leadership of all jurisdictions involved before a settlement bill can go to Congress. Recent history has shown that achieving unanimity among the residents of whatever area is chosen for a new reservation site is unlikely, but as litigation costs mount and the court case draws closer to a trial date, state, local, and federal leaders will face increasing pressures to risk offending some constituents if the title threat and the drain of the defense costs are to be lifted from the community at large.

If the Rowley-Horton task force effort fails, however, the claim may have to run its course—through a lengthy and expensive jury trial in which the issue of what political leaders had done almost 200 years ago will again be debated and the consequences of those actions again weighed. As the trial pushes on, it is likely that banks and title insurance companies may become unwilling to do business in the claim area. That is a scenario that all involved in the settlement talks say they want to avoid, but those talks—like Indian policy throughout New York State's history—continues to be slowed by federal, state, and local political snags.

7

The Historical Background to the Present-Day Seneca Nation— Salamanca Lease Controversy

LAURENCE M. HAUPTMAN

INTRODUCTION

In 1985 the *New York Times* featured a story on Salamanca, New York, a city housed entirely on the Allegany Reservation of the Seneca Nation of Indians. Claiming that a crisis of momentous proportions was now at hand, the newspaper reported that ninety-nine-year leases made by non-Indians with the Senecas were to expire in 1991 and that tensions were building between the two communities about the terms of renewal and even whether the Seneca landlords should issue new leases.[1] Much of the reporting of this controversy surrounding the future of Salamanca has failed to bring out the long and complex history of the leases, a factor that still shapes both the Indian and non-Indian positions in today's negotiations.

HISTORICAL SURVEY: THE FIRST HUNDRED YEARS

In the mid-nineteenth century, the Senecas began leasing rights-of-way through portions of their reservations to several railroads, including the Erie Railroad and its component spur lines. White farmers, persons in service occupations for the railroads, and their employees began to occupy tracts of land within the Allegany Reservation. They subsequently leased these reservation lands at low rentals from the

Seneca tribal council or from Senecas who claimed individual possessory rights to such lands in conformity with ancient usages and
customs. Because some of these leases were of highly dubious legality,
and because of the significant economic investment of whites on the
reservation, Congress officially confirmed the leases in 1875. This date
marked the beginning of the major thrust by non-Indians for allotment
of Seneca lands by these same lessees and their representatives.

By 1875, some of the non-Indians had already made sizeable
profits by subleasing Indian land; 420 leasing arrangements had been
made and the total white investment on the Allegany Reservation had
reached $1,359,775. Approximately one-third of this reservation was
leased to non-Indians. By 1900, Salamanca's white residents outnum-
bered the Indian population on Allegany by five to one.[2] Consequently, several non-Indian communities, including the City of
Salamanca, were founded within the Allegany Reservation.

To make matters more complicated, an oil and natural gas rush
soon took place in and around the Seneca lands. In the 1890s, a non-
Indian venture—the Seneca Oil Company—leased parcels of the Allegany Reservation, obtaining a ninety-nine-year lease containing
provison for one-eighth royalty to the Indians. The company proceeded to develop these lands and struck oil in 1897. In 1899, 75,695
barrels were produced. On January 1, 1900, the Seneca Oil Company
sold its leases to the South Penn Oil Company, a subsidiary of Standard Oil, for $2 million, transferring forty wells producing two hun-
dred barrels a day. With "oil fever" in southwestern New York,
pressure for allotting Indian lands reached its zenith in this period, led
by Congressman Edward B. Vreeland, a partner in the Seneca Oil
Company.[3]

In addition, the Allegany Reservation of the Seneca Nation was
also affected by the early nineteenth-century machinations of land
speculators. Although the long history of the Ogden Land Company's
claim to Seneca lands is beyond the scope of this chapter, the company's relationship to these lands needs some elaboration. The Ogden
Land Company has been interpreted as owning the first right to
purchase the Allegany and Cattaraugus reservations if the Indians,
however unlikely, ever decide to sell their lands. The noted legal
scholar Gerald Gunther, of the Stanford University School of Law, has
stated that the "Ogden claim has been a pervasive source of difficulty in
the handling of New York Indian matters."[4] This assertion is an
understatement of one of the most perplexing problems involving
aboriginal land tenure in the United States.

On September 12, 1810, David A. Ogden of New York City purchased for himself and his associates the Holland Land Company's interests in Seneca lands in New York. The Ogden Land Company, not a corporation but comprising the heirs of Ogden and his partners, contributed to Seneca suspicions of the motives of white people. Tempered only by the activities of well-meaning Quaker missionaries, the Ogden Land Company continually interfered in Seneca politics throughout the first half of the nineteenth century. As land speculators, the company sought to remove the Indians from New York State in order to profit from the sale of their lands. It pursued this objective through bribery, whiskey, the threat of force, and deliberate misrepresentation of facts. The company was instrumental in one of the most flagrant land swindles in New York history, the Treaty of Buffalo Creek of 1838, in which a majority of the Iroquois chiefs in New York were prevailed upon to sell the remainder of their reservations in the state to the company. Only after considerable agitation by many of the Indians and their white friends were the Senecas able to sign the Second Treaty of Buffalo Creek, the so-called compromise treaty, which returned to the Indians in 1842 the Allegany and Cattaraugus reservations. It was these events and their impact that caused the political upheaval of 1848 that led to the formation of the Seneca Nation of Indians.[5]

Bitter memories of the actions of the Ogdens and other land speculators lingered in Iroquois country throughout the nineteenth century. Nevertheless (and ironically), the Ogden Land Company's preemptive claim had helped to cloud the issue of allotment and let the Senecas keep their land. The question had been raised about how Congress or the state of New York could partition Seneca land and allow for its sale to whites other than the Ogden Land Company. During the second half of the nineteenth century and well into the twentieth both Washington and Albany, pressured by the white lessees and their political representatives, grappled with the issue of buying the company's preemptive right. Congressmen and assemblymen repeatedly introduced legislation to extinguish the claim. Despite the government's recognition of the legality of the claim, the Indians questioned whether the Ogden Land Company had any right to sell their land at all. At the same time, the Senecas resisted government efforts to extinguish the claim because they believed extinguishment would be the first step in separating them from their land. Meanwhile, the Ogden Land Company held out for more settlement money, demanding more than Congress believed they deserved. In this way, the impasse helped the Senecas hold onto their land base, resist the threat of allotment and survive as a people.[6]

The pressure for allotment of Seneca lands did not arise suddenly with the bills that Congressman Edward Vreeland introduced in the House of Representatives early in the twentieth century. From 1875 onward, bills and riders dealing with this question had been submitted almost every other year in Congress and in the New York State Legislature. In Congress, New York representatives drafted legislation to allot Seneca lands outright or attached amendments to Indian appropriation bills calling for the United States government to extinguish the preemptive claim of the Ogden Land Company. In the New York State Legislature, similar attempts had been undertaken. These early attempts eventually resolved the jurisdictional question in favor of Congress, and, at the same time, recognized the official standing of the Ogden Land Company. They also showed that there was little support both inside and outside of Congress for paying out large sums of public moneys to extinguish the company's claim. At the turn of the century, Vreeland discovered a "magic formula" for convincing a large number of his budget-minded colleagues of the advantages of this action. His plan was to have the Seneca Nation itself pay off the Ogden Land Company with part of the $2 million it had obtained in a court decision adjudicating its claims in Kansas. The two reservations would then be divided among individual Indians under an allotment formula that would facilitate land transfer and sales to non-Indians.[7]

Vreeland, who was also the president of the major bank in Salamanca, was the chief architect and promoter of allotment of Seneca lands and led the fight in Congress. The favorable climate for allotment that had produced the Dawes Act of 1887 also aided Vreeland in his numerous attempts to secure allotment of Seneca lands. Through effective public relations work and political finesse, he sponsored two bills—H.R. 12270 and H.R. 7262—and managed them successfully through the House of Representatives, but they were defeated in the Senate. Despite Vreeland's failure to secure passage, interest in allotment of Seneca Nation's lands continued through World War I.

The longevity and strength of Vreeland's movement to allot Indian lands was, in part, a result of support by influential reform groups, such as the Indian Rights Association and the annual Lake Mohonk Conferences of Friends of the Indian. They viewed allotment as part of their four-point plan of forced assimilation: Christian proselytizing; compulsory education in white American ways and values;

the breakup of tribal lands; allotment to individual Indians to instill personal initiative (supposedly required by the free enterprise system); and finally, in return for accepting land-in-severalty, the reward of United States citizenship.[8]

Vreeland was also armed by several studies made by committees of the New York State Legislature, with the most important one headed by James S. Whipple, a Salamanca attorney and friend of Vreeland. In a report of 1888–1889, the Whipple Committee urged the United States government to extinguish the Ogden claim in order to solve the so-called "Indian problem" and begin a "radical uprooting of the whole tribal system, giving to each individual absolute ownership of his share of the land in fee."[9] In this report, which has continued to breed Iroquois resentment toward the New York State government to the present day, Iroquois family life, land claims, lifestyle, and religious practices and traditions were held in contempt to emphasize the "need for the changes in landed patterns and tribal governments."[10]

In the tight-knit power structure of Salamanca politics (which changed little through World War II), the motive for the movement to pass the Vreeland bills was clear. Whipple's son was married to Vreeland's daughter and the congressman's brother served as special counsel for the New York Legislature's Whipple committee investigation. A. W. Ferrin, co-editor of the local newspaper, the *Cattaraugus Republican* (now the *Salamanca Republican-Press*), was also the Indian agent for the New York Agency of the Bureau of Indian Affairs (BIA) and was in favor of the legislation.[11] In 1902, on the day his first allotment bill passed the House, Vreeland openly expressed his objective: "I represent 8,000 people who live upon these reservations; who hold ninety-nine-year leases from these Indians, and want to get a title to their lands."[12]

While the movement for allotment of Seneca lands had died out by the 1920s, a lasting legacy remained. Because of the bitterness caused by the Vreeland bills, the Senecas associated all legislative efforts (such as the Indian Citizenship Act of 1924 and the Indian Reorganization Act of 1934) as renewed attempts to get at their land base.[13] The white leaders at Salamanca, led by the same families as in the 1890s (such as the Vreelands and the Whipples), never completely lost hope of securing title. After a while, many just stopped paying their rents to the Seneca Nation. They took these payments for granted as "inconsequential" obligations, partly because they were infinitesimal and partly because they assumed that the Indians were powerless to force them to pay. By 1939, over 25 percent of the leases within the Allegany Reservation were in default. Moreover, more than two hundred had been delinquent for more than seven years.[14]

Related to the allotment movement and forcible assimilation of Indians into the mainstream was a movement to shift the Iroquois from federal to state jurisdiction. For years, the United States government and the state of New York had frequently clashed over which had paramount jurisdiction over the Iroquois. Although the federal government provided little monetary aid to the Iroquois until the New Deal, the New York Agency of the Bureau of Indian Affairs paid and distributed annuities under federal-Iroquois treaties, collected rentals on leases, provided educational loans and scholarship programs beyond state schools, administered special federal work-relief programs (such as the New Deal Indian Civilian Conservation Corps) and made special investigations and prepared annual reports to Washington.

New York State, through the Department of Social Services in Buffalo, administered the Thomas Indian School, almost all social welfare and work relief programs, and payment of State annuity moneys to the Mohawks, Onondagas, and the scattered Cayugas. The New York State Department of Health was in charge of administering to the health needs of reservation Indians. In the educational realm, the Chief of the Special Schools Bureau of the State Education Department administered district schools on the reservations and worked with public schools that some of the Indians attended in towns adjacent to the reservations. Beyond high school, the state provided aid for students attending state normal schools and colleges. The State Department of Highways financed the construction and maintenance of highways on the reservations. With the expansion of federal government services to the Iroquois in the 1930s and the change from a federal operating budget of the New York Agency of a few thousand dollars, the ambiguities between State and federal jurisdiction became more accentuated.[15]

Despite the opinions of legal scholars (including Felix Cohen, the foremost authority on Indian law and an attorney for the Interior Department in the 1930s and 1940s) that federal-Iroquois treaties of the 1780s and 1790s "had the effect of placing the tribes and their reservations beyond the operation and effect of general State laws," New York State continued to exercise de facto concurrent jurisdiction over Indian affairs from the 1790s onward.[16] New York State legislators and representatives in Congress continued to seek paramount jurisdiction over Indian affairs during the last quarter of the nineteenth century and into the mid-twentieth century. At the time of the Whipple Committee and again in 1906, 1915, 1930, and 1940, legislators attempted to effect this change. The Iroquois waged major battles, especially in 1930, against state jurisdiction. Even though the jurisdiction bill of 1930, introduced by Congressman Bertram Snell of Potsdam, had provided for a formal recognition of property rights guaranteed by treaties, the Six Nations, suspicious of non-Indian motives, feared it as a "contravention of treaty rights" and an effort that would subject them to the uncontrollable whims of state politics.[17] According to Tuscarora Chief Clinton Rickard:

> In 1930 a serious threat faced our Six Nations people in the form of the Snell Bill in Congress, which would give control of our Six Nations to New York State. We Indians have always feared being under the thumb of the state rather than continuing our relationship with the federal government because it is a well-known fact that *those white people who live closest to Indians are always the most prejudiced against them and the most desirous of obtaining their lands*. We have always had a better chance of obtaining justice from Washington than from the state or local government. Also, in turning us over to the state, the federal government would be downgrading our significance as a people and ignoring the fact that our treaties are with the United States.[18] [Emphasis added.]

To the policy makers, jurisdiction and leasing seemed to be separate issues and were viewed by them as unrelated. The Indians however, never viewed them as entirely distinct, largely because the same New Yorkers who had pushed for jurisdictional changes in the past were often the same attorneys or legislators who represented non-Indians in their legal struggle against the Iroquois. For example, the Snell Bill of 1930 had been drafted by Henry Manley, the Assistant Attorney General of New York State. Later, in the early 1940s, Manley was one of the attorneys for the Fornesses and other Salamanca lessees in their legal appeals to stop the Senecas from initiating eviction proceedings. In the 1950s, Manley worked on behalf of the New York State Power Authority in its successful fight to condemn Tuscarora lands for a reservoir. Similarly, Daniel Reed, a Congressman from Dunkirk, New York and a protege of Snell, was the main voice in protecting the interests of his southwestern New York constituents in their legal tiffs with the Seneca Nation. As a highly influential member of the House of Representatives Ways and Means Committee, Reed

108 LAURENCE M. HAUPTMAN

was the legislative "point man" in getting his colleague Hugh Butler of
Nebraska to introduce legislation in 1948 and 1950 leading to New
York State jurisdiction over Indian criminal and civil matters.[19]

In the 1930s, after years of seeking redress, the Seneca Nation
found a favorable ear at the Public Lands Division of the United States
Department of Justice. Aubrey Lawrence and, more significantly,
Charles Cleaves Daniels, the brother of the powerful southern Demo-
crat and FDR supporter, Josephus Daniels, took up the Seneca cause.
During the New Deal, C. C. Daniels was a Special Assistant to U.S.
Attorney General Nicholas Biddle and specialized in Indian legal
matters. In the early 1930s, Daniels had met Lulu Stillman, a non-
Indian activist who had served as a legal advisor and confidante to
Indian traditionalists at the St. Regis and Tuscarora Reservations.
Stillman had served as clerk-stenographer-researcher for the New York
State Legislative Committee (better known as the Everett Commission)
that was investigating the so-called "Indian problem" from 1919 to
1922. The report of Chairman Edward Everett of Potsdam, New York,
though never published, had concluded that the Iroquois were fraudu-
lently dispossessed of over six million acres of land in New York.[20]

Although C. C. Daniels was never involved in the Iroquois
claims movement, he was influenced both by Stillman and by Everett's
report. In a memorandum to the U.S. attorney general in 1934,
Daniels wrote, "However much the conclusions of the Chairman [Ever-
ett] may be questioned, there can be little doubt that he was honest and
sincere in his effort to get at the very bottom of the New York Indian
situation." In this memorandum, Daniels thanked Stillman for helping
him obtain a rare copy of the Everett Report, gave a brief history of the
jurisdictional question affecting the Iroquois, insisted that the Indians
were almost entirely suspicious of and opposed to state supervision
over tribal matters, and enclosed Everett's findings for the Attorney
General's perusal.[21]

In late 1934, after a visit to Salamanca that was preceded by
contact with the BIA central office in Washington, Daniels prepared a
memorandum that suggested it would be proper procedure for the
council of the Seneca Nation to cancel the leases. Daniels' preliminary
investigation suggested that all leases be investigated in Salamanca to
determine whether they warranted cancellation; that legal action be
taken to repossess lots and collect back rent where the facts warranted
it; that after cancellation, new leases more favorable to the Indians be
written; and that all tenants, whether in default or not, be encouraged
to accept new, more equitable leases that would benefit the Seneca
Nation and the growth of the locality.[22]

On March 4, 1939, at a regular session of the tribal council, the Seneca Nation finally decided to take Daniels' advice and cancel all delinquent leases. Two months later, the Lease Committee of the Seneca Nation, composed of Cornelius Seneca, Wilford Crouse, Theodore Gordon, Jr., Cephas Watt, Adlai Williams and Ulysses Printup, held a meeting at the Dudley Hotel in Salamanca which was also attended by Daniels and Lawrence. The Seneca Nation Lease Committee authorized the two Justice Department attorneys to proceed with the "test cases of certain leases cancelled by the Council . . . for the purpose of establishing through proper legal procedure the fact that the Council of the Seneca Nation has legal authority to cancel any and all delinquent leases on the basis of delinquency."[23] Despite the cancellation of over 800 of the leases, the Seneca Nation left open the Indian willingness to negotiate new leases at 2.5 percent of the appraised value of land and insisted that the cancellations were done only when the defaulting lessees refused to enter into negotiations, and that the intention of the Indian action had never been "to work any hardship upon the defaulting lessees or any third persons . . ." Since these ninety-nine-year leases had no accelerator clauses and had been negotiated at bargain-basement rates, the Indians saw federal court cases as the only hope to rectify the abuses of the past.[24]

Although three test cases were originally contemplated by Daniels and Lawrence, only two proceeded to court, with *United States v. Forness, et al.* as the center piece of Justice Department and Seneca concern. The Fornesses, Fred and Jessie, operated a large garage in the commercial center of the city. Under the Seneca Nation formula, the Forness' $4 per year rental of choice commercial property would have been raised to $230 per year. Their lease had been cancelled because they had not paid rent for eleven years.

The Justice Department brought the test case on behalf of the Senecas to determine if the Indians had the right to cancel the Forness' lease and other federally authorized leases because of nonpayment.[25] The Justice Department soon won firm support from a powerful ally, Secretary of the Interior Harold L. Ickes, who saw the issue as righting a terrible past wrong done to the Indians. Nominal rentals of one dollar a year and insignificant rentals in the heart of the business district led Ickes to conclude that the "question should be settled in favor of the protection of the Indians' interests and rights in this matter," not simply the acceptance of past rents due with interest. He recommended that the test cases be prosecuted to a final legal conclusion since it would lead other delinquent lessees to negotiate with the Indians for new, more equitable leases.[26]

The Seneca lease case, however, did not proceed without serious roadblocks. In response to Seneca actions, the leaseholders deposited their rent money ($8–9,000), in the Salamanca banks since the Senecas had refused to accept money from delinquent lessees after lease cancellations. The delay in securing judgment from the federal courts produced extreme hardship on the Senecas since the Nation depended on this lease money to operate. Other problems included the lack of a smooth working relationship between the attorneys of the Nation and the Justice Department. In addition, Daniels and Seneca officials had to contend with large gaps in documenting the case since twenty-five years of tribal records and minutes had been "misplaced" because of a series of corrupt Indian leaders and councils in the early 1900s.[27]

While preparing the Justice Department's case, Daniels discovered that the Senecas had repeatedly sought to deal with the delinquent leases. In 1911, a full-scale investigation of this situation had been undertaken by the Interior Department. Each year, the Superintendent of the New York Agency prepared a list of delinquent leaseholders. In 1931 and 1932, an audit of the books of the Seneca Nation had revealed the seriousness of the problem. Moreover, on several separate occasions prior to the cancellation of the leases, the *Salamanca Republican-Press* had quoted the mayor of the city as urging the prompt payment of rentals.[28]

The Forness case finally reached the United States District Court in 1941. The decision of the lower court rendered by Judge Knight found against the Senecas, but focused largely on the role of BIA Superintendent Charles Berry, rather than on whether the Senecas had the right to cancel delinquent leases. Berry had sent notices on Interior Department stationery to various lessees notifying them that rent was due on February 19, 1939, and that an interest payment would be charged on rents not paid by April 20. Judge Knight insisted that Berry was not simply an agent of the United States government but also "clearly the agent of the Indians." The judge also maintained that the Seneca Nation had implicitly ratified the acts of the agent since this procedure of notice and extension had been undertaken for many years. Moreover, since the tender of payment occurred before April 20, the "right to reenter" a lease under common law protected Forness from ejectment. Despite his emphasis on Berry's role, Judge Knight rejected the laws of the state's application to the Seneca Nation since it "occupies the position of a quasi-independent Nation." He raised the issue of State jurisdiction indirectly in his decision, insisting that "the Indians are not subject to state laws and the process of its courts."[29] As a result, the Senecas had no satisfactory redress and had the added burden of operating without the Salamanca lease money which was now tied up by the court proceedings.

The Justice Department refused to concede and appealed the decision. By November 1941, Daniels was cooperating with the personnel in the Interior Department in preparing supplementary memoranda of law and hinted that he was prepared to take the case to the United States Supreme Court. Frustrated by the setback in the lower court, Daniels accused the United States Attorney's office in Buffalo of not working hard enough on the case and suggested that Judge Knight had made a poor decision and exhibited prejudice in the case.[30] Finally, on January 20, 1942, the Federal Circuit Court of Appeals for the Second Circuit reversed and remanded Judge Knight's earlier decision.[31]

Finding against the Fornesses, the higher court restricted the application of state laws, insisting that the lessees were "customarily lax about paying their rent"; that all too frequently in the past they had been in default; and that the Senecas had attempted to cancel leases in the past. In one earlier instance, the Department of the Interior had blocked the Indians because of restrictions regarding the use of tribal funds in hiring an attorney. To the court, the "present action by the Nation, then, represents the culmination of a long struggle by the Indians to enforce their economic rights."[32]

According to the opinion written by Justice Jerome Frank, the Senecas had made a timely effort as best they could under the circumstances. This noted New Dealer, legal scholar and jurist stated:

Circumstances like these cannot be excused by the lame apology that others were doing likewise, and that the Senecas were known to be long-suffering. Even if such an excuse were not tantamount to an astonishing claim of a vested right in wrongdoing, preventing any correction of an evil condition, it would still fall short of proving laxness on the part of the Indians. It would be both impractical and unfair to require the Indians to bring suit each year for the paltry sum owned on this plot, a suit costing more than the amount which it would yield, and it would be equally impractical and unfair to hold that they must expend part of the rent for badgering defendants and their neighbors into prompt payment. To hold that the Senecas cannot cancel this lease because they have treated defendants and others generously in the past would, in these circumstances, be a miscarriage of justice.[33]

The attorneys for Forness and the lessees in Salamanca argued that the Senecas had no right to cancel the leases since they were procedurally barred by the New York Civil Practice Act. Justice Frank maintained, in overturning an earlier federal district court decision, that the congressional intent in confirming the Salamanca leases in 1892 had to be determined first. Frank had stated: "We cannot believe that Congress intended that, in our times, the rights of American Indians as landlords should be determined by the early 17th century views of Coke—an antique dealer in obsolescent medieval ideal—commenting enthusiastically on the 15th century writings of Littleton, a medieval lawyer."[34] In 1892 when the Salamanca leases had been confirmed, the Congress still had a trust responsibility to Indians as guardians to protect them from exploitation. Thus, since Congress had not permitted application of the New York Civil Practice Act, it did not apply to the circumstances of the case. "State law cannot be invoked to limit the rights in lands granted by the United States to the Indians, because . . . State law does not apply to the Indians except so far as the United States has given its consent."[35]

Even after the United States Supreme Court refused to grant a certiorari hearing to Forness' attorneys, the Salamancans persisted in their efforts to resist the implications of the Federal Circuit Court of Appeals' decision, namely to negotiate new leases at higher rates with the Seneca Nation.[36] In retaliation, Daniels advised the Justice and Interior Departments and the Seneca Nation to "give 'em both barrels" since only then would the lawyers and lessees in Salamanca believe that the "government is dead in earnest to secure the protection of its wards without further delay." He added that the "persons whose leases have been cancelled will fall over each other to secure new leases when they realize the danger of delay—paying heavy costs, attorneys' fees and possible loss of their lots."[37]

The Senecas then began eviction proceedings with the support of the Justice and Interior Departments against the hold-out delinquent leaseholders who had refused to negotiate and sign new leases.[38] The City of Salamanca, at the recommendation of their new attorney Henry Manley, then sought injunctions to stop these evictions. These efforts were denied by judges in both federal and state courts. Through these delay tactics, Manley sought to put economic pressure on the Indians because they needed the $13,000 in rent moneys tied up by the legal dispute.[39]

This Salamanca-Seneca lease war ended in 1944. By that time, most Salamancans had reluctantly accepted new leases. These new leases had been drafted and researched by Superintendent Berry and three BIA personnel who were specially assigned to check hundreds of land descriptions contained in available maps and county records to insure their correctness. From a total of 839 leases, 627 were renegotiated upward. Twenty of the remaining leases were in the process of renegotiations while the remainder were held "by persons whose whereabouts were unknown" or parties uninterested in retaining possession. The United States Attorney's office in Buffalo called a final halt to these proceedings in April.[40]

By that time, an anti-Indian backlash of immense proportions had developed. As early as August 1942, Daniels had seen the potential of a political backlash to the Indian victory in the Forness decision. Looking into his crystal ball, the North Carolinian had predicted that the lessees and their supporters hoped "within three years" to elect a Congress "not in sympathy with the policy of protecting the Indians as the present administration has shown." To Daniels, "they may after numerous failures to do so, have Congress pass an act turning over to the 'tender mercies' of the State, the Indians." He concluded: "The sort of treatment that they would get can be understood when it is remembered that the State becomes a party against the Government in practically every case brought to protect the 'wards of the nation' from graft and exploitation."[41] Daniels' prediction was almost entirely accurate. Instead of Daniels' estimate of a three-year process, Congress passed the so-called jurisdiction bills (seen by the Senecas as "spite bills") six to eight years later in 1948 and 1950, inspired by the political influence of the New York congressional delegation and its major Senate ally, Hugh Butler of Nebraska.

The Forness case had thrown into question the general belief among New York officials that laws passed in Albany took precedent where federal laws left off. The implications of the case were far-reaching since the decision implied that the Iroquois were beyond the reach of state civil and criminal courts and statutes. Consequently, the Iroquois were subject only to the federal Ten Major Crimes Act of 1885. Confusion was everywhere. Could an Indian be arrested by state police for reckless endangerment while driving his car on a state-maintained highway that traversed a reservation? Did state social services statutes apply to problems affecting Indian families on the reservation?[42]

Although there were many legitimate questions about the legal complications that had arisen because of the decision, the Indians were unfairly pictured as threats to whites, especially in Massena, Salamanca and other communities in proximity to large Indian populations. The fear that the Indians were beyond the pale of law enforcement was further intensified by the fact that only two Iroquois nations in New York had their own courts of civil jurisdiction and there was no enforceable codified Indian law for the punishment of criminal offenses except what was contained in the 1885 federal statute. These concerns were combined with the bitterness expressed by many Salamancans and their representatives in Albany and Washington about the Seneca Nation's cancellation of leases. On the other side, the Iroquois distrust of the State caused by New York's past Indian policies produced a near-universal Iroquois belief that "the storm clouds were arising."[43]

The backlash started on November 3, 1942, after the Salamancan leaseholders had exhausted all legal and legislative hope of redressing or delaying the application of the Seneca eviction proceedings. After allocating $10,000 for Indian social assistance in the county, the Cattaraugus County Board of Supervisors—egged on by prominent Salamanca attorney Charles E. Congdon and A. Page Bedell, county supervisor from Salamanca's second ward—recommended the cut-off of additional county and state funds to the Indians on the grounds that the Forness case had ruled against the application of state laws to the Indians. Although New York State never went along with the county's decision, Congdon insisted that the resolution "offers a chance to save money for Cattaraugus County, and also to start a movement that may save a lot of money to the State."[44]

The Senecas attempted to counter the actions of the Salamancans. President Cornelius Seneca on November 26 insisted that "if it is illegal for the State to spend money on our reservations, it is also illegal for the State to collect taxes from railroad property and utilities located on the reservations." According to Seneca, outsiders failed to realize that the state has collected millions of dollars in taxes on railroad and utilities assessments on reservations. The Seneca President blamed the action of the County Board of Supervisors on the part of a "few disgruntled Salamanca people. They are angry because we Indians finally have demanded our just rights and are trying to break the control of a certain element in Salamanca over tribal affairs."[45]

Alarmed by the implications of the Forness decision, especially in challenging concurrent jurisdiction of the State and federal governments in Indian matters, the New York State Legislature, under pressure from southwestern interests in the state, created the Joint Legislative Committee on Indian Affairs on March 8, 1943 to deal with the "more or less continuous state of confusion" about State authority over Indian reservations.[46] The Joint Legislative Committee's intentions were made clear by its makeup and by the way it operated in its first year. Like the earlier Whipple Committee of 1888–1889, the 1943 committee was dominated by New Yorkers from the southwestern corner of the State. Although the committee's membership included nine legislators (including some from Brooklyn, Manhattan, Binghamton and Rochester), its chairman, William H. Mackenzie, its vice-chairman, George H. Pierce, and its most important voice and chief counsel, Leighton Wade, were from southwestern New York. Wade was from Olean as was State Senator Pierce while Assemblyman Mackenzie represented Allegany County. A fourth committee member, Leo P. Noonan, represented Cattaraugus County. The committee quickly scheduled nine hearings throughout the state in 1943, with the first in the series to be held at Salamanca in August of that year.

Indian suspicions about the motives behind the hearings were evident from the beginning. Cornelius Seneca later testified in 1948 that Indians questioned the committee's objective even before the opening of the hearings in 1943: "Why did they come to Salamanca? Why didn't they start in some other part of the State?"[47]

The hearings began on August 4. The committee first heard testimony from Thomas Wilson, mayor of Salamanca; Thomas H. Dowd, formerly a State Supreme Court justice and local attorney for the Home Owners Corporation who had been involved in the original movement for congressional confirmation of leases in 1892; and George H. Ansley, attorney for the City of Salamanca. Numerous Salamancans, including James Whipple and Hudson Ainsley, whose forefathers had been involved in the New York State Legislative Committee of 1888–1889 and the original ninety-nine-year leases, represented the lessees' position and testified at the hearings. The Interior Department was represented by John Reeves, BIA attorney and specialist on New York Indian legal matters. Only Wilford Crouse, the newly elected president of the Seneca Nation, was allowed to present the Indian side of the leasing question.

According to Reeves, the committee's procedures were highly irregular. Besides loading the witnesses in favor of the Salamancans' position, the committee did not even swear in the witnesses before they testified. Moreover, testimony was abruptly suspended at noon on August 5 when Chairman Mackenzie announced that the committee was scheduled to visit the Thomas Indian School that afternoon. According to Reeves' report to the Interior Department, only after

Cornelius Seneca, then the Treasurer of the Seneca Nation and known for his gentlemanly qualities and moderate politics, protested and demanded an opportunity to be heard, claiming he had prepared an extended statement, did the state committee finally agree to return to Salamanca to hear additional Indian testimony.[48]

The Seneca tribal treasurer received his opportunity to counter the efforts of the lessees when the Joint Legislative Committe on Indian Affairs returned to Salamanca on September 7. Seneca enunciated the Iroquois' general feeling that they were opposed to state supervision and changes in the federal-Indian relationship since "our treaty and dealings were originally with the federal government"; that the State's historic coercive policies in the past had only contributed to this attitude; and that Indian suspicions about the State had increased since outstanding Indian land claims had never been settled by Albany.

Seneca also criticized the committee for earlier denying Indians the right to testify against what Salamancans had presented about the Indians: "Now, I feel that we have been misrepresented to some of the people of the City of Salamanca by some of the publicity given us Indian people, the council body, and also the Indian Leasing Commit-tee, of which I happen to be a member." He accused the state and by implication, the Joint Legislative Committee, of favoring the Salaman-cans. Seneca added that the Indians, unlike the testimony and news stories slanted against the Indian position, did not intend to "dis-possess people in Salamanca, run business out of the City of Sala-manca, in plain words tear down the City of Salamanca." He said: "All we are asking for was just rent, not excessive rental."

In an effort to counter what he saw as the inevitable path to legislative action unfavorable to the Indians, Seneca attempted to win favor with the committee by suggesting that the Nation had begun judicial reforms, had approached the federal government for the crea-tion of a tribal police system and had warned its tribal members that "if we Indians don't behave ourselves, some outside agency will come in and make us behave."[49] Seneca, a wise, politically shrewd, self-edu-cated iron worker, looking back into tribal history to the time of the Seneca political revolution of 1848, understood full well that a new era of outside political interference in Indian affairs was brewing and that the Indians had to walk a tightrope to prevent disaster.[50]

As early as December 1943, Wade and the Joint Legislative Committee had drafted in rough form two bills dealing with the state assumption of criminal and civil jurisdiction over the Iroquois.[51] On another front, Judge Dowd lobbied highly placed Justice Department personnel. He insisted that lessees like himself who were not officially in default in payment of rentals to the Seneca Nation should not be treated like those who were delinquent and that the "old rate of rental shall continue without change" to lessees in this category. The elderly attorney, in a manner of Salamancans from a past era, revealed his motive: "If accepted by you [Assistant Attorney General] and the Department, and the Indians, it gives a *permanency of title* [emphasis added] to the property owners here in Salamanca, and without that permanency of title, property values in Salamanca will almost disappear." Although Dowd had alluded to leases, his use of the words "permanency of title" is especially revealing, knowing the past history of the Seneca leases.[52]

Other Salamancans echoed Dowd's concerns and carried the judge's points even further. A leaseholder, in a letter-to-the-editor column of the *Salamanca Republican-Press*, maintained on September 11, 1943, that "what we want and what I am optimistic enough to believe we will actually have, is not a lease of the land but a deed of it." He added that federal government plans for the Kinzua Dam on the Allegheny River was bound to make the Salamanca–Seneca Nation controversy passe. Hence, ". . . the Indians better settle now with the Salamancans before the federal government through condemnation proceedings takes the land anyway." Despite the Ogden claim and obvious Indian opposition to his suggestion, he proposed the simple purchase of Seneca land by the federal government and its resale to the leaseholders of Salamanca.[53]

After the closing hearing in October 1943, the Joint Legislative Committee issued a report in February 1944 that almost entirely focused on the Salamanca lease controversy and the questions of jurisdiction. The report recounted the history of the leases and emphasized the lack of state jurisdiction over reservation Indians as a result of the Forness decision which it characterized as a "reproach" both to the state and the nation. It recommended that Congress take appropriate legislative action and that the Indian tribes, the BIA and New York State officials hold a conference to deal with the dispute. The report suggested that there were two alternatives: an increased recognition of state jurisdiction or an increased awareness that the federal government assume the state's annual burden of $400,000 by taking over education, health, highway and social services to reservation Indians.[54]

The language of the report was loaded in favor of transfer of jurisdiction. The report failed to mention that highways and bridges maintained on reservations were used by all the state's peoples or that "they were not built or maintained for the especial use of the Indians."⁵⁵

Another section of the report was entitled the "Ogden Land Company title." The report concluded about the Ogden's preemptive claim: "The existence of this claim is a *continuing obstacle to purchase* [emphasis added] by the City of Salamanca of the 3,570 acres of Reservation land occupied by the municipality."⁵⁶

As a result of the Joint Legislative Committee's lobbying, Congress awarded New York State criminal and civil jurisdiction over the Iroquois in 1948 and 1950. Adding insult to the indignities already faced by the Seneca Nation, Congress, in 1951, at the urging of Butler, Reed and Wade, passed the Seneca Rental Bill. Because the New York Indian Agency was now closed, leaseholders under the provisions of the Act paid their rental moneys directly to the City of Salamanca; the city would then forward the money to the Seneca Nation. Although this facilitated payment and replaced the role of collection undertaken in the past by the Indian agent, the legislation created the false impression that the city had paramount authority over "its residents" and that the Indians were simply ordinary landowners, not federally recognized quasi-sovereign Indian nations.

CONCLUSION

This brief survey of the history of the Seneca Nation-Salamanca lease controversy reveals much about New York State's past policies toward the Iroquois as well as Indian perceptions of State policy makers and their approaches to native people. As a result of the unyielding political pressures from non-Indian residents of the southwestern part of the state, New York legislators led the way in lobbying before Congress for bills that affected the Seneca Nation and all Iroquois. These legislative actions were largely perceived by most Iroquois as contrary to their interests or needs.

Albany policy makers should realize that the state's past approaches to this controversy were less than even-handed and that the American Indian's position was largely ignored. Present-day policy makers have a clear responsibility to all Salamancans, both Indian and non-Indian, and cannot simply "wash their hands" of the entire controversy. They must encourage the two sides to sit down at the table for serious negotiations, understanding that this long-standing controversy cannot be resolved by political rhetoric.

NOTES

1. Lindsey Gruson, "As Lease of Indian Land Expires, a City Worries about Its Future," *New York Times*, February 19, 1985, B-1. The author would like to thank David Jaman of Gardiner, New York, for his helpful comments in the final preparation of this article.

2. Laurence M. Hauptman, "Senecas and Subdividers: Resistance to Allotment of Indian Lands in New York, 1875–1906," *Prologue* 9 (Summer 1977): 106; Thomas S. Abler, "Factional Dispute and Party Conflict in the Political System of the Seneca Nation (1845–1895): An Ethnohistorical Analysis" (unpublished Ph.D. diss., University of Toronto, 1969), viii, 169–73; Thomas E. Hogan, "A History of the Allegany Reservation: 1850–1900" (unpublished M.A. thesis, SUNY Fredonia, 1974), 8; and Hogan, "City in a Quandary: Salamanca and the Allegany Leases," *New York History* 54 (January 1974): 79–101.

3. Ibid.

4. Gerald Gunther, "Governmental Power and New York Indian Lands—A Reassessment of a Persistent Problem of Federal-State Relations," *Buffalo Law Review* 8 (Fall 1958): 9.

5. Hauptman, "Senecas and Subdividers," 107.

6. Ibid.

7. U.S. Congress, House, *Congressional Record*, 57th Cong., 2d sess., 1902, 36, pt. 1: 337; Edward B. Vreeland to Merrill E. Gates, January 10, 1902, Records of the U.S. Board of Indian Commissioners, 1899–1918, RG 75, NA.

8. *Proceedings of the Twentieth Annual Meeting of the Lake Mohonk Conference of Friends of the Indian, 1902* (Lake Mohonk, N.Y., 1903), 57–61, 101–6.

9. New York State, *Assembly Document 51—Report of the Special Committee Appointed by the Assembly of 1888 to Investigate the "Indian Problem" of the State* (Albany, N.Y., 1889), 59–79.

10. Ibid. Interview of Keith Reitz, May 3, 1983, New Paltz, N.Y.; interview of Orens Lyons, September 8, 1984, Syracuse, N.Y.

11. Hauptman, "Senecas and Subdividers," 112.

12. U.S. Congress, House, *Congressional Record*, 57th Cong., 2d sess., 1902, 36, pt. 1: 337.

13. Laurence M. Hauptman, *The Iroquois and the New Deal* (Syracuse: Syracuse University Press, 1981), chapters 1, 3, and 4.

14. Arch Merrill, "Salamanca Lease Settlement," *American Indian* [New York City] 1 (Spring 1944): 3.

15. W. K. Harrison and William N. Fenton, Report: "The New York Agency Problem," December 30, 1936, William N. Fenton MSS. In Dr. Fenton's possession at

Slingerlands, N.Y. (Indian Service Records, 1935–1937). These records have recently been transferred to the American Philosophical Society Library in Philadelphia, Pa.

16. Felix Cohen, *Handbook of Federal Indian Law* (Washington, DC: U.S. Government Printing Office, 1942; reprint edition, Albuquerque, NM: University of New Mexico Press, 1972), 419; see also Gunther, "Government Power," 1–26; James W. Clute, "The New York Indians' Rights to Self-Determination," *Buffalo Law Review* 22 (Spring 1973): 985–1019.

17. United States Congress. House Committee on Indian Affairs. *Hearings on H.K. 9720: Indians of New York*. 71st Cong., 2d sess. (Washington, DC, 1930), 1, 19–20, 154–65, 199. For the 1940 attempt to transfer jurisdiction, see "Indians O.K. Wanted," *Buffalo Courier-Express*, April 18, 1940; David C. Adie to Senator Robert F. Wagner, March 25, 1940, BIA Central Files, 1940–1952, acc. #53A 367, Box 1055, File #22649-1940-013 (N.Y.), RG 75, NA.

18. Barbara Graymont, ed., *Fighting Tuscarora* (Syracuse: Syracuse University Press, 1973), 95.

19. Ibid.; "Salamanca Seeks to Enjoin Indians from Taking Lands," *Buffalo Evening News*, August 28, 1942; "Defendants File Answers in Indian Lease Cases," *Salamanca Republican-Press*, November 25, 1942.

20. New York State Assembly, (Unpublished) *Report of the Indian Commission to Investigate the Status of the American Indian Residing in the State of New York Transmitted to the Legislature, March 17, 1922* (Albany, N.Y., 1922), pp. 2, 303–4, 324; Hauptman, *The Iroquois and the New Deal*, 11–12; and Helen Upton, *The Everett Report in Historical Perspective: The Indians of New York State* (Albany, NY: New York State American Revolution Bicentennial Commission, 1980).

21. *New York Indians*, Memorandum of C. C. Daniels, Special Assistant to the Attorney General, Relating to the Everett Report, November 21, 1934, memorandum found in Everett Report file copy, Akwesasne Museum, Hogansburg, N.Y.

22. John Collier to W. K. Harrison, March 4, 1935, Records of the New York Agency, 1938–1949, Box 7, #380, RG 75 NA.

23. "Indian Landlords Insist Palefaces Pay," *Rochester Times-Union*, March 10, 1939; Wilford Crouse, Chairman, "Resolution of the Lease Committee of the Seneca Nation of Indians," May 23, 1939, Records of the New York Agency, 1938–1949, Box 7, #380, RG 75, NA.

24. Seneca Nation Resolution of May, 1940 attached to letter of C. C. Daniels to Charles E. Berry, May 27, 1940, Records of the New York Agency, 1938–1949, Box 7, #380, RG 75, NA.

25. C. C. Daniels to Charles E. Berry, March 12, March 22, July 3, 1940, Records of the New York Agency, 1938–1949, Box 7, #380, RG 75, NA.

26. Harold Ickes to the Attorney General, May 21, 1940, Records of the New York Agency, 1938–1949, Box 7, #380, RG 75, NA.

27. C. H. Berry to John R. Reeves, February 12, 1940; John Van Aernam, July 3, 1940, Records of the New York Agency, 1938–1949, Box 7, #380, RG 75, NA.

28. C. C. Daniels to Charles H. Berry, March 19, 28, 1940; Daniels to Frank A. Archambault, June 20, 28, 1940, Records of the New York Agency, 1938–1949, Box 7, #380, RG 75, NA.

29. 37 F. Supp. 337.

30. C. C. Daniels to Charles H. Berry, November 14, 1941; Berry to Daniels, Nov. 24, 1941, Records of the New York Agency, 1938–1949, Box 7, #380, RG 75, NA.

31. *U.S. v. Forness et al. (Salamanca Trust Co. et al., Interveners).* 37 F. Supp. 337 (February 14, 1941), 125 Fed. Rep., 2d Ser., 928 (January 20, 1942). "Our Indian Landlords Finally Get a Break," *New York Times,* January 21, 1942.

32. 125 Fed. Rep., 2d Ser., 931.

33. Ibid., 940.

34. Ibid., 938.

35. Ibid., 932.

36. *City of Salamanca et al. v. United States,* 316 U.S. 694 (June 1, 1942), "Defendants File Answers in Indian Lease Cases," *Salamanca Republican-Press,* November 25, 1942; "Knight Dismisses City Suit Against Seneca Nation," *Salamanca Republican-Press,* November 18, 1942; "Salamanca Seeks to Enjoin Indians from Taking Lands," *Buffalo Evening News,* August 28, 1942.

37. C. C. Daniels quoted in Frank A. Archambault to William Zimmerman, Jr., August 5, 1942; Daniels to Attorney General, August 3, 1942; Records of the New York Agency, 1938–1949, Box 8, #380, RG 75, NA. Daniels had been relentless in his crusade to help the Senecas. C. C. Daniels to C. McFarland, September 10, 1937; to Josephus Daniels, October 12, 1937, December 16, 1937, February 5, 1938, July 15, 1938, September 8, 1939, Josephus Daniels MSS., Microfilm Reel 4, Library of Congress, Manuscript Division, Washington, D.C.

38. "Local Indian Office Issues Statement Regarding Leases," *Salamanca Republican-Press,* November 5, 1942. William Zimmerman to Charles H. Berry, June 26, 1942, Records of the New York Agency, 1938–1949, Box 8, #380, RG 75, NA.

39. Daniels to Attorney General, August 3, 12, 1942, Records of the New York Agency, 1938–1949, Box 8, #380, RG 75, NA.

40. "5-Year Dispute Over Indian Land Leases Is Ended," *Buffalo Evening News,* April 5, 1944. Paul L. Fickinger to C. H. Berry, September 7, 1944, Records of the New York Agency, 1938–1949, #380, RG 75, NA.

41. Daniels to Attorney General, August 3, 1942. Daniels' role in the proceedings ended on January 31, 1943. The Seneca Nation passed a resolution honoring him as "one of the unsung heroes in the crusade for righteousness and justice . . ."

42. Upton, "The Everett Report," 147.

43. United States Congress. Senate. Subcommitte of the Committee of the Interior and Insular Affairs. *Hearings . . . New York Indians.* 80th Cong., 2d sess. (Washington, D.C., 1948), 79–82, 213–18.

44. "Move to Stop All State Aid to Indians," *Salamanca Republican-Press,* November 20, 1942; C. C. Daniels to Commissioner of Indian Affairs, November 24, 1942, Records of the New York Agency, 1938–1949, Box 8, #380, RG 75, NA.

45. "State Gets Taxes on Indian Lands, Seneca Contends," *Buffalo Evening News,* November 27, 1942; "Supervisors' Move Draws Criticism of Seneca Leader," *Buffalo Evening News,* December 27, 1942.

46. New York State. *Legislative Document #52* (Albany, N.Y., 1944), 32.

47. U.S. Senate. *Hearings, 1948,* 195.

48. John Reeves, Memorandum to Mr. Zimmerman, August 11, 1943, BIA Central Files, 1940–1952, Acc. #53A 367, Box 1055, File #22649-1940-013 (NY), RG 75, NA.

49. New York State. Joint Legislative Committee on Indian Affairs, *Public Hearing Held at Salamanca . . . September 7, 1943* (Buffalo, NY, 1943), 3, 7–18, 23.

50. Interview of Pauline Seneca, July 17, 1982, Cattaraugus Indian Reservation. For the earlier Seneca political upheaval, see Thomas Abler, "Friends, Factions,

and the Seneca Nation Revolution of 1848," *Niagara Frontier* 21 (Winter 1974): 74–79.

51. C. H. Berry to William Zimmerman, Jr., November 25, 1943; Zimmerman to William H. Mackenzie, December 11, 1943, BIA Central Files, 1940–1952, Acc. #53A 367, Box 1055, File #22649-1940-013 (NY), RG 75, NA.

52. Thomas H. Dowd to Normal M. Littell, August 12, 1943; Dowd to Martin McIntyre, August 14, 1943, Franklin D. Roosevelt MSS., Box 296, "Indians," Franklin D. Roosevelt Library, Hyde Park, N.Y.

53. "The Indian Lease Problem," *Salamanca Republican-Press*, September 11, 1943.

54. New York State. *Joint Legislative Committee Report, February 25, 1944* (Albany, NY, 1944). "Forness Case Decision Termed 'Reproach to State and Nation,'" *Salamanca Republican-Press*, August 5, 1944.

55. Arch Merrill, "Salamanca Lease Settlement," *American Indian* 1 (Spring 1944): 7.

56. Quoted in Ibid.

8

The New York Indian Land Claims
The Modern Landowner as Hostage

ALLAN VAN GESTEL

Four sovereignties exercising the constituent political powers of the United States, the state of New York, the Oneida Indian Nation and the Cayuga Indian Nation are locked in a monumental legal struggle to see which of them will govern, control—indeed, own—the land now occupied by thousands of wholly innocent persons in a vast area of central New York. The successors to the governments of the Oneida and Cayuga Indian nations claim that the government of the state of New York illegally purchased over nine million acres of Oneida and Cayuga land, while the government of the United States stood by and failed to intervene on the Indians' behalf. New York's purchases all happened over 190 years ago—for the most part before the effective date of the United States Constitution. It would be interesting history with little current application except for the fact that those who are threatened with the greatest loss are not any of the governments involved, but rather the innocent and law-abiding citizens of fourteen or more New York counties who live under the cloud of these claims. None of these people, whose land is the target of these cases, were even born until decades after the purchases were completed. They do not deserve this procrustean treatment.

In 1970, a group claiming to be descendants from the aboriginal Oneida Indian Nation filed suit in the United States District Court for the Northern District of New York against the New York counties of Oneida and Madison, asserting that the counties were trespassers on Indian-owned land. Although this suit only claimed as relief money damages from the counties for their "trespasses" on county-owned land for the two years before the start of litigation, it was in actuality a test case, a stalking horse, used by the Indians to establish legal principles to support later claims. That case has twice been before the United States Supreme Court,[1] each time producing astonishing results with potentially devastating consequences for those people who live and work in the claim area.

Two other Indian land claims that cloud the title to almost six million acres of land in central New York were filed in 1978 and 1979, and a third that threatens another three million acres was filed in 1980. The ultimate relief sought in these later claims is the order to restore the Indians to immediate possession of the land—orders that would cause enormous and unmanageable dislocations. The areas that are the subject of these later claims are vast, encompassing geography half again as great as the entire state of Massachusetts, or the states of Rhode Island, Delaware, and Connecticut combined. Innumerable homes, businesses, municipal facilities, schools, colleges, universities, hospitals, public services, and state and local taxation programs could be cast into immediate disarray, with consequent disruptions extending far beyond the claims area, throughout the entire Northeast. If the Indians' claims are successful, the financial consequences would be disastrous and widespread. Security for personal, business, and governmental obligations could be fatally impaired or wiped out. The hopes and investment-backed expectations of thousands, indeed hundreds of thousands of innocent citizens, would be dashed. What was vacant and unimproved land when the Indians "owned" it is now enormously valuable property benefiting, and benefiting from, the industry, investments, and development of hundreds of thousands of individuals, businesses, and governmental bodies who did not even exist when the asserted wrongs were committed.

The Indians proceed with superficial simplicity. They demand to be "restored" to "immediate possession," a situation that disguises the fact that no single or simple order could be fashioned to grant such relief. Given the dislocations and disruptions that would inevitably result, and assuming the order of the court that made it would be obeyed, the federal judge would have to provide for and oversee innumerable contingencies and ramifications. In effect, the court would have to establish itself by judicial fiat as a kind of "transitional government" and appoint its officers as unelected vice-regents to manage a transfer that could take years. It is not "merely" a restoration of possession to real estate that would flow from the ultimate judgment. Because of peculiarities in Indian law, the court, in actuality, is being asked to create entirely new sovereignties out of a major portion of the

State of New York, with political ramifications of inconceivable complexity.

Once before, the Supreme Court faced the issue of deciding on the question of the rightful government of one of the states. In declining to do so it pointed out some of the pitfalls involved.

> [I]f this court is authorized to enter upon this inquiry as proposed by the plaintiff, and it should be decided that the charter government [of Rhode Island] had no legal existence during the period of time above mentioned—if it had been annulled by the adoption of the opposing government—then the laws passed by its legislature during that time were nullities; its taxes wrongfully collected; its salaries and compensation to its officers illegally paid; its public accounts improperly settled; and the judgments and sentences of its courts in civil and criminal cases null and void, and the officers who carried their decisions into operation answerable as trespassers, if not in some cases as criminals.
>
> When the decision of this court might lead to such results, it becomes its duty to examine very carefully its own powers before it undertakes to exercise jurisdiction.[2]

The Indians also seek from the present-day landowners the "fair rental value" of the land claimed "for the entire period of [their] dispossession." This amount, if it could be determined at all, would be staggering. The result of an execution on such a judgment could only be countless personal, business and municipal defaults. These are not cases where the treasury to be tapped is that of the United States[3] or the sum to be paid is large but manageable. Execution on the judgments would dwarf the largest and most complicated, expensive, and time-consuming bankruptcy proceedings and business reorganizations on record. It would constitute, by judicial order, some of the greatest transfers of wealth ever seen, and the transfers would be from the present-day landowners to the "successors in interest" of Indian nations, themselves of doubtful existence when the Constitution became effective in 1789. The problem facing the court in these cases was thoughtfully and sensitively addressed by Chief Judge Warren K. Urbom of the District of Nebraska:[4]

> [White Americans] may also ask themselves questions: How much of the sins of our forefathers must we rightly bear? What

precisely do we do now? Shall we pretend that history never was? Can we restore the disemboweled or push the waters upstream to where they used to be?

Who is to decide? White Americans? The Native Americans? All, together? A federal judge?

Who speaks for [the Indians]? Those traditional people who testified here? Those [Indians] of a different mind who did not testify? The officials elected by [the Indians]?

Feeling what *was* wrong does not describe what *is* right. Anguish about yesterday does not alone make wise answers for tomorrow. Somehow, all the achings of the soul must coalesce and with the wisdom of the mind develop a single national policy for governmental action.

The 1970 case challenged the legality of a purchase from the Oneida Nation by the state of New York in 1795 of approximately 100,000 acres of land. The land later became parts of Madison and Oneida counties upon their creation in 1806 and 1798. The Indians claimed, successfully, that this purchase by New York State was illegal because it failed to comply with the Indian Trade and Intercourse Act of 1793.[5] In this case only the counties were sued and therefore, technically at least, only the county-owned lands in the claim area (a park, a gravel pit, a radio tower, and some county highways) were in jeopardy. The suit, however, sought a court determination that the 1795 purchase itself was illegal. In 1977 the court ruled in the Indians' favor.[6] The result of that ruling, ultimately upheld by the Second Circuit Court of Appeals and the United States Supreme Court, is that although only the counties were sued, it has been determined that the State of New York never legally acquired title to any of the 100,000 acres in the 1795 purchase and all of that land is now in jeopardy.

In 1978, a group calling itself the Oneida Indian Nation of New York brought a claim against the state of New York, the New York State Thruway Authority and, by later amendment, the counties of Broome, Chenango, Cortland, Herkimer, Jefferson, Lewis, Madison, Oneida, Onondaga, Oswego, St. Lawrence, and Tioga, seeking to recover approximately six million acres of land. In December, 1979, two groups of Indians calling themselves the Oneida Indian Nation of Wisconsin and the Oneida of the Thames Band of Southwold, Ontario, brought an almost identical claim in the same court against a class of defendants that included most of the landowners, public and private, in the claim area.[7] In November, 1980, yet another group of Indians calling themselves the Cayuga Nation brought a third claim seeking 64,000 acres in Cayuga and Seneca counties which, by a unique twist of legal pleading, includes a threatened claim for an additional three million acres of land acquired by the state of New York in February, 1789.

The plaintiffs in each case characterize themselves as Indian nations or tribes who are "the direct descendants" of the aboriginal Oneida and Cayuga Indian nations. The Indians claim to be the owners of, and to have the exclusive right to possession of, all of the Oneida and Cayuga Indian nations' aboriginal territory. This aboriginal territory is located in the portion of central New York State that runs from the Pennsylvania border in the south to Canada in the north and comprises primarily the counties of Broome, Cayuga, Chenango, Cortland, Herkimer, Jefferson, Lewis, Madison, Oneida, Onondaga, Oswego, St. Lawrence, Seneca, and Tioga. The Oneida and Cayuga Indian nations are alleged to have "owned and occupied" this land "[f]rom time immemorial to the time of the acts complained of."

The parties being sued are literally thousands of individuals, business entities, municipalities, governmental agencies, schools, colleges, and others who presently assert various interests in and occupy the land.

The more recent Oneida complaints begin their story with reference to a treaty executed on November 5, 1768, between the British Crown and the Six Nations, a confederation of six Indian nations including the Oneida, Tuscarora, Mohawk, Onondaga, Cayuga, and Seneca. In that treaty, certain boundary lines are claimed to have been designated between the Indians and the New York and Pennsylvania colonies.

The Treaty of Paris of 1783, concluding the American Revolution, made no provision for the Indian allies of either Britain or the United States. Thus, it is further alleged, the Continental Congress took separate steps to adjust relations with the Indian tribes pursuant to authority delegated under Article IX of the Articles of Confederation.

A significant portion of Article IX provides:

> The United States in congress assembled shall have the sole and exclusive right and power of determining on peace and war, except in the cases mentioned in the Sixth Article [having to do with the invasion of a state] . . . entering into treaties and alliances . . . of regulating the trade and managing all affairs with Indians, not members of the States, provided that the legislative right of any State within its own limits be not infringed or violated.

According to the complaints, in an effort to implement its Indian policy, Congress created Indian departments and on September 22, 1783, passed a "proclamation" prohibiting and forbidding all persons from making settlements on lands inhabited or claimed by Indians "without the limits or jurisdiction of any particular state" and from purchasing or receiving any gift or cession of "such lands" without the express authority and directions of the United States in Congress assembled. The 1783 Proclamation further provided that every "such purchase or settlement" not having the authority of the United States would be null and void and that no right or title would accrue in consequence of any "such purchase, cession or settlement."

On October 22, 1784, the Continental government concluded a treaty at Fort Stanwix with the Six Nations that provided, among other things, that the Indians "shall be secured in the possession of the lands on which they are settled." It is asserted that the lands referred to in that treaty included approximately six million acres "owned" by the Oneida Indians.

New York State's interest in negotiating its own land cession treaties with the Indian nations began during the period of the Articles of Confederation. As early as March, 1783, the New York Legislature instructed its appointed commissioners to accomplish an exchange of land with the Oneida and the Tuscarora. In 1785, the New York Legislature authorized its commissioners to make a second attempt to obtain land cessions from the Six Nations. After negotiations with the Oneida Nation, a treaty was concluded on June 28, 1785, wherein the Oneidas ceded some 300,000 acres off their southern border.

In the following three years there were efforts by individual non-Indians to lease and purchase Oneida lands. For the stated purpose of protecting their land from these speculators, it is alleged, the Oneidas in 1788 were induced to enter into a 999-year lease of all of their land to one John Livingston, himself a speculator. No consideration under this agreement ever changed hands, however, and the New York Legislature immediately declared the lease void for failure to secure the state's approval. Thereafter, the state of New York entered into new treaty negotiations with the Oneidas and, on September 22, 1788, a major treaty was concluded whereby approximately five million acres of Oneida land were ceded to the state of New York.

The Cayugas claim that on February 25, 1789, the state of New York made a similar, unfair and oppressive treaty with them that had the effect of stripping the Cayuga Nation of almost three million acres of land. They further charge that in 1795 and 1807 the state acquired almost all of their remaining land. It is these latter two transactions that form the basis for the current suit. The 1789 transaction is the predicate for the next claim threatened in the complaint.

The United States Constitution became effective on the first Wednesday of March, 1789.[8] It contained language that, unlike Article IX of the Articles of Confederation, made clear the absolute power of the federal government to regulate affairs with Indians. The debates at the Constitutional Convention reflect the fact that the Framers intended to commit the sole and exclusive power to manage Indian affairs to the federal government, thereby freeing the Constitutional Charter from the conflicting claims of state power that had plagued the Confederation. The Constitution vested the power to regulate "commerce . . . with the Indian tribes" in the Congress.

In 1790, the First Congress passed the first of a series of Indian trade and intercourse acts, codifying federal jurisdiction over Indian land transactions under the new Constitution. This act, with modification, has been reenacted over the years such that there has been a form of Indian trade and intercourse act continuously in force from July 22, 1790, to the present.[9]

It is asserted that the United States did not authorize or participate in the negotiation of the treaties with either the Oneidas or the Cayugas, nor did it ever ratify the purchases.

The Indians in these cases seek to overturn almost two hundred years of real property law and transactions to recover "immediate possession" or the "fair market value" of millions of acres of land. They seek to do so despite the fact that the later Oneida cases and the threatened 1789 Cayuga claim involve transactions that took place before the government that established the court in which the cases are pending was founded, at a time when there was no national government worthy of the name and when the only laws to apply and the only courts to apply them were the laws and the courts of the thirteen original states, whose sovereignty was unimpaired by membership in anything like the present federal system established by a constitution deriving its powers and legitimacy directly from the American people. Further, they seek to do so despite the enormous changes to the parties and the land that have occurred in the intervening years.

The Indians who are suing are twentieth-century groups composed of twentieth-century individuals who do not themselves claim to have been cheated or defrauded by the present landowners. They claim instead to be "successors in interest" to eighteenth-century Indian nations that in the eighteenth century, they claim, were cheated and defrauded by an eighteenth-century political sovereignty. The Oneida and Cayuga governments ceded vacant, wild, and for the most part uninhabited land on the frontier of a new and struggling country; their successors now want to "recover" vastly improved and fully inhabited property in the heart of a stable and prosperous state.

Large numbers of the present landowners can trace their ancestry only so far back as Ellis Island or other ports of debarkation for America's great immigrant population. Even those with roots that reach to the *Mayflower* or the *Half Moon* can hardly be charged with active malice toward the Indian nations of the eighteenth century. All current landowners acquired their property in utter innocence of these ancient Indian claims. Not a single man or woman who has been sued had any hand in the motives or methods of the land purchases by the state of New York occurring almost two centuries before their birth. Today's landowner/defendants are nothing less than hostages in a power struggle between three governments—federal, state and Indian.

That the landowner/defendants have been seized as hostages in the political battle between the Indian, state and federal governments was candidly admitted by Indian apologist Professor Robert N. Clinton of the University of Iowa Law School. In August of 1981, Professor Clinton replied to the predecessor to this chapter,[10] which criticized there, as here, the use of innocent landowners as pawns in this intergovernmental struggle. Commenting on the Oneida and Cayuga lawsuits, he said:

> The litigation is necessary to afford the tribes the necessary bargaining leverage to achieve their not unreasonable demands in a political arena which has historically ignored them and even now is structured in a fashion antithetical to their interests. . . . [T]he threat of the eastern Indian tribes to actually litigate and enforce their seemingly valid claims to large land areas in the east is necessary to create the required bargaining strength needed to have long ignored demands redressed. No country and no good attorney should be expected or required to negotiate from a position of weakness by unilaterally giving up or being forced to abandon a major bargaining strength.[11]

The Indians' claims present an unusual and complex set of problems for the courts. Difficult issues of first impression have been raised and addressed; complicated, sometimes confused and often foreboding areas of the law have been surveyed and traversed. And all the while, a strange and unusual guilt complex derived from notions of past maltreatment of Native Americans by the "invading" Europeans clouds the ability of modern courts to see clearly and apply legal and equitable concepts to protect the innocent landowners. There is with these Indian claims no better example of the oft-quoted maxim that hard cases make bad law.

That these Indian land claims must be taken seriously is apparent from the settlement of the Passamaquoddy/Penobscot claim in Maine. There, the Indians, by settlement, were granted 350,000 acres of land and a monetary package of $81 million.[12]

Another indication of the seriousness of Indian land claims appears in the December 17, 1980, opinion of Judge Lumbard in *Mohegan Tribe v. Connecticut.*[13] There, speaking for the Second Circuit Court of Appeals, he said:

> In the past few years numerous suits have been brought by Indian Tribes still residing in eastern parts of the United States.[14] These tribes have asserted claims to large tracts of land in the East, thereby throwing into uncertainty the validity of land titles throughout the area. . . . To date, the Indians have been largely successful in their legal battles regarding their claims to eastern lands. Defenses based upon state adverse possession laws and state statutes of limitations have been consistently rejected. The only grounds upon which the states have thus far succeeded in defeating Indian claims is in demonstrating that plaintiffs in these suits do not properly represent an existing tribe which can be proved to be the legitimate descendant of the original landholding tribe.[15] (Footnotes omitted.)

In order to appreciate why these claims must be taken seriously and need to be vigorously defended by those whose land is in jeopardy, some basic concepts of Indian land law must be understood. Very early in our judicial history Indian tribes became recognized as "distinct, independent, political communities" qualified to exercise powers of self-government and having other prerogatives by reason of their tribal sovereignty.[16] In *Worcester v. Georgia,*[17] the Supreme Court determined that a weaker power does not surrender its independence by associating with a stronger power and taking its protection. Conquest of the Indians did, however, render tribes subject to the United States, which by the Constitution generally vests in Congress the ultimate power of dealing with Indian tribes.

The relationship between the federal government and the Indians is characterized as being in the nature of that existing between guardian and ward. As a direct result of these concepts, a tribe has at one and the same time certain aspects of a sovereignty as well as certain protected rights with regard to the United States. Conversely, the United States has broad authority to deal with a tribe and its interests, and certain obligations to provide protection against any invasion of those interests by third parties, including the individual states. This special relationship has led the courts to find state-created limitations on the enforcement of property rights to be inapplicable to the property rights of Indian tribes.[18]

The State of Connecticut has argued with some considerable vigor that the Trade and Intercourse Acts had geographical applications limited to "Indian country" and consequently did not apply to lands within the states. This contention, however, was rejected by the District Court;[19] the Court of Appeals, on December 17, 1980, affirmed that holding.[20]

Another twist in Indian law that presents serious problems in presenting a defense relates to the allocation of the burden of proof. A little known federal statute, first enacted in 1822, purports to allocate the burden of proof in all trials about the rights of property in which an Indian may be a party. That statute mandates that when an "Indian" is on one side and a "white person" is on the other—and those are the precise words of the statute—the burden of proof shall rest upon the "white person" whenever the Indian shall make out a presumption of title in himself from the fact of previous possession or ownership. In 1979 the Supreme Court construed the word "Indian," as used in the statute, to include Indian tribes, and the word "white person" to include all non-Indians regardless of color and status, or as either human or non-human such as a corporation.[21] Peculiarly, however, the Court excluded from the reach of "white person" the sovereign states of the United States. Thus, the burden of proof, which in cases involving facts that occurred 150 to 200 years ago can often be determinative, has been thrust upon the only truly innocent party in these Indian land claims—the present-day landowner. At the same time the individual states, which if any wrongdoing ever occurred were the perpetrators, do not suffer the same impediment in defending the claims.

A fundamental and pervasive difficulty with the Indians' claims is that they ask the court to decide issues not well suited to judicial resolution, and to grant relief not appropriate for an appointed tribunal and incapable of judicial administration. Thus, a question was initially faced by the courts was whether these cases are justiciable. The courts were asked to decide whether the claims presented and the relief sought are of the type that admit of judicial resolution. These difficult issues relating to justiciability and limitations on the bringing of actions were squarely faced by the United States Supreme Court in its second decision in the 1970 *Oneida* case. As noted earlier, in 1977, Judge Port, in the District Court, ruled that New York had violated the Trade and Intercourse Act at the time of the 1795 purchase of 100,000 acres from the Oneidas. Later, in 1982, Judge Port assessed damages against the counties for trespassing on the Oneida lands in the years 1968 and 1969. Finally, in 1983, Judge Port ruled that the counties were entitled to indemnification and reimbursement from the state of New York for any amounts that they may ultimately have to pay to the Indians. The basis for Judge Port's ruling was that the state of New York, and not the counties, which did not even exist at the time, was the ultimate wrongdoer and, therefore, in equity, the state should bear the burden. The Second Circuit Court of Appeals affirmed all of the rulings by Judge Port.[22]

The case was finally presented to the United States Supreme Court on October 1, 1984.[23] On March 5, 1985, the Supreme Court handed down its decision. In an opinion supported by five justices and dissented from by the remaining four, the high court ruled that Indian tribes and nations have a common-law right to sue in the federal courts for the recovery of land illegally appropriated from them, that claims of that nature (even though they may create new sovereignties) are justiciable in the federal courts, and that there is no state or federal statute of limitations that bars these claims even though they may be brought 180 or more years after the facts on which they are based.[24]

Justice Stevens wrote a dissent that was joined in by the Chief Justice, Justice White, and Justice Rehnquist. The theory of the dissent was that the equitable doctrine of laches should be interposed to bar a claim that is brought so many years after the facts on which it is based. Under the theory of laches a court must look at the relative equitable positions of the parties and attempt to determine whether it is any longer fair to permit a claimant to bring suit after a long passage of time between the date of the incident and the date of filing suit. Part of the consideration includes whether there were open and innocent changes of circumstances on the part of the person being sued in reliance on the assumption of validity of his position. Justice Stevens closed his dissent with the following words:

> The Framers recognize that no one ought be condemned for his forefather's misdeeds—even when the crime is a most grave of-

fense against the Republic. The Court today ignores that principle in fashioning a common law remedy for the Oneida Nation that allows the Tribe to avoid its 1795 conveyance 175 years after it was made. This decision upsets long-settled expectations in the ownership of real property in the Counties of Oneida and Madison, New York, and the disruption it is sure to cause will confirm the common law wisdom that ancient claims are best left in repose. The Court, no doubt, believes that it is undoing a grave historical injustice, but in so doing it has caused another, which only Congress may now rectify.[25]

Remarkably, seven justices joined in a portion of that decision, which reversed the trial court findings in favor of the counties against the state for indemnification. The seven justices held that the Eleventh Amendment to the United States Constitution barred a suit in federal court by the counties against the state of New York. Since there is no right or law permitting such a suit in a state court in New York, it appears that this part of the Supreme Court's ruling effectively prevents the innocent counties from recovery from the wrongdoing state.

The result of the Oneida decision in March of 1985, together with earlier rulings on other points of Indian law, is that an Indian tribe or nation now has a common-law claim to recover land wrongfully taken hundreds of years ago, without any limitations or similar time bar, against innocent present-day landowners. Those landowners have no effective right to sue their state government, the real wrongdoer, in the same court for reimbursement even though that government is the entity that committed the wrong toward the Indians' predecessors. The state government, it should be noted, forced the private landowners, under the state's modern laws, to pay taxes and abide by its laws and regulations, which it would have had no right to impose if the land really belonged to the Indians. One could hardly be critical of those landowners who, when attempting to make sense out of the rulings by the Supreme Court, conclude that Charles Dickens' Mr. Bramble was right when he said that "the law is an ass, a idiot."

The legal absurdity of the recent decisions is highlighted when it is noted that these kinds of claims can only be brought by an Indian tribe or nation. An individual Indian has no legal standing to sue for tribal land.[26] Indeed, even if he brought suit for land he claimed to be his own, he would face the same legal requirements that apply in non-Indian cases, including the bar of laches if he waited too long before starting suit.[27] Thus, an Indian government can sue an individual and take his land away if two hundred years ago the state government bought the land from the Indian government without the permission of the Unites States government. And, the landowner who loses his land because of the state's ancient transgression has no right to sue the state.

Why the Supreme Court must play judicial brinksmanship with the lives and fortunes of the hostage landowners must be left for those with better insight than that of your author here. Even it, however, after making its extraordinary and far-reaching ruling in the Oneida case, seems to realize where the true responsibility lies. After stating the law, the five justices added an intriguing final footnote to their opinion:

> The question whether equitable considerations should limit the relief available to the present-day Oneida Indians was not addressed by the Court of Appeals or presented to this Court by petitioners. Accordingly, we express no opinion as to whether other considerations may be relevant to the final disposition of this case should Congress not exercise its authority to resolve the far-reaching Indian claims.[28]

Legal scholars have already begun to scratch their heads in an effort to interpret the meaning of that footnote. What guidance, if any, does it give to a trial court faced with one of these kinds of claims? Does it mean that in some way a judge, even if ruling in favor of Indian claimants, can nevertheless apply "equitable considerations" to limit the relief available? What does it mean to suggest that the relief may be limited? Can the trial judge say to the Indians that they win but they can't have the land back? If so, what do they get from their victory?

It would seem that this footnote is a stunning example of the dilemma faced and brinksmanship played by modern-day courts in attempting to struggle with ancient Indian land claims. On the one hand, the court wants very much to compensate Native Americans for ill-treatment in the past. At the same time, the Court seems, albeit in a somewhat abstruse way, to recognize that it isn't fair to place the burden on the innocent modern-day landowner. Thus, it agrees that these cases call for decisions by an elected Congress, not an appointed judge. Again, it was Chief Judge Urbom who made the point perhaps as eloquently as it can be in the *Wounded Knee* cases. He said, in the part of his opinion that is pertinent to the issue immediately at hand:

I feel no shirking of duty in saying that formulation of such a national policy should not be made by a federal judge or the handful who may review his decision on appeal. Four reasons press me to that conclusion.

First, a strength of the elective process is that the citizenry may choose those who mirror their thoughts, and an amalgam of many thus elected is more likely to reflect the conscience and wisdom of the people than a few who are appointed.

Second, legislative bodies have investigative tools for listening to a wider community then do courts for ferreting out the deeper consciousness of the body politic.

Third, relations with American Indians are rooted in international relations. . . , including the laws of conquest and of treaties developed over centuries, not by courts, but by executive heads of nations through negotiations. The United States in its early history accepted in its dealings with other nations the European concepts. Perhaps it should not have done so in its relations with the American Indians. But it did. Changing now, after nearly two centuries, is a matter of massive public policy for broader exploration than courts are able to provide. Essentially, the issues here have to do with the methods of shifting power from one group to another—by war, threat of war, economic pressure or inducement, verbal persuasion, election, agreement, or gradual legislative encroachment. The acceptability of each method should be decided by the citizenry at large, which speaks directly or through its elected representatives.

Fourth, the people of the United States have not given me or any other judge the power to set national policy for them. By the Constitution the people have assigned governmental powers and have set their limits. Relations with Indian tribes are given exclusively to the executive and legislative branches. Perhaps it should be otherwise, but it is not. When and if the people amend the Constitution to put limits on the executive and legislative branches, in their affairs with Indian tribes the federal courts will uphold those limits, but in the meantime the courts cannot create limits. In short, a judge must hold government to the standards of the nation's conscience once declared, but he cannot create the conscience or declare the standards.[29]

In appraising the Indians' complaints, based as they are on eighteenth-century actions and eighteenth-century "laws," it is important that their clear meanings not be distorted by the gloss of twentieth-century perceptions. These are not instances of current wrongs measured by statutes or a Constitution whose meaning has evolved

NEW YORK INDIAN LAND CLAIMS

over the passage of time. The "justifiable expectations" of the land-owners must not be ignored because a court today may regard the actions of our ancestors in a manner different from the accepted views and practices of the times.[30] In considering the claims presented by the remaining Oneida and Cayuga cases, the courts must be ever careful to view the law and the actions alleged with a sensitivity to how they would have been viewed at the times of their occurrence and to the justifiable expectations of the current landowners, whose total inno-cence must be acknowledged.

Courts are not free to give untrammeled effect to their personal or policy preferences. As Justice Cardozo succinctly said: "The judge, even when he is free, is still not wholly free. He is not to innovate at pleasure. He is not a knight-errant, roaming at will in pursuit of his own ideal of beauty or of goodness. He is to draw his inspiration from consecrated principles."[31]

An obvious question that cries out for answer is: what is the position of the federal government in these cases? After all, it was the federal government that, if anyone, failed the Indians generations ago, and it is the federal government that is today the embodiment of the national conscience. Regrettably, the federal record is dismal, con-fused, inept and almost wholly unresponsive. To date it has done little to assume the responsibility for and burdens of the Indian land claims. When the Indians sought relief, the government ignored them. When the beleaguered landowners seek to join it as a third-party defendant it hides behind the doctrine of governmental immunity. And even in those few cases that have been settled, such as Maine and Rhode Island, the federal government has played a reluctant role, joining in only after the parties themselves have, because of the enormous bur-dens of the litigation, negotiated a settlement with concessions by innocent landowners. In addition, the United States has, in the in-stance of the Oneida cases, provided funding to the Indians' attorneys for purposes of bringing the suits.

There is something fundamentally wrong in the stance taken by the federal government. "By standing on the sidelines as Indians and non-Indians fight these bitter court battles, the federal government has encouraged the impression that Indian advances can be made only at the expense of non-Indians who did not commit the acts alleged as the basis of the suit."[32] There is a basic inequity in forcing present-day landowners to defend themselves against ancient claims that are in no sense based upon any wrongdoing on their part while the United States sits on the sidelines or assists in the prosecution. It is time for

Congress to live up to its representative responsibility and enact legislation that will resolve these issues in a way that is fair to all parties and will clear away once and for all the clouds on title by these kinds of Indian land claims.

NOTES

1. *Oneida Indian Nation of New York v. County of Oneida*, 414 U.S. 661 (1974) and *County of Oneida v. Oneida Indian Nation of New York*, 84 L.Ed. 2d 169 (1985).
2. *Cf. Luther v. Borden*, 48 U.S. (7 How.) 1, 38–39 (1849).
3. *See Yankton Sioux Tribe v. United States*, 272 U.S. 351 (1926).
4. *United States v. Consolidated Wounded Knee Cases*, 389 F.Supp. 235, 238–39 (D.Neb. and S.D. 1975).
5. 1 Stat. 329.
6. *Oneida Indian Nation of New York v. County of Oneida*, 434 F. Supp. 527 (N.D.N.Y. 1977).
7. *Oneida Indian Nation of Wisconsin v. State of New York*, 85 F.R.D. 701, 703 (N.D.N.Y. 1980).
8. *See Owings v. Speed*, 18 U.S. (5 Wheat.) 420, 5 L.Ed. 124 (1820).
9. The current version of the act provides in part as follows: "No purchase, grant, lease or other conveyance of land or of any title or claim thereto, from any Indian nation or tribe of Indians shall be of any validity in law or equity unless the same be by treaty or conveyance entered into pursuant to the Constitution." 25 U.S.C. section 177.
10. Allan van Gestel, "The New York Indian Land Claims: An Overview and a Warning," *New York State Bar Journal* (April 1981): 182–85, 212–16.
11. "The Eastern Indian Land Claims: A Reply," *New York State Bar Journal* (August, 1981): 374–75.
12. See Maine Indian Claims Settlement Act of 1980, Pub. L. No. 96-420.
13. 638 F.2d 612 (2d Cir. 1980).
14. *See, e.g., Oneida Indian Nation v. County of Oneida*, 414 U.S. 661 (1974); *Mashpee Tribe v. New Seabury Corp.*, 592 F.2d 575 (1st Cir. 1979); *Epps v. Andrus*, 611 F.2d 915 (1st Cir. 1979); *Oneida Indian Nation v. County of Oneida*, 434 F. Supp. 527 (N.D.N.Y. 1977); *Schaghticoke Tribe v. Kent School Corp.*, 423 F. Supp. 780 (D. Conn. 1976); *Narragansett Tribe v. Southern Rhode Island Land Development Corp.*, 418 F. Supp. 798 (D.R.I. 1976); *Joint Council of the Passamaquoddy Tribe v. Morton*, 528 F.2d 370 (1st Cir. 1975); *Chitimacha Tribe v. Laws*, Civ. No. 77-0772-L (W.D.La.); *Catawba Indian Tribe v. South Carolina*, No. 80-2050-C (D.S.C.).
15. 638 F.2d at 614–15.
16. *Cherokee Nation v. Georgia*, 30 U.S. (5 Pet.) 1 (1831).
17. 31 U.S. (6 Pet.) 515 (1832).
18. *See Western Pequot Tribe v. Holdridge Enterprises, Inc.*, CA H-76-193 (D. Conn. 1977); *Oneida Indian Nation v. County of Oneida*, 434 F. Supp. 527, 541–43 (N.D.N.Y.);

Schaghticoke Tribe v. Kent School Corp., 423 F. Supp. 780 (D. Conn. 1976); *Narragansett Tribe of Indians v. Southern Rhode Island Land Dev. Corp.*, 418 F. Supp. 798 (D.R.I. 1976).

19. *Mohegan Tribe v. Connecticut*, 483 F. Supp. 597 (D. Conn. 1980).
20. *Mohegan Tribe v. Connecticut*, 638 F.2d 612 (2d Cir. 1980).
21. *Wilson v. Omaha Indian Tribe*, 442 U.S. 653 (1979).
22. *Oneida Indian Nation of New York v. County of Oneida*, 719 F.2d 525 (2d Cir. 1983).
23. The case was argued on behalf of the counties by Mr. Van Gestel and on behalf of the Indian claimants by Attorney Arlinda Locklear of the Native American Rights Fund in Washington, D.C.
24. *County of Oneida v. Oneida Indian Nation of New York*, 84 L.Ed.2d 169 (1985).
25. Id., 203–4.
26. *Epps v. Andrus*, 611 F.2d 915 (1st Cir. 1979); *Mashpee Tribe v. New Seabury Corp.*, 592 F.2d 575 (1st Cir.), *cert. denied*, 444 U.S. 866 (1979).
27. *Schrimpscher v. Stockton*, 183 U.S. 290 (1902); *Felix v. Patrick*, 145 U.S. 317 (1892).
28. *County of Oneida v. Oneida Indian Nation of New York*, 84 L.Ed.2d 169, 191, n.27.
29. *United States v. Consolidated Wounded Knee Cases*, 389 F.Supp. 235, 239 (D.Neb. and S.D. 1975).
30. *Rosebud Sioux Tribe v. Kneip*, 430 U.S. 584, 605 (1977).
31. *Nature of the Judicial Process* (New Haven: New York University Press, 1921), 141.
32. Hutchins, "Righting Old Wrongs," *The New Republic*, August 30, 1980, 14.

9

The Oneida Land Claims
A Legal Overview

ARLINDA F. LOCKLEAR

$\mathbf{M}$any words have been spoken and written about the unsettling social and economic effects of the Oneida and other Indian land claims. Generally, these statements are based solely on anecdotal information and tend toward the hysterical. Such statements also generally ignore the obvious and great moral justness of the claims. As a result, these statements of the problem provide no real basis for understanding or addressing the social and economic issues that arise from Indian land claims.

To develop a rational view of the claims and a reasoned approach for resolving them, the entire context of the claims must be examined. A significant part of that context is often overlooked by the public— i.e., the legal merit of the claims. It is the purpose of this chapter to discuss in general terms the legal basis of the claims as a group and the demonstrated validity of the Oneida land claims specifically. One hopes this discussion will further balance the public's consideration of the Oneida controversy.

GENERAL PRINCIPLES

The Indian land claim cases are based on sound and well-established principles of federal Indian law. These principles have no relation to the Indians' law, i.e., law developed and applied by the

Indian tribes to govern their affairs. Rather, these are principles of American federal law found in decisions of federal courts, statutes enacted by the United States Congress, and treaties signed by the United States with Indian tribes. As one might expect, these federal Indian law principles were developed primarily to serve the interests of the United States, not to protect the interests of Indian tribes. It so happens that a number of these principles are protective of tribes, but only because the United States believed such measures to be in its own long-term interest, primarily that of avoiding war with the tribes. Despite the one-sided nature of these legal principles, however, tribes have successfully invoked them as the bases for substantial land claims.

The development of these legal principles predates the founding of the United States. When European countries first arrived upon the North American continent, they found large parts of the continent occupied by Indian tribes. In order to establish relations with the tribes and avoid conflict among themselves, the European nations formulated the doctrine of discovery. The doctrine consisted of two important parts: first, that the Indian tribes found in possession of country were admitted to have the legal right to continued possession; second, the Indians' right to possession could be extinguished and tribal lands claimed only by the "discovering" European nation. [1] Thus, all European nations acknowledged the tribes' right by law to occupy exclusively their lands. The tribes' right of occupancy was not full legal title in the sense that it could be freely sold by them. But it was the complete right to use the land exclusively. That right to the soil is known as Indian title. [2]

The United States acceded to the doctrine of discovery, recognizing the Indian tribes' "unquestioned right" to exclusive possession of their lands. [3] That accession to the doctrine of discovery by the United States is one of three major theories supporting the land claim cases— the federal common law.

The body of federal common law is a relatively narrow exception to the usual rule that, in the absence of an act of Congress, the governing law in a civil dispute is state law. The federal common law exception is limited to those instances where a federal question is presented, but cannot be answered by reference to federal statutes alone. In those instances, a federal court may look to the common law in formulating an answer to the federal question. [4] Examples of federal common law subjects other than Indian relations are foreign relations, interstate disputes, and admiralty.

By virtue of the United States' accession to the doctrine of discovery, Indian title became an issue of federal law. The Supreme Court decided this point in 1974:

> It very early became an accepted doctrine in this Court that although fee title to the lands occupied by Indians when the colonists arrived became vested in the sovereign—first the discovering European nation and later the original States and the United States—a right of occupancy in the Indian tribes was nonetheless recognized. That right, sometimes called Indian title and good against all but the sovereign, could be terminated only by sovereign act. Once the United States was organized and the Constitution adopted, these tribal rights to Indian lands became the exclusive province of the federal law.[5]

As a result, any issue concerning Indian title is one of federal common law to be answered by reference to general common law. Of course, the common law provides a number of avenues of recourse for a property owner who is denied possession of his or her land. The ousted owner can sue for trespass damages and/or ejectment of the trespasser.[6] When these remedies are adopted by a federal court to vindicate the federal common-law right known as Indian title, the federal court creates a federal common-law claim for relief in the Indian land claim cases.[7]

The second basis for the claims is perhaps better known; it arises from a provision of the federal Indian Trade and Intercourse Act of 1790. The particular provision of that act relied on by tribes is the Nonintercourse Act. Roughly paraphrased, it provides that no public or private entity could acquire Indian title without the consent of the United States. Any attempt to do so was declared void, that is, of no force and effect in law.[8] Although first enacted in 1790, this provision has been reenacted by Congress several times and has been in effect continuously since 1790.[9] The Nonintercourse Act effectively codifies the second important principle of the doctrine of discovery that holds that only the United States can extinguish Indian title.[10]

In the early days of litigation in the Indian land claim cases, most of the parties' energies were focused on interpreting the Nonintercourse Act. The defending landowners raised a number of issues in defense of specific claims that were by and large rejected on the basis of a literal reading of the Nonintercourse Act. For example, it was argued that tribes that were not otherwise federally recognized could not file suits under the act. The court found, when two Maine Indian tribes claimed land, that no limitation existed on the tribes that were covered by the act, and rejected that argument.[11] As a result of this important decision, redress for loss of land was made available to non-federally recognized as well as federally recognized tribes so long as the plaintiff could sustain the burden of proving its tribal existence.[12] Defendants in the land claim cases also argued that the suits were barred by the application of state statutes of limitations and other passage-of-time type defenses. Again, these arguments were rejected because of the simple directive in the Nonintercourse Act that tribal title could be extinguished only by Congress.[13] These early procedural victories were important ones. They demonstrated that the land claims could not be knocked out of court early by a swift legal blow. But these proceedings did not test the ultimate merits of the claims.

The actual merit of the Nonintercourse Act-based claims was tested in one of the Oneida suits. This suit—*Oneida Indian Nation v. County of Oneida*[14]—was the first of the modern-day claim cases to be filed in federal court. It was brought by all three present-day Oneida tribes in 1970 against county-owned land, and challenged the legality of a land transfer of 100,000 acres from the Oneidas to New York State in 1795. The transaction had not been supervised or approved by the federal government and was, the Oneidas argued, illegal and void. Initially, the 1970 Oneida suit was dismissed on jurisdictional grounds—i.e., on the theory that the claim made was one under state law for ejectment, not one arising under federal law. In an important decision, the Supreme Court reversed this dismissal. The Supreme Court held unanimously that Indian title was a matter of federal law and, therefore, a claim for Indian land was within the federal court's jurisdiction.[15] The Supreme Court sent the case back to the district court where an even more important decision was made. In 1977, the district court, relying on the Nonintercourse Act, ruled that the 1795 transaction was illegal and void. In the words of Judge Edmund Port,

The plaintiffs have established a claim for violation of the Nonintercourse Act. Unless the act is to be rendered nugatory, it must be concluded that the plaintiffs' right of occupancy and possession of the land in question was not alienated. By the deed of 1795, the State acquired no rights against the plaintiffs; consequently, its successors, the defendant counties, are in no better position.[16]

Thus, the first Indian land claim case had been won on the basis of the Nonintercourse Act.

The third principal basis for the Indian land claim cases is the corpus of federal treaties. Unlike the federal common law and Nonintercourse Act, this basis for a claim is not available to all tribes. It is an available basis for a claim only if the particular tribe concluded a treaty with the United States that extended federal protection to the tribe's territory. Although a federal treaty is asserted as an alternative basis for a number of the land claims, there has been little actual litigation of treaty-based claims. In other contexts, however, federal treaties have been proved to be a substantial basis for Indian rights. For example, the Supreme Court has interpreted treaties with the northwest tribes as guaranteeing fishing rights that cannot be lost to or impaired by states and private individuals.[17] In addition, the Supreme Court has held that tribal lands guaranteed by federal treaty cannot be taxed by a state.[18] It follows, then, that tribal lands guaranteed by federal treaty cannot be lost through unsupervised transactions with a state or third parties.[19]

These are the principal bases of the Indian claim cases in general—the federal common law, the Nonintercourse Act, and federal treaty. All the pending land claim cases assert one or more of these as supporting the tribe's right to recover its land. Beyond that common point of departure, however, it is difficult to generalize about the cases. The history giving rise to each case is unique (although there are certain recurring themes there as well), and each claim is subject to different potential defenses. Therefore, a more particular look at the Oneida claims is in order.

THE ONEIDA LAND CLAIM CASES

To understand any of the land claim cases, you must begin with at least a sketchy knowledge of the historic events giving rise to the claim. In the case of the Oneidas, that history begins with this country's revolutionary war.

At the outbreak of the revolutionary war, the Iroquois tribes were a military force to be reckoned with. Despite the United States' efforts to persuade them to remain neutral in the conflict, all the Iroquois tribes took an active part in the revolutionary war. The Oneidas and Tuscaroras fought with the Americans while the other Iroquois tribes sided largely with Britain.[20] The Oneidas in particular gave active military assistance to the Americans.[21] The Americans were, of course, grateful for Oneida assistance and American leaders often noted the Oneidas' favored status because of their allegiance to the American cause. A 1777 statement of Congress to the Oneidas was typical:

> We have experienced your love, strong as an oak, and your fidelity, unchangeable as truth. You have kept fast hold of the ancient covenant-chain, and preserved it free from rust and decay, and bright as silver. Like brave men, for glory you despised danger: you stood forth, in the cause of your friends, and ventured your lives in our battles. While the sun and moon contrive to give light to the world, we shall love and respect you. As our trusty friends, we shall protect you; and shall at all times consider your welfare as our own.[22]

After the conclusion of the war, the Congress again assured the Oneidas of "the just estimation in which Congress continue to hold their fidelity and attachment to the United States, through all the vicissitudes of the late war."[23]

The Treaty of Paris ending the revolutionary war made no provision for former Indian allies and enemies. Thus, Congress settled its relations with tribes directly. For that purpose, Congress concluded the Treaty of Fort Stanwix with the Six Iroquois Nations in 1784 and made special provision therein for its Indian friends: "The Oneida and Tuscarora Nations shall be secured in possession of the lands on which they are settled."[24] This security for their land was given in acknowledgment of the Oneidas' and Tuscaroras' assistance in the war. As explained by the federal treaty commissioners, "It does not become the United States to forget those nations who preserved their faith to them, and adhered to their cause; those, therefore, must be secured in the full and free enjoyment of those possessions."[25]

At the time of the Treaty of Fort Stanwix, the Oneida Nation was in possession of approximately five million acres in New York State. Their territory was a swath about fifty miles wide in central New York that ran from the Pennsylvania border to the St. Lawrence River. This was the land secured to the Oneidas by the treaty of Fort Stanwix. In the 1789 Treaty of Fort Harmar and the 1794 Treaty of Canandaigua, the United States repeated essentially the same security for Oneida lands.[26]

New York State was also aware of the extent of Oneida land. In September 1784, state representatives met with the Oneidas for the purpose, so they said, of ascertaining Oneida boundaries. In their words, "We have no Claim on your lands: its just extent will ever remain secured to You; it is therefore an object of our present Meeting to have the Metes and Bounds thereof precisely ascertained in all its Parts, in order to prevent any Intrusions thereupon."[27] In response, the Oneidas detailed the boundaries of their territory to the state.[28] However, the state proceeded systematically to defraud the Oneidas out of their entire territory over the next fifty years despite the solemn assurances of federal treaties and laws.

There were altogether twenty-seven different land transactions between the state of New York and the Oneidas. The twenty-seven transactions involved varying amounts of Oneida land and took place between 1785 and 1842. Even though state officials were directly advised of the requirements of federal law, all these transactions save two were concluded without the consent or approval of the federal government.[29] Other circumstances surrounding the transactions were also similar. They were obtained, by and large, by threats and coercion and in some cases outright fraud on the state's part.[30] Thus, the solemn promises of the United States respecting Oneida land were all for naught.

The Oneidas have challenged the legality of all the non-federally approved transactions. The first suit filed by the Oneidas involves the first post-Nonintercourse Act transaction. That transaction was concluded in 1795 and affected 100,000 acres. A second suit filed by the Oneidas challenges all the other post-Nonintercourse Act transactions and involves an additional 100,000 acres. In both those suits, the Oneidas sued only Madison and Oneida Counties for county-owned lands in the claim areas. No private parties are involved. The first suit, also known as a test case, was the suit mentioned above that has gone to final judgment in favor of the Oneidas. The second suit filed by the Oneidas has been on hold pending the outcome of the first suit since it raises the same legal issues as the first.

A third suit (or more precisely, group of suits) was filed in the late 1970s and challenges the two pre-Nonintercourse Act transactions. Those deals were concluded in 1785 and 1788 and involved the bulk of Oneida land, approximately 4.5 million acres. The claims arose before the passage of the Nonintercourse Act and involve different legal principles from the first and second suits. For that reason, those claims were sued upon separately.

The Oneida test case is in the forefront of Indian land claims litigation, outside the jurisdiction of the Indian Claims Commission. It was the first of all the suits to be filed and it was the first and only of all the suits to go to final judgment. That judgment was recently reviewed by the Supreme Court and in an important decision was upheld by the Court. That opinion—*Oneida II*—was the Court's first and only opportunity to review the actual merits of an Indian land claim case. A primary issue raised by the landowners in the Supreme Court was the legitimacy of the federal common law or the Nonintercourse Act as a basis for the claim. The Court found a solid basis for the suit in the federal common law and, as a result, did not reach the question of whether the Nonintercourse Act will support a claim.[31] In addition, the Court agreed with the numerous lower court rulings that rejected the defenses of statute of limitations, abatement, implied ratification and nonjusticiability.[32] Thus, the Oneidas have prevailed completely in that suit and in doing so paved the legal way for the other Indian land claims.

The Oneida suit challenging the 1785 and 1788 state transactions is also in the forefront of Indian land claims litigation. It is the only pending suit that arises out of events that predate the U.S. Constitution and the Nonintercourse Act. For that reason, it raises unique legal issues respecting the authority of the federal and state governments in Indian affairs during the period. Although nearly ten years old, this litigation is still in its infancy. A hearing was held in September 1984 on the interpretation of relevant laws and treaties. The district court has issued an opinion[33] unfavorable to the Oneidas on those issues, but the Oneidas have reason to be hopeful of a favorable outcome in higher courts. In an earlier appeal in the same case, the Second Circuit Court of Appeals indicated that the Oneidas' claim on its face appears to be a valid one.[34] In addition, the Supreme Court hinted in its recent opinion on the Oneidas' Nonintercourse Act claims that the same rule of law prevailed even before the passage of the act: "We recognized in *Oneida I* that *the Nonintercourse Acts simply put in statutory form what was* or came to be *the accepted rule*—that the extinguishment of Indian title required the consent of the United States."[35] If that rule obtained before the enactment of the Nonintercourse Act, then the Oneidas should prevail in this suit just as they have done in the others.

Overall, the Oneida land claims litigation has been a dramatic legal success story. Despite the obvious economic stakes involved, the

Oneidas have prevailed at every important stage in the litigation. The Oneidas went into non-Indian courts seeking redress under non-Indian law and demonstrated that, sometimes, that system of justice works.

THE PASSAGE OF TIME AND EQUITY

All the Oneida successes have left as a practical matter only one possible defense to the claims, i.e., the equitable doctrine of laches. In its *Oneida II* decision, the Supreme Court expressed doubt about the applicability of that defense, but did not decide the issue. As a result, the issue is still an open one.

The purpose of the doctrine of laches is to prevent the assertion of stale claims. Originally, the defense of laches was available only in courts of equity while the analogous statute of limitations defense was available only in courts of law. Now, there are no separate courts of equity and law. Both equitable and legal actions are heard by a single court. But equitable defenses such as laches are, as a rule, still applicable only to traditionally equitable claims. The land claim cases are considered legal, not equitable actions. For that reason, the Supreme Court in *Oneida II* was doubtful that the defense is available at all.

Even were the defense available, it would not bar the Oneida claims. Unlike a statute of limitations defense, laches does not arise simply from the passage of time. The laches defense depends upon the relative equities of the parties. It bars claims where the plaintiff unreasonably delayed filing suit for an unduly long period of time, resulting in prejudice to the opposing party. That is not the case with the Oneida claims for a number of reasons.

First, the Oneidas have been diligent in the pursuit of their land. As soon as the Oneidas realized what was happening to them in the late eighteenth century, the Oneidas called upon the federal government for its oft-promised protection. The first recorded request was made by an Oneida leader during the negotiations that led to the 1794 Treaty of Canandaigua. The Oneidas were told that the matter would be investigated later. No such investigation took place. Since that time, the Oneidas have persistently raised the issue. Throughout the nineteenth century, the Oneidas in both Wisconsin and New York raised the matter of their New York lands with their federal Indian agent to no avail. In fact, there is evidence that the Oneidas consulted a lawyer in 1874 on the claims, but nothing resulted from that meeting. Protests continued throughout the twentieth century. Numerous letters and petitions were sent to the federal government by individual Oneidas and Oneida leaders. The Oneidas also formally requested the United States to sue on the claims as the Oneidas' trustee. With one exception, discussed below, these requests were also to no avail. Thus, Judge Port concluded in his 1977 Oneida decision that the Oneidas "never acquiesced in the loss of their land, but have continued to protest its diminishment up until today."[36]

Second, the Oneidas' legal capacity to sue on the claims without the United States as co-plaintiff, and the federal court's jurisdiction over the claims, have been doubtful until recently. The United States as trustee for Indian tribes plainly has legal authority to sue to protect tribal property rights. Historically, the overwhelming majority of such suits were filed by the United States when circumstances convinced the United States that such a suit was appropriate or required. It was assumed that the United States' trustee obligations somehow diminished the tribes' right to sue on their property rights themselves. That assumption was first squarely rejected by the Supreme Court in 1968.[37] It was also doubtful whether federal courts have jurisdiction over suits filed directly by tribes. That jurisdictional point was not finally resolved in the tribes' favor by the Supreme Court until 1974 in the Oneida test case itself. In other words, the Oneidas diligently pursued their claims in court once that avenue became available to them.

Third, these cases come as no surprise to the state of New York or its citizens. The state, of course, has been aware of the claims since the transactions occurred. The governor was told plainly by federal officials before the time of the first transaction and afterward that the state had no authority to deal in Oneida land. The State chose to ignore that advice and thus acted at its peril. In 1919 the state legislature appointed a commission to investigate the "Indian problem." That commission, known as the Everett Commission, reported back, among other things, that the Indian/state land transactions had been illegal. The legislature did not like its commission's report and suppressed publication of it.[38] There can be no doubt that state officials have actual knowledge of the claims from the state's own records.

Earlier litigation should have brought home knowledge of the claims to private landowners (i.e., actual knowledge as opposed to constructive knowledge arising from county land records). In 1919, the federal government filed suit on a thirty-two-acre parcel of the Oneida claim on behalf of the Oneidas. Based on its determination that the federal government had sole authority to dispose of Indian lands, the court ordered eviction of the non-Indians then in possession of the parcel. On appeal the decision was upheld.[39] The Boylan decision is generally known in the community as the origin of the present-day thirty-two-acre reservation in Oneida. In a contest about leases of Seneca lands in 1942, the same court again affirmed the general principle that New York State had no authority over tribal land.[40] Thus, the existence of outstanding Indian claims is or should be known by the current landowners.

The Oneida claims, then, are not a bit of history dusted off by a clever lawyer and sprung upon an innocent state and citizenry. The Oneida claims arise out of a blatant and knowing violation of the dominant society's own law for which Oneidas have sought redress by every means available to them. The story of the claims is one of conscious neglect of a former ally by the United States. The story is one of fraud and overbearing by the state of New York. And the story is one of self-imposed ignorance of others' rights by the present land-owners. The equities plainly weigh in favor of a remedy for the Oneidas.

One final word about responsibility for the Oneida claims. It is true that the original sin here was committed by the United States and the state of New York. It is also no doubt true that there are a number of innocent landowners in the claim area, i.e., individuals who acquired their land with no knowledge of the Oneida claim to it. But those facts alone do not end the inquiry respecting ultimate responsibility. Whatever their knowledge of the claims before then, the landowners have certainly been aware of the Oneida claims since 1970 when the first suit was filed. Since that time, the landowners have done nothing to seek a speedy and just resolution of the claims. Instead, they have as a point of principle denied the validity of the claims and pursued the litigation, determined to prove the claims to be frivolous. Now that the landowners have failed in that effort, they loudly proclaim their innocence in the entire matter. The Oneidas, on the other hand, have since 1970 repeatedly expressed their preference for an out-of-court resolution of the claims. Had the landowners joined with the Oneidas sixteen years ago in seeking a just resolution, the claims would no doubt be resolved today. For that reason, the landowners share responsibility for the situation in which they find themselves today.

Now that the legal merit of the claims has been demonstrated to a large extent, perhaps enlightened self-interest will convince all parties to deal fairly with the Oneidas. The parties to the claims must cooperate if an amicable solution to the claims is to be found. If that does not happen, then all parties will bear responsibility for the failure. As the Oneidas have learned, it cannot be done by one party alone.

NOTES

1. *Johnson v. M'Intosh*, 21 U.S. (8 Wheat.) 543 (1823).
2. *Oneida Indian Nation v. County of Oneida—Oneida I*—414 U.S. 661 (1974).
3. *Cherokee Nation v. Georgia*, 30 U.S. (5 Pet.) 1, 17 (1831).
4. *D'Oench Duhue & Co. v. Federal Deposit Ins. Corp.*, 315 U.S. 447 (1942).
5. *Oneida I*, 667.
6. *Green v. Biddle*, 21 U.S. (8 Wheat.) 1, 75–76 (1823).
7. *Oneida Indian Nation v. County of Oneida—Oneida II*—84 L. Ed. 2d 169 (1985).
8. 1 Stat. 137.
9. It is now found at 25 U.S.C. section 177.
10. *Oneida I*, 667.
11. *Joint Tribal Council of Passamaquoddy and Penobscot Tribes v. Morton*, 528 F. 2d 370 (1st Cir. 1975).
12. See *Mashpee Tribe v. New Seabury Corp.*, 427 F. Supp. 899 (D. Mass. 1977), *dismissed* 447 F. Supp. 992, *affirmed* 592 F. 2d 575 (1st Cir. 1979), *cert. denied* 444 U.S. 866 (1980).
13. *Schaghticoke Tribe of Indians v. Kent School Corp.*, 423 F. Supp. 780 (D. Conn. 1976); *Narragansett Tribe of Indians v. Southern Rhode Island Land Development Corp.*, 418 F. Supp. 798 (D. R. I. 1976).
14. 70—CV—35 (N. D. N. Y.).
15. *Oneida I*.
16. *Oneida Indian Nation v. County of Oneida*, 434 F. Supp. 527, 548 (N. D. N. Y. 1979).
17. See *Washington v. Fishing Vessel Assn.*, 443 U.S. 658 (1979); *Antoine v. Washington*, 420 U.S. 194 (1975).
18. *Fellows v. Denniston*, 72 U.S. (5 Wall.) 761 (1867).
19. See *Wilson v. Omaha Indian Tribe*, 442 U.S. 653 (1979).
20. Barbara Graymont, *The Iroquois in the American Revolution* (Syracuse: Syracuse University Press, 1972).
21. Ibid., pp. 129–43.
22. Washington C. Ford et al., eds., *Journals of the Continental Congress, 1774– 1789*, 34 vols. (Washington, D.C.: United States Government Printing Office, 1904–1937), 9:996, December 1777.
23. Ibid., 24:492, August 1783.
24. 7 Stat. 15, Article II.

25. Minutes of Ft. Stanwix negotiations, October 1784, in Neville Craig, ed., *The Olden Times*, 2 vols. (Pittsburgh: Wright & Charlton, 1847–1848).

26. See 7 Stat. 33; 7 Stat. 44.

27. Franklin B. Hough, ed., *Proceedings of the Commissioners of Indian Affairs Appointed by Law for the Extinguishment of Indian Titles in the State of New York*, 2 vols. (Albany: Joel Munsell, 1861), 1:41.

28. Ibid., 45.

29. See *Oneida Nation v. United States*, 26 Ind. Cl. Comm. 138 (1971).

30. See, e.g., *Oneida Indian Nation v. United States*, 37 Ind. Cl. Comm. 522 (1976).

31. *Oneida II*, 180.

32. Ibid., 182–89.

33. See Claire Brennan, "Oneida Claim to 6 Million Acres Voided," *Syracuse Post-Standard*, November 22, 1986, 1.

34. See *Oneida Indian Nation of New York v. State of New York*, 691 F. 2d 1070 (2nd Cir. 1982).

35. *Oneida II*, 182 (emphasis added).

36. *Oneida Indian Nation v. County of Oneida*, 434 F. Supp., 541.

37. See *Poafpybitty v. Skelly Oil Co.*, 390 U.S. 365 (1968).

38. See Helen M. Upton, *The Everett Report in Historical Perspective: The Indians of New York State* (Albany: New York State American Revolution Bicentennial Commission, 1980).

39. *United States. v. Boylan*, 265 Fed. 165 (2nd Cir. 1920).

40. See *United States v. Forness*, 125 F. 2d 928 (2nd Cir. 1942).

10

The Sovereignty and Land Rights of the Houdenosaunee

IRVING POWLESS, JR.

L et us thank the Creator that we are well, and we are able to meet. I am going to speak to you, and I would just like you to pay close attention to what I say.

There are many issues before us. I reflect upon the things that have been happening to our people, not two hundred years ago, but yesterday. Termination, genocide, a move to remove our people from the face of the earth. Court hearings, jurisdiction, judges sitting in the courtrooms, making decisions that formulate or change our lives.

The Onondagas had a case on evictions a few years ago, and because of what was happening nationwide in the territories of our people, non-Indians within the territories of the Sioux, the Cheyennes, the Arapahos, the Blackfeet, the Seminoles, and the Senecas, were making decisions that were affecting the landowners, the Indian owners of the land. So there was a move on our part not to get into the situation where non-Indians would be telling us what to do. So we asked these people to remove themselves from our territory. Some of them did, and some of them didn't. The action of the Onondaga Council was to escort them out of our territory.

These individuals, five of them to be exact, went to court, and after a long process, the judge ruled that those non-Indians who left Onondaga were trespassers; those who remained were not. When you try to rationalize what kind of judge makes a statement like this, I have to agree with Allan van Gestel when he says that the laws are idiots.

Nevertheless, such decisions are being made constantly; in Albany such decisions change our lives, and have an impact upon the future of our people. And the people who are making these decisions don't even know who we are. Not too many years ago some Albany legislature subcommittee members went to each of the territories, and they came to Onondaga. One of the subcommittee members, as he traveled through our territory, said, "Where are the tepees?" Now, this man was going to make legislation that was going to change or domi-nate Iroquois life, tell me what to do, and he came to my homeland expecting to see a tepee. Those of us who have studied know that the tepees were out West, and that the Iroquois, or Six Nations, or as we refer to ourselves, the Houdenosaunee, did not live in tepees.

These people who come into our territories and make these kinds of decisions represent what most of this is all about: land claims, court decisions, laws. Last year I received a telephone call from a secretary for the Albany legislature; she said to me, "Do you support the Oath Bill?"

I said, "Yes, I support the Oath Bill."

She said, "Do you support the Library Trustee Act?"

I said, "What is it?"

She said, "Presently, the Library Trustee Act has to be amended so that members of your nation can become trustees to the public library system."

I said, "Well, that's very odd to me. One law, the Oath Bill, has to be amended to *exclude* me, and the law of the library trusteeship has to be amended to *include* me."

And she said, "I really don't understand what you're talking about."

So, I said, "Since I haven't read the Library Trustee Act, I will reserve comment."

This year she called me again, and she said to me, "Do you support the Oath Bill?" The Oath Bill is a requirement that everyone who is a teacher in the state of New York in any of the institutes must sign an oath of allegiance that he or she will support the New York State Constitution. We feel that in our territory, the territory of the Onondagas, Cayugas, Senecas, Oneidas, Mohawks, and Tuscaroras, that we should not make that allegiance. We are a sovereign nation; we are citizens of *our* nation, and we should not have to make an allegiance to the state of New York in order for us to teach within our territory.

So, I said to her, "Yes, I do support the Oath Bill." I said, "What about the Library Trustee Act?"

She said to me that in April 1985 it was passed by the Assembly. In May it was passed by the Senate, and in June it was signed by the governor. In July it went into effect.

I said, "Here we have a law that we did not ask for, did not support, made no comment on, that went right through with no problem whatsoever. That is saying to us that the law did not include us so they had to make an amendment to include us. The Oath Bill," I said, "where is that?"

"Oh, that's tied up in committee."

This is the law that we support even though we don't understand why one law includes us and the other law excludes us. But these are the things that are going on today. Lands are being taken away from us, rights are being taken away from us, but to understand who we are and where we come from, we have to go back.

Somewhere back there in our history, not a myth, not a legend, but in actuality, a person came amongst us, and he said, "We must live in harmony. We must live in peace. We are all brothers."

This concept was portrayed by the Tree of Peace, which was uprooted, and the weapons of war between the nations were buried beneath it. We would live in harmony with each other. This concept of the Confederacy included the Mohawks, the Oneidas, the Onondagas, the Cayugas, and the Senecas (with the Tuscaroras added later).

He put before us a system by which we would be able to choose leaders among our women and among our men. These leaders would then represent the clans in our community. We have Bear, Deer, Wolf, Turtle, Snipe throughout our communities. These clans are all related. As a member of the Wolf clan you can go to the Senecas, the Onondagas, the Oneidas, and the Cayugas and be among your family. Within this family, representatives of the family sit together and they choose their leaders. These leaders then are spokesmen at those council meetings. And when the Grand Council is called, all of the nations come together.

The Mohawks have nine representatives. The Oneidas have nine. The Onondagas have fourteen. The Cayugas have ten, and the Senecas have eight. When this person came among us, he gave us names, and he gave these names to individuals. He sought out those who were not the most respected persons in the community; in fact, he picked out the most devious, the one who was doing the most harm, and he made him the leader among leaders. He changed these people, so that they would have a good mind, and they would be able to show that these people can change. You don't have to be bad people, you can live in harmony.

This was the system that he set down, and the names that he gave at that time, whenever it was, two, three, four thousand years ago. To the Onondagas he gave the name Tadadaho. Sitting next to him, Dehatkadons, Arirhonh. These names still exist. The process by which these people sit in Council still exists.

The rights of the Houdenosaunee do not come from any treaty. They do not come from any court decision or law. The rights of the Houdenosaunee came long before your people came here. We have not changed. I am still Dehatkadons, left-hand man. My name is Dehatkadons, and when I leave this earth, another person shall take my name.

A name you're familiar with, made famous by Longfellow, is Hiawatha, which is a way of saying Ayonhwathah in Onondaga. This person was helpful to the Peacemaker who came about and set up this League of Six Nations. And the name Ayonhwathah still exists among the Mohawks; he is one of the chiefs. When the Grand Council meets, Ayonhwathah sits in Council.

When the Peacemaker came to the Onondagas and he named these people, Dehatkadons was one of the names. Dehatkadons has duties. He sits to the left side of Tadadaho.

There are special duties, special processes that we go through, and we carry with us a badge. This is called wampum. It is not an artifact, as portrayed by some of the anthropologists and others who oppose the Houdenosaunee and say we do not exist. When a Council is called, wampum is used. We send runners to the Mohawks, to the Oneidas, to the Cayugas, to the Senecas, to the Tuscaroras, and we invite them to a meeting. With a runner carrying a string of wampum, the whole process goes through of sending out the message and returning the message. It takes a long time for this to happen, but this was a process that was set down thousands of years ago. And this process still exists today.

There is a meeting coming up, and coming to that meeting are the Dené people, Navajos as you know them, and they come to the western door. It's a process by which you come through and get audience with the Houdenosaunee. These people are concerned, because they are being removed from their territory. Millions of dollars are being expended by the federal government to move these people from the lands that they have been living on these thousands of years, all so that Peabody Coal Company can strip mine, and they can get at the natural resources. Instead of spending millions of dollars to preserve the tradition and culture of the Navajos and Hopis, they are spending this amount, millions of dollars, to remove them from their territory so that they can exploit the natural resources. That is not two hundred years ago; that's today. Hearings are being held down in Washington, D.C., today on these issues.

Our people are fighting for existence. It's not fun and games. We sit in a fight every day. The legislatures, the lawyers in Washington who lobby against us, these clubs—rod and gun clubs, outdoor people, hunting and fishing rights clubs—every day we are confronted with the possibility that maybe we'll end up in court like the Mashpees did a few years ago, when a jury said, "You are no longer Indians. You have no claim."

Can you imagine if a law were passed that Colgate University no longer existed, that the alumni and students now belonged to Cortland College? But you have limitations to being a part of Cortland. Cortland will dictate to you, how you will use your diplomas or whatever you want. You know that this is funny and you laugh, and it is good that you can laugh, but it is a reality I fight every day. These are the things that we face.

Houdenosaunee, that means People of the Longhouse. And when this League was set down these many years ago, the Mohawks were designated the keepers of the eastern door. The Onondagas were the fire-keepers. And the Senecas were the keepers of the western door. Anybody wishing to have audience with the Houdenosaunee had to go through one of these two doors, before he sat in Council with the Houdenosaunee. That process still exists, and it will happen again when the Navajos come to Onondaga, to explain to us what is happening to them in their territory. In the People of the Longhouse, if you will, the process still exists, because the Mohawks are still at the eastern door, and the Seneca people are still at the western, and this Longhouse covers what is now called New York State.

The Houdenosaunee, having such a large house, are not able to live in every room. And so, when the Europeans came into our house, they saw empty rooms, and they said, "Oh, what a nice room! I think I'll set up residence here. And since I'm setting up residence here, whom shall I notify that I've done this? Apparently, these people who are running around in buckskins and feathers, they don't know what to do with that. So, I will go over here to the Thirteen Colonies, and I will say to them, 'I've found a beautiful room, and I'm going to call it Oneida County. Is that all right?'

" 'Sure.' "

So, Oneida County became existent. Onondaga County became existent. Because these people are moving into our rooms, they're filling up our house, and claiming these rooms. We still own that house. That house belongs to us. We are the owners. You are occupying one of our rooms.

If you look at it another way, over here I see a beautiful building, and there are empty rooms in there. Suppose I went into an empty room and said, "What a place! Why, it's got a TV; I'm going to call it home. Onondaga Council, guess what I found? I found a beautiful home. How about passing a law that says I can live there?"

And Onondaga Council says, "Sure."

Now I move in. And guess what happens? The hostile landowner comes down to me, and he says, "What are you doing here?" See? The hostile landowner—the building superintendent—says I can't do this.

"Why not? It was empty. There was nobody here."

He says, "But I own it."

"No. I passed a law with the Onondaga Council that says I can live here."

Now we'll have to get a lawyer, and what will the lawyer say? He will argue the point. I bet you, if we asked Allan van Gestel, he would say that I was wrong, that I couldn't move into the room as I have described.

We go back to our first beginnings, when the Peacemaker and Ayonhwathah went among us, and explained to us how we should live together in peace and harmony. I wish to leave you with this thought, that under the Tree of Peace has sat the Dutch government, the French government, the British government, and the United States. George Washington came and sat under our Tree. Thomas Jefferson sat under our Tree, in peace, as we tried to formulate ways that we could settle our disputes.

George Washington gave promises. It was he who set down the 1790 Nonintercourse Act, on behalf of the Houdenosaunee, to show his good faith to the Houdenosaunee that our lands would not be taken away from us. George Washington has a special place in the history of the Houdenosaunee, as he has with you. To you, he is the father of your country, a very reputable man. But during the American Revolution George Washington said to Colonel Sullivan, "Go out and kill every one of them. Extinguish the Six Nations people." Sullivan started his raid, and he went to our villages, and he burned them. He burned our crops, in an attempt to extinguish our people—a policy that exists today, a policy that we are always defending against; we are always looking out for our people.

It must be set down today, solid, as it was three, four thousand years ago, that we are the landowners. This house is ours. This must be set down, so that my grandchildren's grandchildren will be safe, and they will still be able to conduct the ceremonies of our people. They will still be able to sing their songs and speak their language. And they will still be able to teach you people about peace and harmony and living together.

You are not hostages in our house. We don't hold you here. But we do recognize the fact that you are in our house. We have people who are working on settling the dispute as to how you should live in our house.

The Creator has given us a mind. He has given us the ability to sit and think. And we hope that we are intelligent enough to sit down and negotiate a solution to the problem that faces us today. I think that, sitting under the Tree of Peace with the Houdenosaunee, we can come to a solution to the problem.

11

Epilogue

WILLIAM A. STARNA

It has been nearly two decades since the Oneidas brought their initial land claim action in New York State. This, and the filing of subsequent claims by other Iroquois tribes, has drawn the attention of the legal community, other Indian tribes and organizations, historians, anthropologists, and local, state, and federal governments and their non-Indian citizens. Reactions to the suits have been mixed, to say the least, and range from those of vociferous detractors and "nay-sayers," to unquestioning supporters. Unfortunately, the polemics that emerge from such oppositional positions hide the realities of the land claims. This book of essays is one attempt to bring these realities home.

CURRENT STATUS OF LAND CLAIMS

As of September 1, 1987, Indian land claims in New York stood as follows:

Oneida

The pre-1790 Oneida claim was dismissed in Federal District Court in November 1986. It was appealed to, and argued in, the Second Circuit Court, United States Court of Appeals, on June 3,

1987. In March of 1985, the United States Supreme Court affirmed a lower court's opinion that the Oneidas had a possessory right to land claimed in their post-1790 suit. Further action will be required to assess the amount of damages and fair compensation to be awarded. In September 1986, negotiations commenced between the state of New York, the federal government, and the Indian parties.

Cayuga

The Cayuga claim is also in a negotiation stage, albeit a "new one," and has been so for over four years. In 1980 a settlement was reached after three years of negotiations, but failed to receive Congressional approval. While negotiations continued, cross-motions for summary judgment were filed. On April 29, 1987, the state's chief negotiator announced that an agreement was near. The details of the pact and the Cayuga's response have not been made public, although further negotiations appear to be in order. On August 21, 1987, the United States District Court, Northern District of New York, denied the cross-motions for summary judgment. Further proceedings will be limited to the issues of federal government ratification and alleged abandonment by the plaintiff tribes.

Mohawk

There is a stay on further proceedings, which includes a defendant's motion to dismiss, pending negotiations. Formal discussions began in 1986.

Stockbridge-Munsee and Seneca

The Stockbridge-Munsee and Seneca land claims are in the early stages of the litigation process at this time. Meanwhile, there have been settlement talks between the state and the Senecas, and very preliminary explorations into beginning a dialogue regarding the Stockbridge-Munsee suit.

THE ROAD TO NEGOTIATIONS

Negotiated settlements, or more directly, out-of-court resolutions of claims brought, were, from the outset, the primary strategy of the Indian litigants. This was clearly the stance taken by the Oneidas in 1970. Assuming the position that their cases were not only morally worthy and just, but legally compelling and justiciably sound, offers to negotiate instead of litigate were made explicitly to the defendant class, i.e., those sued by the Oneidas. Similar offers have been made by the Cayugas, Mohawks, and others. For the Cayugas, the near-settlement reached in 1980, evolving from lengthy and good-faith negotiations, was torpedoed by then Congressman Gary Lee, and it was only at this point that the tribe had little choice but to bring suit.

The state of New York, at least in recent years, has also portrayed itself as preferring to negotiate rather than litigate. Notwithstanding this assertion, the record tells another story. In the 1970s, the early stages of land claims, negotiations were not under any active or serious consideration by state officials. For what are, in all fairness, under-standable reasons, the state of New York instead decided to fight the complaints. Initially, the state had no reason to believe that the Indians' suits would go anywhere in the courts, basing this judgment on the perceived strengths of its legal defenses and prevailing legal precedent. The obvious supposition on the state's part was to litigate and win. Nevertheless, subsequent legal victories by the Oneidas, and the concomitant pressure to negotiate settlements brought by the courts, forced the state to take out-of-court resolutions seriously.

Although state parties to the claims continue today to profess a policy of negotiations first, and litigation as a last resort, they chose the latter when confronted with the most recent claim, that of the Stock-bridge-Munsees. This was in the face of a request by the Indians' attorneys to explore a non-hostile and equitable solution outside of litigation. And it is not as if there is a different theory of law involved in the plaintiff's action, or even new defenses being considered by the state. The Stockbridge-Munsees are claiming relief arising under the

Commerce Clause, Article I, Section 8, United States Constitution, 25 U.S.C. Section 177 (Indian Trade and Intercourse Act), the federal common law, and the Treaty of Canandaigua, 7 Stat. 44. Although other federal and state treaties and agreements are involved, this is essentially the same claim to relief successfully brought in the Oneidas' actions and which is fundamental to the other land claims. For its part, the state will undoubtedly bring to bear one or all of its few remaining defenses in the aftermath of the Oneida decisions; for example, that of abandonment, used in the Cayuga claim; laches, not reached in *Oneida II*; and whether or not the Stockbridge-Munsees have enjoyed continuous tribal status or political continuity throughout their history. It remains to be seen whether or not these defenses are viable and compelling, and if the refusal to negotiate was a sound strategy.

THE NEGOTIATIVE PROCESS

It would be inappropriate, and at best, speculative, to comment on those claims that are currently under active consideration or litigation. What is worthy of examination, however, is the context in which negotiations are taking place, the process itself, and the possible outcomes.

There is a complex network of interested parties involved in the negotiative process, not to mention the number of "players." To a certain extent, this process and its constituent elements can be generalized into a pattern. That is, there is a constancy in this process that can be identified and schematized.

For its part, New York State's involvement is directed from the executive department and ultimately, the governor's office. There are ten individuals in this department, including the governor, who offer counsel, form policy, and participate in making decisions affecting the claims, both those in litigation and those in negotiation. Part of this total of ten is a key player, an attorney who acts as the governor's representative not only in land claims, but also in the full range of Indian issues occupying state business.

Acting in an attorney-client relationship with the executive is the Department of Law. Although there are just a few individuals involved, about nine, only three have what could be described as intimate, day-to-day knowledge of the claims; the remainder are kept informed through routine departmental protocol and are peripheral to the issues. Of the three, two are essentially litigators, one of whom is directly involved in the negotiative process, while the third "monitors" their activity and reports to an individual in the state counsel division in the department.

The state legislature is, in a less direct fashion, also involved in negotiations. In the assembly, efforts are coordinated through the governmental operations committee and its one staff member assigned to the Indian land claims. This individual also sits on the negotiating team or "task force," and reports directly to the committee chairman and then to the speaker of the assembly. In the senate, the majority leader has an appointed representative at the negotiating table who reports directly to him and his counsel. The remainder of the legislature is not only outside of the negotiative process, but has not been kept informed, in any formal way, of the issues at hand. In fact, a very large majority of the members of the state assembly and senate representing the claims areas did not know negotiations were in process, were not familiar with the status of the claims, had no real input into the settlement process, and had virtually no insight into the claims issues or the Indian communities involved. Several members spoke forcibly, and with some rancor, arguing that they were being kept out of the process on purpose, a perception that is not altogether inaccurate. Individuals both in the Department of Law and representing the executive, in addition to several staffers, have indicated that the legislature would be brought in "at some point" in the negotiative process, but seeking their counsel now was unnecessary.

At the federal level, New York's congressional delegation is involved in the settlement efforts. These individuals include New York's two senators and congressional representatives, and members of their staffs. Coordinating these activities, and occupying a powerful position in terms of developing a settlement "package" that will be acceptable to all, is a *pro bono* facilitator from Rochester Gas and Electric, a major utility in upstate New York. Also participating at the federal level are a number of individuals from the Department of the Interior and its solicitor's office.

Local governments involved in the two major claims are represented at negotiations by county officials, as in the Cayuga claim, or by counsel, in the Oneida and Mohawk cases.

Finally, there are the various Indians tribes, members of their leadership, and their attorneys and consultants. These include three

Oneida groups; namely, the Oneida Tribe of Indians of Wisconsin, Inc., the Oneida of the Thames Band of Canada, and the Oneida Indian Nation of New York. Intervenors in Oneida, the Houdenosaunee, do not presently sit at the table. In addition, there is the Cayuga Indian Nation of New York, and three groups representing the Mohawks through a tri-council structure; that is, the Mohawk Council of Akwesasne, the St. Regis Mohawk Tribal Council, and the Mohawk Nation Council of Chiefs.

In any examination of this negotiative process and hoped-for settlement, there must first be recognition of the tensions that exist within government bureaucracy, which are then compounded when linked to tribal governments and other competing interests. These are expressed in political rivalries, territorial disputes over jurisdictional or regulatory powers, struggles between policy formulators and administrators, alliance formations and cleavages, interagency friction, personality conflicts, and other bureaucratic pathologies.

Contributing to these tensions are contradictions operating in the system. One such contradiction is revealed in the posture taken by New York State and federal officials in the context of the land claims. The state, through its spokespersons, has repeatedly maintained that its primary focus and abiding interest is settling the claims through negotiations; that is, reaching closure on these complex issues and, importantly, obtaining a "clear release," i.e., extinguishing any further claims. The state has further asserted that insofar as it is concerned, resolving the claims is not a "win or lose proposition," thus, its intentions are honorable. Similar statements have been made at the federal level. Nonetheless, this apparently positive stance is countered by the inherent adversarial or antagonistic principles that underly the bureaucracy and its components. The state government's interests are directed first toward self-protection. For example, it has entered land claims litigation with the sole intention to win. It will not effect a settlement unless, from its point of view, the federal government contributes its "fair share." And it fought, at every turn, counties' efforts to be relieved of expenses incurred in defending themselves against the Oneida claims. For its part, the federal government has insisted that the state pay its "fair share" of any settlements, which, it says, must amount to 50 percent of any total package. It vacillated on the issue of whether or not it should exercise its trust responsibility in protecting the interests of the Indian parties. And today, it has distanced itself from the claims and the attendant negotiation proceedings, maintaining that they are "local issues." In the meantime, the

affected counties and municipalities have had to protect themselves by
hiring attorneys, bringing an action against the state to be indemnified
for their legal expenses, and, in Cayuga, held culpable for aborting the
1980 settlement.

The point is, any suggestion by government, whether at the
federal, state, or local level, that they have entered the negotiations
putting aside the pivotal issue of whether they win or lose, is simply
untrue. The inherent tensions and adversarial nature of government
bureaucracy and its legalistic underpinnings lay false this notion.
Thus, government's expressed intent is knowingly unrealistic, and has
been promulgated for public consumption and other, self-serving purposes.

Sitting outside the government bureaucracy, and clearly affected
by its dynamics, are the Indian tribes and their governments. Not
unexpectedly, a certain degree of discord exists in these communities
as well. Given the kin-based nature of most Indian tribes, disputes that
do arise can sometimes be traced to family disagreements, which are,
in turn, ramified into the sociopolitical structure of the society. Traditional means of resolving such conflicts are no longer a viable alternative for Indian tribes. For example, in the past, a dissenting group
would simply split off from the main body and form its own social
unit. Reservation boundaries and, in many cases, Indian tribes being
introduced to elective political structures through the Indian Reorganization Act (1934), have removed such an alternative from consideration.[2]

It goes without saying that there is a great disparity in size
between Indian tribes and the dominant non-Indian society surrounding them. For example, the largest tribe to bring a claim against New
York is the Oneida Tribe of Wisconsin, with an enrollment of approximately 9,000 individuals. There are some 2,500 Oneidas in Ontario,
and about 700 in New York State. The Cayugas number fewer than
500, while the Mohawk combined enrollment (Canadian Band and
American Tribe) is about 7,000. There are some 1,000 Stockbridge-
Munsees and 6,800 Senecas (all reservations).

The total Indian population in New York State is about 38,000,
residing on seven federal reservations, two state reservations, a specially leased parcel of land, and within five major urban communities.
The State of New York has a population of 17.6 million non-Indians.

The recitation of these population figures provides a clear indication of scale when discussing the current land claims conflicts. It also
furnishes persuasive evidence supporting the view historically and

commonly held in government circles that Indians in the state do not constitute a political threat to those in power, and are not regarded as an important political constituency.

At the same time, Indians in the state and elsewhere generally do not view themselves as participants in the political process of the larger, dominant, non-Indian society. This is in spite of being made U.S. citizens by statute in 1924. Instead, they see themselves as sovereign nations, on equal footing with the United States in essentially all matters, and standing, for all intents and purposes, outside of its jurisdiction. This view is firmly rooted in federal Indian law and supported by political theory and legal precedent. Thus, there are historical and cultural reasons why Indians, by choice, do not form political constituencies of any consequence to the dominant society.

All of this background is brought into focus in examining the ongoing land claims negotiations. One of the first observations to be made by those who follow the process is its interminable slowness. From all quarters come complaints, sincere and otherwise, of inaction and delay. And each party blames the other.

The state contends that its task in the negotiations has been made more difficult because, and this is in reference primarily to the Oneida case, there was disarray and factionalism within the New York tribe and there was no federally recognized polity with which to talk. As a consequence, said state officials, negotiations could not move forward with dispatch, and unless and until the Indians settled their internal strife, a resolution of the claim would not soon be in the offing. What the state fails to mention or consider in this situation is the fact that in 1975, the Department of Interior withdrew its recognition of the Oneida Indian Nation of New York's executive committee, the govern- ing body of the tribe. Reacting to pressure from a dissident group within the tribe, and without benefit of notice or due process, a BIA functionary advised the committee that it was no longer recognized. If the tribe had remained a federally recognized body, the disputes and differences of opinion pointed out until very recently would have to have been described as nonpartisan or bi-partisan politics, rather than factional disputes as they have been. They would have little bearing on who sits at the table, or better yet, would have given the state little excuse but to proceed in good faith with the negotiations. On July 29, 1987, the Department of Interior recognized the traditional govern- ment of the New York Oneidas. It remains to be seen what will transpire now that there is a federally recognized body representing this group.

In other instances, however, the state has chosen to deal extensively with the Grand Council at Onondaga, representing the Houdenosaunee or Iroquois confederacy, a group that has never been a federally recognized body. This, in and of itself, has been a source of controversy in virtually all Iroquois communities. Many elected leaders of the duly constituted and recognized tribal governments point to this apparent anomaly in the state's behavior and suspect that it is a deliberate move intended to perpetuate, if not create anew, internal tribal conflicts, thus stalling land claims settlements. Such a Machiavellian scheme is denied vehemently by state officials. Nevertheless, it is the Grand Council that has a direct line to the governor's office, and it is this group that sits in conference in the executive chambers in Albany. It also actively opposes any Oneida settlement.

In the Cayuga claim, the state has steadfastly maintained that the federal government is the culprit, holding itself at a distance from the negotiations and acting the part of an observer rather than a participant. The state wants the federal government to be fully involved in the process, and refuses to go it alone or obligate itself for what it perceives to be more than its share of any settlement. Underlying this position is a curious conviction among many state officials, including some in the Department of Law, that the wrongs committed in the past were as much the fault of the federal government as they were the state, since the federal government did not enforce the Nonintercourse Act.

The state has also tended to fall back on a philosophical rationale to explain the protracted nature of the land claims negotiations. This is most often couched in phrases like, "things like this take time," "these are complex issues and must be approached with caution," or, "we don't want to shove anything down anyone's throat." Alluding to a perceived cultural difference, one official noted that "the Indians don't like to be rushed." Further, an individual in the governor's office has asserted that the Cuomo administration has had to adjust slowly to the responsibilities of leadership, and that there are still legislators with "Indian-hating attitudes," a not inaccurate observation.[3]

The Cayugas and their leaders are concerned with the inaction that has characterized the current settlement attempts. More than two years ago, they and their attorney presented a package to the state that addressed the details of their terms of settlement in land, cash award, and services. There has since been no substantive response from either the state or the federal government. The state contends that the issue is in the hands of federal officials and their *pro bono* facilitator. This explanation, however, is somewhat flawed and requires discussion.

The facilitator, who ostensibly represents the congressional delegation, is described by some individuals in the Executive Department as a "close personal friend of the governor," and is known to visit the governor's chambers to confer with members of the executive staff. This is in the face of assertions by other state government officials that he "does not report to the governor," or that he "does not work for the executive" in the area of land claims.

In the meantime, delay has raised the specter of political discord among to the Cayugas. Cayuga chiefs, having acted in good faith at the bargaining table, have begun hearing complaints from exasperated tribal members who have lost patience with the state and federal governments' inaction. And as in most communities, local leadership bears the burden of explaining the delay, and will ultimately suffer the political costs. State and federal officials show little concern for the difficulties faced by the Cayuga chiefs and the threats posed to the community and their political system by government bureaucracy and inaction.

The Oneida's concerns emanate from a historically justifiable mistrust of the government that is expressed in suspicions that the state is stonewalling negotiations, that the Cuomo administration is operating with a hidden agenda in mind, and that individuals in state government are not serious in their efforts in reaching a settlement. At the federal level, the Oneidas are wary of the activities and loyalties of the *pro bono* facilitator and his known link to the governor's office and also to the Grand Council at Onondaga.

Recalling that the Oneidas have been in the courts and in a struggle with the state for nearly two decades, and that at every turn, the state has used the law as an obstacle and delaying tactic to thwart their efforts at settlement, it is no wonder that they believe the state is stonewalling. Coupled with this is the fact that many of the governor's advisors stand in an adversarial position to the Indians, including his secretary, who earlier in his career had prepared legal research for the state of Maine in their land claims.[4] The difficulty with this is that the Maine claims settlement, for all of its positive results, has its flaws, and the Oneidas and their attorneys are determined to avoid a settlement structured in a similar fashion. For example, the Maine settlement provides for considerable state regulatory jurisdiction. The concern of the Oneidas is that the state will develop a mindset or model of settlement based on the Maine case because of this person's influence and policy directives.

A critical eye has also been cast on the effect the governor's aspirations for national office might have on resolving the Oneida land claims through negotiation. Questions have arisen as to whether or not Cuomo will risk offending upstate, non-Indian voters and political contributors with an unpopular and possibly unwanted land claim settlement.

The actions of the federal government to distance itself from the negotiations, and its enigmatic, noncommittal stance at negotiations, has deeply concerned state officials, the Indian parties, and their counsel. For its part, the state would like to see more federal involvement and initiatives in bringing the claims to a resolution, and of course, an increased level of financial contribution to any settlement. The Indians, in turn, are eager to see the pace of the settlement process picked up, and for the state and the federal parties to come to an agreement on their responsibilities. From its perspective, the federal government is content to maintain its distance, arguing that the land claims are a local issue. Further, it has suggested that the state and the Indian tribes negotiate an agreement, at which time they will take an active role in assuring the passage of enabling federal legislation.

Contributing to the difficulties surveyed above is the ambiguous legal status the Iroquois have occupied throughout the history of their relationship with the national and state governments. This status has been marked by periods of benign neglect alternating with assertions of jurisdictional rights by both the federal and state governments. Characteristically, the federal government has continually asserted its right to exercise control over Indian affairs, while the state of New York, time after time, has rejected this position. There were frequent legal and legislative struggles fought in Congress, and, because of the constitutional issues raised, in courts. Few resolutions have been forthcoming, and today, New York and the national government continue to disagree as to their responsibilities regarding the sovereign indian tribes within the state.

During the past century, four major concerns have dominated Iroquois-federal-state relations: (1) the continuing issue of who has ultimate jurisdiction over Indian lands in the state, (2) whether or not New York State's criminal and civil laws can be applied to Indians on a reservation without the express authorization of Congress, (3) the meaning of the land guarantees embodied in the federal-Iroquois treaties of the eighteenth century, and (4) in view of the constitutional and congressional prohibitions, whether or not the state's early transactions with the Iroquois can be considered valid.[5] Although each of these concerns has, in one form or another, been addressed, they remain essentially unresolved and continue to be sources of controversy and conflict.

One example is the issue of civil and criminal jurisdiction. In 1948 and 1950, Congress authorized and transferred first criminal and then civil jurisdiction to the state of New York over Indians on reservations.[6] In doing so, the federal government reasserted its supremacy in Indian affairs. Since that time, however, the state has exercised this jurisdiction in a rather arbitrary and peculiar manner.

In general, the state has taken the position that the federal statutes empowering the state to exercise jurisdiction are permissory in nature; that is, the state will not act unless there is a specific request for assistance by a tribe or the Indian residents on a reservation. This questionable interpretation has become mythologized to the extent that virtually no one involved with Indian issues in the Department of Law or the legislature is aware that New York State, by statute, has civil and criminal jurisdiction. Nevertheless, in other instances, the state chooses to exercise its jurisdiction in a highly selective fashion, one that is dictated, in part, by political pressure exerted by non-Indian residents living near reservations. For example, New York has attempted to set policy and enforce the collection of sales taxes from purchases made on Indian reservations. However, it was unsuccessful in a recent action taken to collect such taxes on gasoline sales.[7]

What is of greater concern, however, is the apparent failure by the state to keep separate two different issues related to the tax question. The state obviously believed it was acting within the law in its attempts to assess tax levies on sales by individual Indian entrepreneurs to non-Indian consumers. Nonetheless, it seemed less interested in distinguishing this question from that of a potential violation of tribal sovereignty; that is, it cannot assume to extend the logic of its taxing efforts to tribes and their operations, which, under federal law, are sovereigns, and stand outside of state jurisdiction.

THE FUTURE

Although the preceeding chapters and discussion have provided some answers to the questions raised in the introduction, a number of pressing and difficult problems remain. In general, these can be placed within the framework of whether or not the land claims can be resolved in the foreseeable future and what their determination will hold for Indians and non-Indians alike.

It is difficult to envision the claims being settled any time soon. Given the political nature of the claims, e.g., periodic changes in local, state, and federal government, and the involvement of multiple parties often at odds with one another, added to the requirements and ritual of the negotiating process, most observers believe it will take at least ten years, or longer, for settlements to be reached.

In order to do so, it will be important to establish and promulgate a program aimed at informing the public fully and effectively about the land claims and the meaning and significance of their resolution. Throughout the process, a large part of the difficulty has been to overcome the ignorance and negative propaganda that obscures, at times intentionally, the circumstances and facts of these cases. This is not to deny, however, that the issues are complex. They concern, after all, the multifarious history of federal Indian policy and law, and run the gamut from political partisanship and struggles within the government bureaucracy, to Indian mistrust and internal strife, to racism.

The impact of a settlement on both the Indian and non-Indian communities will be great. In at least the Oneida and Cayuga cases, there will be two new Indian reservations in New York State, while for the St. Regis Mohawk and Senecas, their current reservation lands may very well be enlarged. Contrary to innumerable rumors and disinformation, private landowners will not be deprived of their property; nor will Indians run lawless through local communities and about the state.

Instead, for non-Indians, there will be new neighbors, a return to the homeland from which they have long been separated, and an eagerness to determine their own future. It goes without saying that adjustments and accommodations will have to be made, facilitated by federal, state, and local governments, to assure minimizing any potential disruptions in either community. However, the benefits to the surrounding non-Indian population can be significant in terms of economic development and improved living standards, to name two. Nevertheless, to what extent such benefits are realized is contingent on the relationship that develops between the two communities. If racism is allowed to raise its ugly head, as it has at times in the Cayuga case, then there is the potential for serious problems.[8]

For the Indians, the impact of a land claim settlement on their communities will be profound. In the Oneida and Cayuga cases, having a land base will enable them once again to exercise tribal jurisdiction, and it will provide a means by which economic development, improved quality of life, and self-determination can be realized. All of this will go far in assuring the cultural survival of these people.

Cayugas will no longer be dependent on the good graces of the Senecas who have allowed these landless people to reside on their reservation over the years. There will also be the possibility that Oneidas, scattered in communities in central New York, will return to a common ground.

Much of this is dependent upon whether or not the Indians can resolve existing internal disputes that have kept the communities, to a degree, in a state of turmoil and dissention. It is a chance for Indian leadership to demonstrate its wisdom and strength, and to give real meaning to the Iroquois tradition of caring for the next seven generations.

By virtue of time and importance, the land claims have become a vital part of the modern day Iroquois world view. A key question is whether or not a resolution will be accepted and integrated into the Iroquois consciousness, or rejected so that the claims continue, at least in the minds of the people.

The answer to such questions will be determined largely by two factors—the nature of the negotiating process itself and the terms of settlement. Unless the negotiations are conducted in a dignified and respectful manner, it may be impossible to ever resolve the claims issues. And unless the final terms reflect the seriousness of the claims and the ambitions of the Iroquois people, the settlement, even though ratified by Congress, will rankle and cause great bitterness among the Indians.

Thus, it is especially critical that New York's officials, and those at the federal level, develop more than their presently superficial understanding of the Indian communities to assure that the appropriate ritual and respect is observed, and carried forth as one sovereign to another. As it now stands, many individuals in New York State government are insensitive to the fact that they are dealing with people from another culture. They see no reason to develop insight into the Indian communities, their history, or their politics; and in a number of cases, they exhibit behavior that is at best patronizing, and at worst, racist. There is much to be learned.

It is also true that the Indian participants must proceed with care and forbearance in their interactions with state and federal governments, although the point could be taken that this is precisely what they have done for some two centuries. New York's record in dealing with the Indian populations within its borders is not a good one.[9] There is no reason why this unfortunate historical fact cannot be reversed.

NOTES

1. Unless otherwise cited, information contained in the epilogue is based on an examination of New York State Indian policy and land claims carried out by the author while a Senior Fellow at the Nelson A. Rockefeller Institute of Government in 1986–87. See William A. Starna, "Indian Land Claims in New York State: A Policy Analysis," report submitted to Governor Mario M. Cuomo and the Nelson A. Rockefeller Institute of Government. Albany, New York, August 1, 1987.

2. Nancy Oestriech Lurie, "Money, Semantics, and Indian Leadership," *American Indian Quarterly* 10 (1) (Winter 1986): 47.

3. Laurence M. Hauptman, "Circle the Wagons," *Capital Region* (February 1987): 53. See also Hauptman, *Formulating American Indian Policies in New York State, 1970–1986: A Public Policy Study.* Report submitted to the Governor of New York and American Indian Nations September 1, 1986. Manuscript on file, The Nelson A. Rockefeller Institute of Government, Albany.

4. Hauptman, "Circle the Wagons," 52.

5. Jack Campisi, "National Policy, States' Rights, and Indian Sovereignty: The Case of the New York Iroquois." In *Extending the Rafters: Interdisciplinary Approaches to Iroquoian Studies,* ed. Michael K. Foster, Jack Campisi, and Marianne Mithun (Albany: State University of New York Press, 1984), 105.

6. 25 U.S.C. Sec. 232 and 233.

7. *Herzog Bros. Trucking, Inc. v. State Tax Commission* (New York State Court of Appeals, May 7, 1987 [514 New York Supplement 2nd No. 3, p. 21, June 3, 1987]).

8. Michael Winerip, "Perennial Hope of the Scattered Cayuga Nation—Land," *New York Times,* August 10, 1984.

9. See New (York) State Commissioners of Indian Affairs, *Proceedings of the Commissioners of Indian Affairs, Appointed by Law for the Extinguishment of Indian Titles in the State of New York,* by Franklin B. Hough 2 vol. (Albany: J. Munsell, 1861); New York (State) Assembly, (unpublished) *Report of the Indian Commission to Investigate the Status of the American Indian Residing in the State of New York Transmitted to the Legislature, March 17, 1922* (Albany, 1922); Laurence M. Hauptman, *The Iroquois and the New Deal* (Syracuse: Syracuse University Press, 1981); *The Iroquois Struggle for Survival* (Syracuse: Syracuse University Press, 1986).

Index

IROQUOIS LAND CLAIMS
was composed in 10½ on 12 Janson on a Mergenthaler Linotron 202
by Coghill Book Typesetting Co.;
with initial capitals and chapter numbers set in Post Mediaeval Medium
by Dix Type, Inc.;
printed by sheet-fed, offset on 50-pound, acid-free Glatfelter Natural Hi Bulk,
also notch-bound with paper covers,
with dust jackets and paper covers printed in 2 colors
by Braun-Brumfield, Inc.;
designed by Vicky Welch;
and published by

SYRACUSE UNIVERSITY PRESS
SYRACUSE, NEW YORK 13244-5160